Charlotte Hampton 3:

City CO-BNV East

How To Sell Fashion

How to Sell Fashion

ANNALEE GOLD

Second Edition • Fairchild Publications, New York

Standard Book Number: 87005–201–2

Library of Congress Catalog Card Number: 78–51903

Printed in the United States of America

It's a New York tradition

Our Christmas windows have brought 150 years of joy. Today, they'll take you back to olde
New York of 1826. The modes of the day! The horse-drawn carriages! Scenes from
our first little store at 47 Catherine Street and all the others that followed. A pageant through
New York's history and ours. Accompanied by old-time songs, marches, and carols.

Oh, come with us, come with us as we travel through time!

Lord & Taylor

Fashions of the past, an appropriate advertising theme for Christmas. This full-page newspaper ad tied
in with window displays at Lord & Taylor, celebrating the history of the store, an example of institutional
advertising.

I have some clothes in my closet that are attractive and not at all worn out. They are about ten years old, the same age as the first edition of this book. Clothes and books have a way of aging—they reach a certain point, and there is no hope. One must go on to something new.

So, I have gone on to the second edition of *How To Sell Fashion.* I hope *it* will wear well and last for quite a few years.

Wardrobes are easier to manage than books. They can be discarded gradually, refurbished, and adjusted. But a book, once written and published, is final. There is no hem to take up, no seam to let out. It must do for a while.

I do not like that finality, and I have dawdled over finishing this new edition. As I write, I am wondering about woven mesh jewelry, and some new styles of boots, and a great department store that is about to do over its fashion floors, and, and, and . . . and yet, it is time to write, "the end."

As in the previous edition, I have written for two audiences; people in store management, and students of retailing who have not yet entered the field of fashion.

Because of women's liberation, I have been very conscious of personal pronouns. I have used "he," or "she," and "they" alternately.

Much of what I have written was drawn from the ideas of many people who helped me, and who gave generously of their time.

Among the retailers and people in related fields to whom I owe warm thanks are: Howard Abrahams, television advertising consultant; Phyllis Bernstein, Attitude; Richard Blume, Kenneth Siegal, R.H. Macy; Stephen Bruce, Calvin Holt, Serendipity; Eve Cooley, Marion Lewis, Virginia Palmer, Village Casuals; Susan Comito, Susan Weisel, The Silver Plum; Alfred Eisenpreis, Newspaper Advertising Bureau; Jack Eugster, The Gap Stores, Inc.; George Frei, Sheridan Associates; Linda Friedman, Lonia; Gloria Geis, Belk Stores Services, Inc.; John Glasser, No Name Stores, Inc.; Janet Goff,

Eleanor Lambert, Inc.; Allan Johnson, Paul Le Blang, Ross Bonanno, Saks Fifth Avenue; John Lucas, J.C. Penney Co.; Myrna Masoff, A & S.; Chuck Miller, Target Stores, Inc.; Gene Moore, Tiffany & Co.; Milton Negrin, Alexander's; Rita Perna, A.B. Dalrymple, Montgomery Ward & Co.; Eric Peterson, Shopping Center World; Roger Rice, Television Bureau of Advertising; Anne Saum, Anne Saum and Associates; Diane Scott, Galleria; Laurence J. Straus, Strouss; Geraldine Stutz, Henri Bendel; Nancy Vardakis, Kings Plaza Shopping Center; Wilmer Weiss, Dayton-Hudson Corp.

I also appreciate the help of the International Council of Shopping Centers.

Special thanks are due to members of the Fairchild News Staff: Bernie Lett, New York City, for cooperation in photography assignments; Karen McNeill, Atlanta, for contact work with Rich's and Davison's; Jeff Melvoin, Miami, for contact work with Burdine's. Also, to Barbara Scholey, book designer.

And last but far from least, I am deeply grateful to Olga Kontzias of Fairchild's Book Division, who was my long-suffering editor, Without her, I could not have completed this book.

Annalee Gold
New York

Contents

What Is Fashion?

Fashion is a way of dressing that is currently accepted. To say that fashion is current is to say that it changes constantly. We may not be conscious of the change from season to season, or year to year; it is like a low hum in the background that we ignore because it is always there.

Designers show their collections and new ideas burst upon the scene; some disappear, some are gradually absorbed and become part of the mainstream of change.

We have only to look backwards to realize how change has come about. If we pick up an old magazine, or look at an old movie, or glance at an old photograph, we immediately exclaim that it is old-fashioned, even before we have picked out the details of silhouette, hair and makeup that are out-of-date.

The word, "fashion" is used in other ways, some overlapping, some ambiguous. Fashion may refer to clothing in general, which is also called *apparel*. A "fashion" may refer to a specific item or piece of clothing, which may also be called a *style*.

Style is a word with many meanings, including fashion and beyond it. Style may describe a cluster of characteristics that we associate with an era, a group of people, a place, or a person.

When we think of the style of the 1920's, we conjure up images of short, straight dresses without waistlines, bobbed hair, cloche hats and other characteristics that go beyond clothing—Model-T Fords, silent movies, the Charleston, to name a few. They are all part of the style of the 1920's.

We may have experienced that style indirectly, through movies or books, or personal recollections of our parents or grandparents. The style of the 1920's is quite different from the style of the 1940's and the style of the 1890's.

We also have definite associations with phrases such as peasant style, Mexican style and English style.

The personal style of men and women in the public eye is often individual and

2

Many designer fashions are inspired by ethnic themes. Philippine bag worn over the shoulders is a first cousin to Bonnie Cashin's beige cotton jacket with back pocket. *(Left, courtesy of The American Museum of Natural History. Right, courtesy of Eleanor Lambert.)*

4

distinguished—and imitated. Jacqueline Kennedy Onassis, when she was the wife of the late President John Kennedy, had great personal style. Her pillbox hats, bouffant hair and simple dresses and coats were widely imitated. Brigitte Bardot, the French actress, had quite a different style. Her long, tousled blond hair and ruffled, little-girl dresses were also imitated. Famous rock musicians expressed their personal style in spangled and sequined costumes, or tattered rags.

But it is not only celebrities who have style—though the personal style of a celebrity may influence fashion.

Many men and women in all walks of life have personal style, and express it in their clothing, as well as in everything else they do.

The woman with a personal sense of style takes fashion and adapts it to her own needs. She will not wear a fashion that is not becoming to her. She will add some special twist that is hers and hers alone; it comes from within. It is as much a part of her as her smile and her eyes.

There are other women—and they are a larger group—who always dress fashionably but never look really chic. They conscientiously wear the latest styles but add nothing of their own. Fashion is put on; it comes from without.

Style comes from within. Fashion is universal. Style is individual.

As still another example of confusing terms, we add *flair for fashion* to our list of phrases. It is sometimes used to describe a woman with personal style. It also refers to a woman with an awareness of what is happening in the world of fashion.

Then, there is the much-overworked phrase, *life style*. We shall avoid it.

Fashion changes are echoed by changes in the way women shop. In Chapter 2 we will examine some changes in shopping habits that developed while hemlines rose in the 1960's and fell in the 1970's.

New Shopping Habits

"Where did you go?"
"Shopping."
"What did you buy?"
"I didn't buy anything, I just went shopping."

Traditionally, it was the well-to-do woman with plenty of time and money on her hands who made an occupation of shopping. Sometimes she bought, sometimes not. The more money she had, the more probable it was that her casual shopping would turn serious.

But in the 1970's, most women had other occupations. Shopping for the sake of shopping dropped below work, sports, social life, hobbies, travel, and a host of other activities. New ways of life developed new shopping habits.

Women no longer confined themselves to women's departments. Back in the 1960's, young girls found that they often preferred men's jeans. They began to shop in men's departments. Petite women complained of a lack of merchandise in their size range. Sometimes they found sophisticated styles that fit them in teenage departments, where prices were lower, too.

This was typical of the new attitude toward shopping; women were perfectly willing to ignore tradition if they could find the merchandise they wanted in another department.

Young men and women shopped together. As men became more interested in their clothes, and more knowledgeable about fashion, shopping became a joint venture for young couples. Often, the woman would turn to the man and ask, "What do you think?" She was not deferring, in the old-fashioned sense, she was consulting. The man could be depended on to tell her that a style or color was becoming or unbecoming; he knew what he was talking about.

This was a far cry from the traditional husband-wife shopping situation that always had comic overtones. The husband accompanied his wife in a state of irritation, squirming uncomfortably while she hesitated and made her choices. He might object to something "crazy" or to a plunging neckline with too much plunge. He might object to price. But he knew nothing about fashion, and cared less.

More women shopped by mail order. The catalogues of the great mass merchandisers, Sears, Roebuck, Montgomery Ward and J.C. Penney prospered even as their retail stores expanded. Catalogue merchandise was more sophisticated and up-to-date. Presentation improved, too. Good photography and professional attention to layout enhanced the appearance of catalogues.

At the same time, other retailers joined the catalogue parade. Some specialty chains produced catalogues that looked like fashion magazines, with full color photographs printed on good quality paper.

The reasons why women shopped by catalogue went beyond catalogues themselves. In the stores, they found poor service. Armchair shopping was a convenience. With several catalogues on hand, they could "visit" different stores easily and make their selections.

Store loyalty declined. This, too, spurred catalogue shopping, but it had more far-reaching connotations. The mystical bond that often linked a woman to one special store was gone. Perhaps she had depended on "her" saleswoman to pick out styles for her. That favorite saleswoman was no more.

Perhaps the customer counted on finding the collection of a particular designer in one store only. Such exclusivity virtually disappeared. So women moved from store to store picking up one item here, another somewhere else.

Young people shopped without their parents. Parents gave them a clothing allowance and the young people chose their own clothes. The age of independence dropped. It was not unusual to see 12-year-olds shopping alone, or with their friends.

Families shopped together. This was a suburban development tied to the shopping center. As more women worked, they did not have free time during the day. Seven-day weeks in some states encouraged family shopping; if stores stayed open on Sunday, the whole family could hop in the car and drive to a shopping center. Heavy loads of packages were no problem; everything went in the car, and the garage was directly in the center.

Family shopping often focused on hard goods as well as fashion merchandise and other soft goods. The children wanted to have something to say about the new living room couch, and the new color television set.

While they were there, it was convenient to pick up a pair of shoes, or a dress or a sweater.

While shopping attitudes were changing, morality was changing, too. Stealing became a way of shopping. This was not limited to women; it applied to men as well. People seemed to have a strange new attitude towards stealing—often, they did not consider it immoral because they were stealing from a store, which was a large, impersonal entity. That was different than stealing from a person—or so they felt. While internal theft, and executive theft, continued to account for more losses than customer theft, customer theft did increase sharply.

7

Affluent women sometimes bought merchandise from expensive stores and then, on their way out, "lifted" a little something else, adding it to merchandise they paid for. Young people sometimes vied with each other in shoplifting.

Retailers installed expensive security systems, for example, a special merchandise tag that "beeped" if the merchandise was stolen.

If a thief tries to walk out of the store with merchandise he has not paid for, the special tag sets off the beep, alerting security guards. When a customer pays for merchandise, the cashier removes the special tag.

In one shopping center, the manager of a store that had not adopted this system reported that customers were saying, "Oh, let's go shoplifting in Store Z, and then let's go shopping." The same manager reported catching a thief in the act. "Why did you have to pick on me? I only took one shirt!" the thief wailed.

Salespeople in accessory departments reported ingenious tricks. Said one veteran saleswoman, "I am always suspicious when a woman says, 'I'm just going to walk over to the window so I can see the color in natural daylight. And now that men carry handbags, we have to watch them, too. A man carrying a bag just doesn't look funny anymore."

Sometimes quick thinking saved the day. A case in point concerned a large department store with a busy, crowded main floor. An alert service manager noticed a dignified, well-dressed woman pick up a pair of expensive sunglasses and slip them down the neckline of her dress. He stepped up and said to her politely, "Madam, will that be charge or cash?" The woman flung the glasses on the counter and fled.

Thieves can do their work more easily when there are fewer people on the floor to watch, and more racks to hide behind while slipping a garment under a coat or into a handbag.

As more men and women shopped together, and more men became interested in fashion, those changes set off a chain reaction of still other changes. Shopping habits are closely linked to changes in the fashion marketplace itself. In our next chapter, we will examine the different kinds of stores in which fashion merchandise is sold.

Where Fashion Is Happening Today

I n the Far West, American Indians come "to market" on specific days, spread out baskets and beads on their blankets, prop themselves against a wall, and wait for tourists to ask, "How much?"

3

The outdoor market is as ancient as the Bible. It was the first store. Something very much like it still exists today in many parts of the world.

Farmers' markets, as they are called, may be located outdoors but are often indoors. Imagine an old loft or warehouse crammed with merchandise of every kind —not just clothes, but hardware, tools, equipment, and many other items. Decor, display, sales help and other refinements of modern retailing are virtually unknown. Each "owner" has rented an area of space. The stand is piled high with merchandise helter-skelter. The clothes are mostly work clothes, housedresses, and other strictly functional apparel. Despite the lack of glamour, this is where fashion begins for as soon as a woman has selected a pink dress instead of a blue, she has expressed a fashion preference.

The farmer's market grew out of a rural society that is rapidly declining. It has given way to more organized, sophisticated forms of retailing that meet new customer needs. Some of these forms of retailing are:

- The discount store
- The junior department store
- The franchise store
- The franchised line
- The leased department *Run & operate by someone other than the store must follow all of stores policy's*
- The supermarket
- The national chain store

The stores are often located in a new retail complex, the *shopping center.*

Briefly, here are some basic facts about these outlets and ways of distribution that everyone interested in fashion retailing should know.

10 THE DISCOUNT STORE

The discounter moves large quantities of merchandise and sells at low prices because the cost of his operation is low. Modern discounting evolved after World War II, when there was a tremendous population shift to the suburbs. The department store was slow to follow its customers to suburbia, but the discounter was on the spot, buying up land before land costs went up sharply.

In the beginning the discount store was usually a one-floor operation with the simplest of fixtures that were flexible and could be rearranged easily. Service was kept to a minimum. There were very few salespeople.

The discounter was able to move large quantities of merchandise because his location was convenient for people living in the neighborhood, because the merchandise was openly displayed and easy to get at, because he offered better parking facilities than the downtown stores, and because he offered mostly staple merchandise with mass appeal.

Most discounters started out by selling hard goods, small and major appliances. Later, many moved into staple fashion merchandise. It was at this point that discounting began to compete with department stores and specialty stores in the area of fashion. (A department store is a large store that carries every category of hard goods and soft goods. For the purposes of this book, a specialty store is a store that carries soft goods, mostly fashion merchandise.)

There are two forms of discounting with unusual characteristics that are worth noting, although they are not major volume factors in the total discount picture.

The rural discounter sprang up in small towns after World War II, where he competed with catalogue business, particularly the operations of Sears, Roebuck and Montgomery Ward. Discounters usually depend on moving large quantities of merchandise; the rural discounter cannot, because his location limits him to a relatively small group of customers. The urban discounter is unusual because of his location. Discounters generally settled in suburbia, following on the heels of the suburban-bound population.

Given the elements of discounting, the crowded space, lack of service, and the need to keep costs down, it is hard to see how discounters can handle true fashion merchandise although they have been successful in moving staple fashion.

Based on performance in 1977, discounters were recording mixed results from their fashion presentations. Korvettes, for example, showed losses during that year and new units were featuring records, cameras and non-fashion merchandise. K-mart, on the other hand, appeared to be expanding rapidly and profitably, and was sticking to the traditional discount fashion formula—racks and racks of staple merchandise—and doing it successfully.

THE JUNIOR DEPARTMENT STORE 11

The junior department store has become much more important as a distributor of fashion merchandise since the late 1940's. Many junior department stores grew out of the variety store chains, and located in suburbia. (The term, "variety store" refers to stores like F.W. Woolworth Co. and McCrory Corporation, that were informally called five-and-tèn's, or five-and-dime stores.) The old variety stores were located in cities in downtown areas. They were mostly one-floor stores that carried stationery, cosmetics, kitchenwares, notions, sweets and some packaged staple fashions. They had soda-and-sandwich counters.

The new stores were larger; some were multi-level. They have traded up to higher price lines and moved into more women's and girls' ready-to-wear. Some carry sportswear, dresses and shoes. Packaging is more sophisticated. Often, these units are anchor or main stores in moderate-sized shopping centers. They have rack displays as well as counters.

Though the largest customer group for this merchandise is made up of women looking for low prices, some young people have taken to shopping in junior department stores and variety stores as a way of expressing their independence of more traditional retail outlets. Fads for accessories attract them; in the early 1970's, it was a fabric shoe. Some years later, a fad for bobby socks drew young customers to chains like Woolworth's and Kress & Co.

THE FRANCHISE STORE

The franchise store is a retail operation that is relatively new as a distributor of fashion merchandise. The merchandise is mostly staple and basic. Prices are usually in the low to medium range. The franchise store is managed by the owner, who is known as the franchisee. He is responsible for the operation of the store, for its relationship to the community, and for its image.

The franchisor provides merchandise and often promotional and selling aids. In short, he provides the selling know-how that the owner, or franchisee, lacks.

Not all franchise stores carry staple fashions. Shoe stores like Capezio and Pappagallo are known for their young, up-to-date styles.

The word "franchise" has other meanings. A *franchised line* is a line of merchandise that is confined to one store in an area. It is exclusive with that store. Sometimes, this merchandise is collected in one spot, which becomes a department in itself. It may have its own sign, and its own special displays. In this way, the franchised line becomes a franchised department.

THE LEASED DEPARTMENT

The leased department is not a new retailing technique, but it should be mentioned because it is so widespread. When a store finds that its staff is not capable of buying and selling a special type of merchandise—furs and shoes are typical—an outside source is called in to take over the department. This outside source has expertise that store management lacks; however, store management must watch a leased department very carefully. Merchandise, sales staff, and presentation in a leased department should be fully in accord with the total store image. If they are not, the store will suffer.

THE SUPERMARKET

The supermarket is primarily a distributor of food, but many supermarkets have moved into non-food products including fashion merchandise. Their fashion merchandise is generally low-priced and staple. Some supermarkets display fashion merchandise on shelves adjacent to food; others house fashion in a separate building. Supermarkets sell sportswear and dresses as well as packaged hosiery and intimate apparel.

THE NATIONAL CHAIN

The national chains include three organizations each unique in its own way: Sears, Ward's and Penney's. Some of their stores are like department stores, except that their buying is not local or autonomous; it is centralized. Merchandise goes from a central point to stores all over the country. All three sell from mail order catalogues as well as stores. Sears and Ward's started with catalogues and moved into general merchandise stores. Penney's started with stores that sold women's and children's apparel, expanded to hard goods, and then introduced its catalogue operation.

What is most important for our purposes here is that all three have traded up their fashion image. They have moved into higher price lines. They are selling more diversified, sophisticated merchandise that follows fashion trends closely. They sell to a mass market, but today's mass market demands increased sophistication.

Of the three, Sears is by far the largest. After World War II, Sears was quick to grasp the significance of the population shift to the suburbs. Sears bought up land and followed the population, expanding tremendously. Ward's did not begin its expansion until the late 1950's and has grown at a much slower rate, though its rate of growth increased sharply in the sixties.

What happens when a national chain starts looking for a fashion image? What has happened at Ward's is typical. Old standards for fashion merchandise change. Thrift and value are no longer enough. Ready-to-wear is smartly styled. Merchandise diversifies, and includes luxury items such as furs and diamonds.

Diversification applies to merchandise, timing, price ranges, and other aspects of merchandising in both the catalogue and the stores. (In 1977 Ward's had just under 500 stores across the country.) Rita Perna, Ward's assistant vice president and national fashion coordinator, explains how she regulates the fashion pace for a national audience.

"We have maintained our traffic builders, or low-end categories, even though we have traded up," notes Ms. Perna. "If, for instance, our best-selling jeans are $17, we will also have jeans that sell for less. And we will have other styles at prices up to $27, even though our greatest strength is at $17.

"Timing is different in different parts of the country. Florida does very little in back-to-school and fall fashion, and what they do is early. Our Florida stores might go into rust, earth and leaf tones, and they would have that merchandise in August. By October, they're back into pastels. Fall comes early in Dallas, too.

"Some styles seem to catch on and hold on in a part of the country; it may have to do with climate, or ethnic background, or some other regional factor. Texas always takes little black dresses; that may be because of the Mexican-American population. In Los Angeles, women are still wearing maxi-coats over dresses. Double knit polyester pantsuits are still popular, especially in the Southwest and the Midwest.

"Then there are always new customer groups coming up to add to the diversity. There is a young half-size customer who isn't on a diet, although she may have a bust measurement of 37 to 50 inches and a waist measurement of 29 to 44 inches. She wants sportswear and separates and pantsuits; she wants to dress fashionably, regardless of her weight."

With all this variety, Ms. Perna must pull fashion together with themes; for example, folkloric motifs, knits, sweaters, plaids.

Ward's catalogue accounted for about 25 percent of total volume in 1977; stores chalked up the remaining 75 percent. With a total volume of about $4 billion, Ward's places high in the ranks of giant retailers.

The giant national chains set new patterns of merchandising, opening units in many states in all parts of the country. Other retailers, seeing the advantages of chain store operations, copied the idea within more limited geographical areas.

Regional chains grew along with national chains. There were discounters, department stores and specialty chains, carrying fashion merchandise, and, sometimes assortments of fashion merchandise plus linens and domestics, furniture and appliances. Some were small, and limited to two or three states. Others spread throughout a larger area. Some did not even call themselves chains, but preferred the term, "groups" or "regional groups."

Belk Stores Services Inc., a family-owned organization, refers to itself as a regional grouping of privately owned stores in 18 southeastern states. (In 1977, Belk included some 400 stores, mixing fashion and other merchandise in varying proportions.)

14

A Montgomery Ward store in a shopping center in Springfield, Illinois. The rack is the basic fixture. A jacket hung by nearly invisible wire seems to float in mid-air. Facing page: the junior department is defined by ceiling grid, change of floor covering, and two mannequins on pedestals. Simple layout with all merchandise on display is typical of mass merchandising.

"We carry fashion at all price levels, from budget to designer names," comments fashion director, Gloria Geis. "Our budget departments are simply fixtured with racks. Our better fashion departments are arranged with more island displays and architectural details, such as arches and multi-level departments.

"Each store has the right of refusal—we do not force it to accept merchandise that would be wrong for its customers."

But flexibility is tempered with central control. Ms. Geis goes into the fabric and leather markets and holds meetings with buyers twice a year, outlining trends for the coming season. Fashion buyers have her information and direction before they go into their markets.

Regional chains, like giant national chains, must mix local independence and centralized control carefully. The Fashion Director, or Fashion Coordinator—there are other titles—sets a framework; within this framework, individual stores develop their own successful formulas. "Success" is the key word; most chains will allow member units leeway as long as they show a profit.

The chains, like all other retailers, have borrowed freely from each other, mixing, changing, improvising, and learning by trial and success, as well as trial and error.

With all this borrowing, it is sometimes difficult to label a retailer clearly. Discounters added services like charge accounts and improved their decor as they moved into fashion. Department stores, on the other hand, eliminated sales help in some departments, and cut prices to meet competition from discounters. Variety stores added more fashion lines. Ward's and Sears started with catalogues and added retail stores. Penney's started with retail stores and added a catalogue. All these retailers meet and compete in a shared marketplace—a marketplace that hardly existed before 1950, yet is now a vitally important outlet for fashion—and other—goods and services.

The shopping center is a group of stores in suburbia ranging in sizes from a small "strip" center of perhaps 10 or 12 stores to a large regional center of more than 100 stores. A few centers are located in downtown areas. (We will discuss shopping centers fully in Chapter 4.) For the purposes of this chapter, it is enough to say that the shopping center is a reproduction of urban downtown moved out to the suburbs. In the moving process, there were some changes, but much of the character of downtown shopping was preserved.

In both downtown and suburbia, it seems that more different types of stores are carrying fashion merchandise; not the high fashion designer styles that magazines and newspapers like to publicize, but basics. Sportswear and separates, accessories and bodywear, T-shirts and jeans, packaged hosiery and bras. It is the mass market that retailers pursue most eagerly; that is where the greatest potential profit is to be found —by those who can find it.

In summary, here are brief definitions of the most important kinds of retail operations that sell fashion merchandise.

An underselling store. One that offers merchandise below conventional prices.

A discount store. One kind of underselling store. Its key characteristics are prices below those of conventional stores, limited sales help and other services, concentration on price promotions, and minimal fixturing.

A promotional store. A store whose image is based on price promotions.

A general merchandise store. One that carries both hard goods and soft goods.

A junior department store. One kind of general merchandise store. It carries some furniture and some soft goods, but in limited assortments.

A department store. Another kind of general merchandise store. It carries a full line of hard goods, including major appliances, such as washing machines and furniture, and a full line of soft goods, including apparel in wide assortments.

Five-and-ten or variety stores. Mostly one-floor operations concentrating on inexpensive items—many years ago, needles and thread, stationery, cosmetics, candy and children's toys actually sold for five cents and ten cents; hence, the name. Prices rose to one dollar, two dollars and more; but the old name stuck.

A specialty store. A store carrying soft goods with strong emphasis on various categories of fashion merchandise. (The Federal government sometimes classifies large specialty stores as "department stores" because they carry so many different categories of merchandise. But, strictly speaking, a department store is one that carries a full hard goods line as well as soft goods.)

A national chain. A store grouping which has some form of centralized management and whose units are located throughout the country.

A regional chain. Units in a section of the country; the Midwest, the Northeast, or the Far West. There are also *local chains,* some with as few as two or three units. Chains are described as local when all their units are in one state.

A shopping center. A cluster of stores in a clearly designated area which includes parking facilities. In most cases, the center will also include recreational and commercial facilities so as to simulate a downtown shopping area.

Three definitions of categories of merchandise belong with our store definitions:

Hard goods. Major and small appliances, such as television sets, washing machines, toasters, hardware, wall accessories and china; also furniture and equipment, such as lawn mowers.

Soft goods. Linens, domestics, piece goods (fabrics) and all fashion merchandise.

A big-ticket item. An item that sells for a high price. A refrigerator is an example of a big-ticket item in hard goods. A fur coat is an example of a big-ticket item in soft goods.

Two more terms are important and should be defined:

Trading up. The policy of adding merchandise in higher price lines. For example, a store that carries sweaters in a range of $15 to $25 is trading up when it adds sweaters that sell for $35.

Trading down. The opposite: it refers to a policy of lowering price ranges. The store that carried sweaters ranging up to $35 lowers its top price to $25.

Besides changing upper and lower limits of price ranges, a store may also trade up or trade down by changing the concentration of its strength in a price range. Using a sweater department as an example again, a store might trade down by carrying only one or two styles at $35 where it previously carried eight or ten styles. It might show the most styles in a price range of $15 to $20.

Stores trade up or trade down because they are adjusting to new customer needs or new customer groups. A formerly poor neighborhood with a new middle-class population calls for trading up.

Stores may feel that they can persuade their customers to trade up one price range. In a large store with many customers, a few dollars added to each sales ticket means a substantial difference in total volume.

Many of the stores described above are often found together in the shopping center. In our next chapter, we will see how the shopping center has become, in effect, one giant store, and how its growth and development have affected fashion.

Shopping Centers: The Suburban Marketplace

Shopping centers chalked up some $200 billion of retail sales in the United States in 1977. Fashion merchandise accounts for nearly half of those sales, according to many experts. This is very big business, and yet, the shopping center was virtually unknown 30 years ago.

4

Where did shopping centers come from? Why are they so important as distributors of merchandise in general and fashion merchandise in particular? The answers to these questions can be summed up in two words: *suburban life.*

The suburbs are communities outside of metropolitan city areas that began to grow and develop rapidly in the late 1940's, after World War II. People bought homes in the suburbs, leaving the city for these new frontiers where land was often cheaper and air was always fresher.

As the shift of population continued, it was clear that the modest stores of the suburbs, geared to pre-war population, could not meet the needs of suburbanites.

The discounters, a new breed of retailers, opened up stores in the suburbs. Early discounters concentrated on hard goods.

A second wave of discounters balanced off hard goods with soft goods, and a still later group of discounters concentrated on soft goods.

National chain stores, department, specialty, variety and supermarket chains opened branch units, following their customers into the suburbs.

Smaller regional and local chains, and independents followed. Suburban retailing began to keep pace with suburban growth.

The earliest shopping centers were rows or "strips" of a few stores along the highway, adjacent to a parking lot. They were called *strip centers.* The parking area was and is essential, for the car links the suburban shopper to the shopping center.

The early strip center, or neighborhood center as it was sometimes called, sold little or no fashion merchandise. Typically, it included a small supermarket or superette,

The crowds came to see the famed "Cookie Monster" do his thing at Northwest Plaza Shopping Center, St. Louis. Northwest has three important department store units—Famous-Barr, Stix, Baer and Fuller, and Sears—so it wants to attract mass market shoppers. The "Cookie Monster" appears to be just what the retailers wanted. *(Courtesy of Skate-On, Bridgeton, Missouri)*

a variety store, a luncheonette and perhaps a drug store. This mix of stores was not different from the mix of stores on a city street.

The community center was larger and more varied. Its anchor store might be Woolworth's, or a unit of a supermarket chain, like Food Fair. At this stage, fashion merchandise entered the picture.

The large, regional center was the next phase of growth. The regional center is a total shopping experience, which is sometimes called "one-stop shopping." It includes stores that sell many different kinds of fashion merchandise.

All centers except the smallest have anchor, or main stores, which are the largest stores in the centers. Depending upon the size of the center, its anchor may be a variety store, a junior department store or a branch of a national chain. The largest centers have two or more anchor stores.

Penney's, Ward, Sears, Macy's, Lord & Taylor, Saks Fifth Avenue and Neiman-Marcus are examples of chains that may anchor a center.

The character of the anchor store or stores set the tone of the center and help determine what kinds of customers it will attract. The character of a center anchored by Sears will be quite different from the character of a center anchored by Neiman-Marcus; this applies to fashion and all other merchandise.

During the 1960's, the large, regional center went indoors. Merchants had been looking for a way to circumvent bad weather. The answer was enclosure. Large centers became *malls* with roofs and walls, heated in winter and air-conditioned in summer.

The large, regional center built as an enclosed mall is a total shopping experience paralleling downtown shopping with added conveniences.

The customer does not have to put up with streets crowded with traffic. Once inside the center, rain, snow, heat or cold no longer matter.

Shopping center hours are longer than downtown city store hours. Families often find it most convenient to shop in the evening, while mothers of children may shop during school hours and teenagers shop after 3 P.M.

Typical center hours are 10 A.M. to 9 P.M., six or seven days a week; a schedule that can accommodate the needs of all customers.

Inside the enclosed center, stores face inward, opening on the central mall.

Many malls have two or more levels, connected by stairways and escalators. Sometimes, anchor stores in a two-level mall are built to four levels, so that the first two floors of the four-floor anchor store open on to the two levels of the mall.

Some regional centers have a free-standing store as a neighbor. The free-standing store is one which is located right next to the center, drawing the same customers. It is not enclosed, and is not part of the center.

The growth of suburban population is reflected in the growing number of shopping centers in the United States.

In 1950, there were about 100 centers in the country. In 1960, there were 4,000. By the mid-1970's, the total rose to 16,000 for the United States, Canada and 26 other countries, according to the International Council of Shopping Centers.

According to a 1977 issue of *Shopping Center World*, a monthly magazine covering the shopping center industry, centers in the United States ". . . cracked the magic $200 billion barrier at the end of 1976, reaching an annual sales rate of $217,454,000,000 . . ."

A chart from the same magazine, reports on 12 years of growth from 1964 to 1976.

In 1964, 7,600 centers chalked up $78.7 billion gross sales.

In 1976, 17,523 centers achieved gross sales of more than $217 billion.

Fashion retailers in shopping centers have their share of problems; some unique to centers, others similar to problems of downtown.

Limited space, limited assortments. Most branch stores are smaller than downtown flagship stores. Floor space is extremely valuable; any merchandise category that does not produce a good return must be eliminated. Hard goods, like furniture and appliances, take up a great deal of floor space, and are offered in limited assortments.

As for fashion merchandise, it is true that a rack of skirts or pants does not take up very much space. But there are many styles, sizes and colors. Some must be eliminated. So the store offers fewer styles in fewer colors and a limited size range. Slow-moving categories like evening wear may be eliminated entirely, or given token representation.

In some cases, where downtown neighborhoods deteriorated seriously, the suburban branch store became more important than the downtown flagship store.

Elimination of traditional window displays. The windows of many stores open directly on to the mall, so that the window becomes the interior display. Poor interior display becomes poor window display, as well.

The problem of the store interior on display, unprotected by a traditional window, is unique to shopping centers. This exposure of the store interior places a heavier burden on fixturing, signage, and old-fashioned neatness. It is very difficult to keep a store neat when customers are continually pulling clothes off racks and tables, yet the effect of messiness is unappealing, to put it mildly.

Tables piled high with "specials," poor lighting, rows of racks, dirty floors—these are a few examples of bad housekeeping that goes on display when the store window opens directly on to the mall.

Side-by-side neighbors can look monotonous. This problem is unique to centers. Downtown stores alternate with other, non-retail buildings. The center, however, is one continuous vista of stores. Sometimes, too many stores selling one kind of merchandise are clustered together—for instance, shoe stores. The shopper sees shoes to the point of boredom. The same thing happens when fashion stores offer merchandise that looks very much like the merchandise next door.

When each store finds its unique personality, instead of imitating its neighbors or looking for a common denominator, then the shopper entering the mall is interested and intrigued as she passes from store to store.

Personnel problems. Shopping center merchants face problems similar to the problems of downtown merchants. There is a shortage of qualified people who are willing to work at selling. Many salespeople are marginal; they will work for a short time only. It is difficult to motivate and train a transient staff.

The long hours of shopping centers intensify personnel problems; stores must find salespeople who are willing to work evenings. The advent of the seven-day shopping week in many parts of the country has created more problems; not many people are willing to work on Sunday.

Fashion on ice: Shopping center malls give an extra lift to fashion promotions by offering sufficient space to permit all types of fashion shows, including the icy variety. Here at Plaza Frontenac, St. Louis, models of varying ages show off fur coats, parkas and other sporting goods to an attentive audience. Better-priced furs reflect the carriage trade draw at the center which has units from Neiman Marcus, Saks Fifth Avenue, and Gucci's. *(Courtesy of Skate-On, Bridgeton, Missouri)*

Decline of the small, independent store. Small stores are always affected by their larger, more powerful neighbors. In the center, the small store is extremely dependent on the large anchor store. If the anchor store decides to open seven days a week, the small store must reluctantly do the same. Because the large anchor store pays the most rent, it tends to dominate the overall policy of the center.

Because of this too-close relationship, as well as rising rents and some other problems, many small independent stores were forced to close down in the early 1970's. Sometimes they left empty spaces behind them; there were no newcomers to take their places.

While the small store is under intense pressure from the anchor store in a shopping center, it would be unfair to say that this problem is unique to shopping centers. Many small stores have closed in downtown city areas, too. Their reasons for closing have been similar: high rents, personnel, and security problems.

In the center, as in the downtown shopping area, the decline of the small, independent store is a loss for all retailers, for the independent adds variety, and some offer a special kind of merchandise that improves the total merchandise mix of the center.

Attacks from environmentalists. Large shopping centers with their multi-level garages were singled out as sources of pollution, caused by masses of cars coming, going and parking. Developers began to consider the possibilities of smaller rather than larger centers in order to minimize pollution.

While large regional centers continued to open during the 1970's, their rate of growth slowed. The slowdown was attributed to a variety of causes.

Some observers noted that there had been over-expansion in the 1960's.

One aspect of this slowdown was the failure of small independent stores.

Rising fuel costs in the 1970's hit two ways. Shoppers paid more for fuel for their cars. Casual driving became less casual; this affected shopping patterns in centers.

Enclosed centers had to pay more to maintain their elaborate energy systems which included heating and air-conditioning.

All these factors developed in an atmosphere of recession. The combination of inflation, or rising costs, and recession, tightened budgets and limited spending in all retail stores, in shopping centers and downtown as well.

In spite of slower rate of growth, centers expanded in another direction. The suburbs inspired downtown. Reaching for success, downtown began building its own shopping malls.

But on the whole, the shopping center remained a suburban phenomenon. The large regional center, with its service operations as well as stores, was a way of life and a place to go.

If we want to understand what a shopping center is really like, and what role fashion plays in its overall scheme, we must go beyond abstract ideas and examine a real shopping center in some detail.

First, we turn to Kings Plaza, Brooklyn, New York. It is typical of large, regional centers yet it has its unique features.

Our observations were made during the mid-1970's, and were supplemented by on-the-spot interviews.

Kings Plaza is a completely enclosed mall with its own heating and cooling systems, enclosed garages and an open parking lot. It is a two-level center with four-level anchor stores; Macy's and Alexander's.

Macy's is a national department store chain, carrying hard goods as well as soft goods. The Kings Plaza branch is strong in home furnishings as well as moderate-priced fashion.

Alexander's is a regional promotional chain that emphasizes budget-priced soft

Kings Plaza

SHOPPING CENTER & MARINA

FLATBUSH AVENUE at AVENUE U, BROOKLYN, N.Y.

DIRECTORY

Welcome to Mass Merchandising: At Kings Plaza Shopping Center, this directory greets shoppers who have many stores to shop from, but who will clearly recognize the dominant role played by the two anchors, Alexander's (left) and Macy's (right). While there are scores of other stores selling fashion merchandise at the center, including fairly large units for Bond's and Lerner's, the two anchors loom very large, and have a major influence on shopping center promotional efforts.

goods. Hard goods are limited; there are no major appliances, though there are small appliances.

Kings Plaza is a middle-class center with little high fashion merchandise. It has the wide variety of service operations characteristic of a regional center, including a photography shop and a travel agency.

There are more than 35 clothing stores (including stores that carry clothing for men and children as well as women). Of those 35, about 15 are shoe stores.

Fashion weaves in and out of the program of special events that are part of the center's year-round activities. The mall, with its open space and protecting roof, is an ideal place for special events. There are fashion shows and demonstrations. There are also special events in individual stores.

Antique shows and art shows are good examples of non-fashion special events that often draw fashion customers.

Visiting "petting zoos" for children may bring families, who stay to shop. Boat shows attract affluent visitors who are interested in clothes as well as boats and boating supplies.

According to figures supplied by the executive staff of Kings Plaza, the center draws on potentially 3,400,000 shoppers from surrounding areas, and may be visited by 375,000 to 400,000 shoppers in a given week. Annual gross sales are estimated at $100 million.

Its marina, an unusual feature, was made possible by the coastline location—an example of how geography influences the development of a center. Customers sail into the marina, disembark to shop, and sail off with their purchases. Instead of "stop and shop," boat customers "dock and shop."

Kings Plaza can be reached by mass transportation. This is not as unusual as it was in the 1960's. Customers travel by bus, and some bus lines connect with subways. Brooklyn is part of the metropolitan area of New York City, a blend of urban and suburban, apartment houses and private homes.

The stores of Kings Plaza do some joint promotion; however, most stores promote independently, using local editions of metropolitan newspapers, or local papers and local radio. Joint promotions are generally limited to flyers that appear at holiday time, or at the beginning of a new season.

We have already described Kings Plaza as a middle-class center with little high fashion merchandise; that description covers its small stores and its two anchors.

A comparison between Macy's and Alexander's sheds some light on differences between anchor stores.

Macy's Kings Plaza is a unit in the Macy's New York division of R. H. Macy, the department store chain, with divisions in many parts of the country.

Alexander's is a branch of a regional chain with eight stores in New York, three in New Jersey and one in Connecticut.

Both stores have four floors.

Macy's is a department store with a full line of hard goods and soft goods.

Alexander's is a promotional store, with little in the way of hard goods.

At Macy's, soft goods represent 50 to 60 percent of total merchandise; there would be more hard goods in the downtown flagship store.

At Alexander's the ratio of soft to hard goods is 85 to 15 percent. There are no major appliances.

Macy's carries wide assortments of up-to-date fashion mixed with basics.

Alexander's concentrates on basics.

Macy's covers a wider price range. Its middle price points are higher than the middle price points of Alexander's.

One summer Macy's carried straw tote bags priced at $5.98 to $20, with strength in the $5.98 to $7.98 range. Alexander's carried similar styles, but the assortment was smaller. Price range was $3.98 to $7.98. The main price point was $3.98.

Macy's uses special fixturing to enhance fashion merchandise, while Alexander's relies mostly on standard racks and tables. For instance, a summer display of straw tote bags at Macy's was set up in a pavillion with uprights and beams of natural wood. Espadrilles at Macy's hung from walls covered with netting of natural-colored rope. Alexander's had nothing comparable.

Macy's has its sales and specials, but they do not dominate fashion merchandise as they do at Alexander's.

Macy's has more sales help; at Alexander's, there is more emphasis on self-selection and self-service.

While anchor stores set the tone of Kings Plaza, they are only part of the whole. Many other stores sell fashion merchandise. There are youth stores like No Name and The Gap. (We will discuss those stores in Chapter 15.)

Young people shop in many stores at Kings Plaza, and many merchants appeal to their tastes. Some of their favorite themes grow out of the basic attitude known as funk. There is the tacky funk of patched, frayed jeans and the pop-art funk of a T-shirt, screen-printed with a message or portrait of a favorite movie star or TV personality.

There is the somewhat toned-down, elegant funk reserved for the woman who is not in her teens; it refers to fashion merchandise that is daring in color or design, but not like funky fashions worn by the very young.

A store that specializes in elegant clothes may add a touch of funk to sharpen its fashion image.

No Problem is an example of a fashion shop in Kings Plaza that specializes in up-to-date designer looks. Prices go well over $100. Long sweater coats and printed chiffon evening separates are elegant; beaded and sequined wedgie shoes add a touch of funk.

This store caters to women with a serious interest in chic. Decor is in keeping with the merchandise. There are attractive chandeliers, contemporary black-and-white carpeting and well-tended wall racks. The racks do not dominate the store. Customers do not feel that every piece of merchandise is on display; on the contrary, there is a pleasing balance between merchandise and decor.

Traditional salespeople offer traditional service. This is not a self-selection store. The atmosphere is low-pressure, and customers are allowed to browse.

Other fashion stores in Kings Plaza pursue their customer with different merchandise. The Silver Plum, an independent store, sells dresses, sportswear and accessories. Prices are lower than the prices of No Problem, but there is a definite awareness of fashion. Many young people shop at The Silver Plum, but it is not a youth store; mature women also shop there.

"We sell pants, but we're not a jeans store," is the way the manager, expresses her sense of the store's fashion image.

Simple evening gowns of crepe and matte jersey with or without matching jackets are a specialty of the store and can be made to order. There is a swatch book, and a choice of some trimmings, including feathers. The shop often puts together bridal parties, working well in advance. Prices are moderate. Evening gowns fall easily into the $65 to $85 price range.

While the atmosphere is informal, The Silver Plum is a service store. Salespeople are ready to help customers coordinate outfits, including accessories. The shop makes a point of specializing in accessories; hats, scarves, bags and jewelry. Upper wall space is used for pinned displays.

One-of-a-kind and antique or semi-antique jewelry is another category that The Silver Plum likes to emphasize; it is good for gift business, and it adds a little something extra to the store's fashion image. Prices range from $20 for a carnelian ring to $85 for an old silver compact. Necklaces of frosted crystal and semi-precious beads, old beaded bags and mesh purses are examples of one-of-a-kind accessories that sell well. There are young customers who are willing to spend $50 or $75 for a mesh purse or a necklace. They are the same young women who live in jeans, T-shirts and other inexpensive separates. The inconsistency of spending is typical of contemporary fashion; each customer concentrates her fashion dollars on a favorite category.

Although jewelry is usually non-returnable, The Silver Plum has worked out a compromise arrangement that encourages gift selling. The salesperson notes on the receipt, "Gift—to be given January 24th." The customer may present the receipt and jewelry for exchange within five days after the date noted on the receipt.

Attitude, another small specialty store, is one of a two-unit chain. The Kings Plaza shop has an advantageous corner location with closed windows. An inventive arrangement of fitting rooms makes good use of space. They are parallel to an outside wall, with shutter doors that open into the store. Fitting rooms alternate with windows. Seen from the outside, the wall of the store presents a view of window strips alternating with blank panels, which are the backs of the fitting rooms. In this way, one wall fills two functions.

Attitude is something like The Silver Plum in that it is a service store with salespeople who sell, make suggestions, help customers assemble and coordinate outfits, and in general do more than take money and wrap.

Attitude focuses on daytime wear, emphasizing sportswear and separates. There are few accessories. In summer, there is beachwear, including swimsuits. Typical moderate-to slightly-higher-prices include a $23 beach shift and a $63 smock in an unusual ombré cotton fabric. The fashion tone is smart in a casual way—this is not a store for drop-dead chic. Like The Silver Plum, Attitude caters to a youngish, sophisticated customer.

The fashion coordinator, who is in effect the manager of Attitude, is involved in many tasks at one time. At a given moment, she may be doing any or all of the following:

1. Examining a $27 blouson top that has just been unpacked. Is it ready to go into stock?
2. Minding a baby in a stroller. The mother left the baby "for just a minute while I do one errand."
3. Answering the phone, saying calmly, "Thank you for calling Attitude" and then going on to talk with a customer.
4. Worrying that the windows have not been changed for two weeks. Corner stores are good for traffic, but people do not like to see the same styles over and over again. It takes many changes to keep them interested.
5. Wondering how she is going to get off the phone to take care of two customers who have just come into the store. There is only one saleswoman on the floor at the moment; the other saleswoman is out to lunch (it is 2:30 P.M.).
6. Talking to the writer who is observing all this action, and explaining the nature of the store.

The baby starts to cry, the customer on the phone is insistent, the saleswoman says she has not had lunch yet, the customers are getting impatient and the writer is waiting. The manager keeps her cool, and eventually, everything is taken care of. She will go out to "lunch" at 4 P.M.

Lerner Shops is a national specialty chain that sells women's and children's wear at budget prices. There are 476 Lerner stores in 40 states.

Lerner's has still another kind of fashion image. It represents an assimilation of contemporary trends that are passing into basic fashion. Styles are clean and simple, with a minimum of fussy details. This is in contrast to many inexpensive clothes that pile on fussy details and look the worse for being overdone. Lerner's manages to steer a fashion course safely between the avant-garde and the dowdy.

Unlike Alexander's, it does not stress off-price promotional merchandise though it does stress value for the money.

Unlike Attitude and The Silver Plum, it is not a service store.

Unlike Macy's, it does not have the assortment and variety of fashion merchandise catering to different sizes, price levels and specific age groups.

Unlike the youth stores, it does not focus on a special customer group. We find merchandise in Lerner's that is similar to merchandise in most or all of these other stores, but despite similarities, and even overlapping, the Lerner image comes through clearly.

30

The Lerner customer will find a long dress she can wear in the evening for $25, and it will be in good taste, not overly fussy or sleazy. It will not be high-fashion or funky. She will find sportswear and separates, and simple dresses. In the winter she will find coats. Lerner's is a clothing store; there are few accessories.

Lerner's proves that neatness and pleasing appearance need not be elaborate. Good, clear-but-not-harsh lighting comes from fixtures that are clusters of simple globes in two colors.

Carousel racks are neatly arranged; merchandise is not packed so tightly that customers cannot pull out an individual garment. The center top of the round carousel rack is used as a base for a dressed mannequin, suggesting a coordinated outfit.

There is one open window opening on to the mall, and another closed window. There are fitting rooms. Signage is clear and simple. Sections of softly colored wallpaper and a few floral decals help create a neat, light atmosphere.

In the summer, knit tank tops under $5 and chenille beach jackets at $9 are good buys. Self-service displays of packaged socks are placed near the cashier's desk to draw last-minute impulse sales.

The differences between service, self-selection, and self-service are finely shaded. Lerner's comes closest to self-selection. There is someone to point out the sweater section, or the size 14 dress rack. But the saleswoman who initiates a sale and moves it along by suggesting, reassuring and presenting is not part of the scene at Lerner's. Customers do not expect it; they are independent, quite willing to look around themselves. Because the store is not large, customers do not get lost—they can find their way around easily. Good displays and well-organized stock are the "silent selling staff."

We started off our discussion of Kings Plaza by describing it as middle-range, with concentration on sportswear. Yet we have seen, in our analyses of stores, how many different fashion images that overall image covers! There are stores that overlap, yet each may have one feature that makes it different, so that women will turn to it for its antique jewelry, or its special bridal service, or its elegant funk, or its clean-cut, budget-priced clothes.

There are also important differences in service and presentation. Merchandise, service and presentation are the ingredients that set the tone of the overall center, as they set the tone of an individual store. The center is a mixture; the sum of its parts.

For a look at a very different mixture, and a very different fashion tone, we turn to "The Galleria" in Houston, Texas. For the sake of clarity, we will refer to it as "Galleria."

Galleria is a three-level enclosed mall patterned on a famous shopping area in Milan, Italy, from which it takes its name, and its high, vaulted ceiling. Neiman-Marcus and Lord & Taylor are its anchor stores.

Houston is a prosperous city, so Galleria is assured of affluent customers. The center has two hotels, each with 500 rooms. These hotels attract many business conventions, as well as other visitors to the city.

Six high-speed glass elevators, a private club with tennis courts and an ice-skating rink are among Galleria's special features. If Kings Plaza customers can dock and shop, Galleria customers can skate and shop.

The fashion image of a center anchored by prestige specialty stores like Lord & Taylor and Neiman-Marcus is very different from the image of a center like Kings Plaza. There is more emphasis on high-priced merchandise and luxuries.

The store list of Galleria includes Bally of Switzerland (shoes), Mark Cross/Cartier (leather goods and jewelry), Tiffany & Co. (jewelry) and Parke Bernet (the internationally famous art auctioneers).

Galleria reflects its Southwest background in fashion and in other goods and services. Jeans were work clothes of the frontier, and were worn by ranchers and cowboys, so it is quite natural that Galleria's list of member stores shows names like House of Jeans and Jeans West, as well as The Gap. The Turquoise Lady specializes in American Indian jewelry. Moving beyond fashion, there is the Sam Houston Book Store, and El Fenix Mexican Restaurant.

The services that Galleria offers include some aimed at affluent customers. Many centers have a bank; Galleria also has a stock brokerage. There are four travel agencies, one in Neiman-Marcus.

It would be unfair to say that Galleria carries only expensive merchandise. Many of its stores cover the important middle-price ranges. But the overall image of this center is an image of affluence.

There are many services available to customers in a large center, some provided by individual stores, and some, by the center, for all customers of all stores. We can get an idea of some of these services by looking at some excerpts from an issue of Galleria's newsletter.

The shopping center newsletter is a useful tool. It helps stores keep informed about each other, and it provides them with information about overall center activities that they can pass along to their customers.

In a Christmas issue of its newsletter, Galleria informed its member stores about a special photo service. A story headlined, "Instant Photos with Santa" told readers that "Santa arrived on ice skates the day after Thanksgiving . . . children or adults can have an instant color photo made with the old gent from 10 A.M. to 8 P.M. . . . for $2.49 . . . please inform your salespeople . . . so that they can tell inquiring customers."

Another item told member stores that "Southern Fabrics (a member store) had a real interest shown in Ultra Suede. Ladies have taken classes in how to sew this wonderful fabric. In November, two fashion shows were presented by Krestine Corbin, a representative of Ultra Suede, who shows a wardrobe valued at $6,000."

One successful, high-price center deserves another. That's what has happened in rapidly growing, oil-rich Houston which produced the Galleria, anchored by Neiman-Marcus and including Tiffany and Cartier/Mark Cross, and has now added on a lush Galleria 2, with its main tenant Lord & Taylor. Photo shows the original Galleria in a dramatic long shot indicating ice skating on the bottom level, and the intricate and expensive ceiling. Facing page: artist's concept shows the projected Galleria 2 as very roomy, very bright, and very attractive as befits a center whose prices say ''oil country.''

Other news items announced an ice show, the location of special holiday gift wrap stations, and the location of a site where shoppers could buy Christmas stockings for stuffing.

We have written of the shopping center as a suburban development of increasing size and diversity. However, the shopping center began to assume new forms in the 1970's.

Spurred by environmentalists, shopping center developers and planners began to "think small." They invented Mini-malls, boutique centers, and small groups of shops that were, in effect, malls within malls.

Shopping centers moved downtown, as city planners looked for ways to revive downtown shopping areas.

Our chapter would not be complete without some discussion of the charges critics have levelled against shopping centers.

Pollution caused by cars was the most serious charge.

Architectural critics described some centers as blight upon the landscape. Others noted that elaborate plans for indoor architectural features dwindled to benches and plastic plants. Piped-in music and poor quality of food in restaurants were among other criticisms.

As for fashion, critics say that clothes in shopping centers look alike to the point of monotony, and that variety somehow flattens out as stores draw closer to each other.

Clearly, shopping centers have critics as well as friends.

Following is a summary of highlights of shopping center growth and development.

- The shopping center is a product of the suburbs. It was invented because it was needed.
- Early shopping centers were strips or rows of stores.
- The large regional center was the high point of shopping center growth.
- The role of fashion in the shopping center is one aspect of the economic level of the center, and the income level of its customers.
- The shopping center is a center of community activity as well as a group of stores.
- Evening hours accommodate shoppers with no free time during the day.
- Anchor stores set the fashion tone, and the overall tone of the shopping center.
- The anchor store of a large center is almost always a branch of a large chain.
- Sportswear is the most important fashion category in most centers.
- Fashion stores pursue the youth market actively in shopping centers.
- Merchandise assortments are limited in shopping centers as compared to downtown because space is limited.
- The traditional enclosed window display is eliminated in many stores in shopping centers. The interior of the stores becomes, in effect, the window.
- The character, and fashion character, of shopping centers is as varied as the communities they serve.
- Centers in affluent communities are tenanted by high-fashion stores selling high-priced merchandise.
- Centers in middle-class communities are tenanted by stores that concentrate on basic fashion.
- Pollution is a serious charge levelled against centers by critics, who are often concerned with the quality of environment.
- The car is the essential link between customer and shopping center.
- Almost half the merchandise sold in shopping centers is fashion merchandise.
- Sameness and lack of diversity of fashion merchandise is a real danger, especially in large shopping centers.

- The small independent store has had a hard time surviving in shopping centers, as it has downtown.
- There are similarities, as well as differences, between retailing downtown, and in the shopping center.

The shopping center has come a long way from the small strip of stores by the side of the highway. It has grown and diversified, keeping pace with suburban growth. It has gone past offering of merchandise to offering of service and entertainment. The largest shopping centers are places where people go when they want to see a movie or a fashion show; a basketball demonstration or a demonstration of how to tie a scarf.

In spite of problems and criticisms, it seems safe to predict that the shopping center will endure because it fills so many needs for so many people.

Image:
How Customers
See the Store

5

People perceive a store in a certain light; that light is the store's image. Image is the sum total of impressions the store leaves in the minds of those who enter its doors, or look at its ads, or hear about it from friends. Everything a store does and is contributes something to its image: sales help, service, decor, layout, advertising, gift wrapping and, of course, merchandise.

Retailing, like any other business, reflects the personality of managers and owners. In the past, merchants built great stores that reflected a point of view. Neiman-Marcus, with its luxury and extravagance, was one such store. Ohrbach's, with its image of thrift plus a touch of fashion, was another.

The late Dorothy Shaver, who was president of Lord & Taylor, made that store into a unique retail operation. She pioneered in discovering and promoting American designers. She was one of the first, if not *the* first, retailer to understand the boutique concept. She discovered artists who created advertising so special that newspaper readers could identify it without reading the store name.

Whatever a store's image is, it starts from the top, and is established as a result of top management policy. Sometimes image is simple and clear-cut, as in a highly promotional store that sells price, or, at the other end of the spectrum, a high fashion store that sells nothing but expensive designer merchandise.

Most stores, especially large stores, have more complex images. Sometimes a store's image is unclear; this is because management has not made clear-cut decisions.

What is our image? What should it be? After store executives have asked themselves these two key questions, many other questions must be asked—and answered.

- Should we depend on assortment? This is a traditional department store image. The store has the best selection of sweaters or swimsuits; it is an image of completeness.
- Should we offer our customers the newest fashions? This is a traditional

specialty store image. Sometimes management will question a new look or a new style, and ask, is this right for our customers? Do they want this kind of look?

- Should we offer clothes in the highest price ranges? Top designer clothes? How high should we go?
- If we are a high-priced store, should we also offer moderately priced fashions? How much of each? Which will dominate?
- Do we want an image of somewhat conservative fashions that will reassure a customer who looks to us as an authority? How much that is new should we show? Are we better off with updated basics than with the very latest styles?
- Are we trying to appeal to young people? Mature women? Are we trying to appeal to too many customer groups? Are we spreading ourselves too thin?
- Should we emphasize our private label merchandise more and brands less? Are our brands and designers different? Are we offering any exclusives? Is there anything in our store that is not available everywhere else?
- What can we do to create exclusivity in some category? What can we offer that is really special and different? Are we doing enough in this direction? Are we playing fashion too safe?
- What kind of sales help do we really have? Can we call ourselves a full service store? Should we concentrate on self-selection because that is more realistic?
- How fast do our lines move at check-out counters in self-selection departments?
- Should we continue services like gift-wrapping? Can we do this efficiently at holiday time?
- Does our advertising reflect our image? Is it distinctive? Do we have a recognizable store logo that is repeated in advertising, on shopping bags, and wrapping?
- Do we live up to our fashion claims? Is our merchandise as attractive as our advertising? Does our merchandise look so much better in our ads than it does in the store that customers are disappointed when they see the real thing?
- Are we changing so that we keep up with the times?
- Have we moved fast enough to keep up with our customers?
- Have we moved too fast for our customers? Traded up too much? Should we slow down a little?

Some retailers change their image frequently; a change in direction may reflect a change in top management. Other stores are afraid of any change; they play it safe and stay with proven successes.

Wilmer Weiss, a top retailing executive with a strong background in both department and specialty store merchandising, believes in change that he describes as "continuing but not radical." (In 1977, Mr. Weiss was senior vice president, corporate fashion and design, Dayton-Hudson, the midwestern department store chain. Earlier, he had been a vice president of Franklin Simon, the specialty store chain.)

"We are in an exciting era of change," comments Mr. Weiss. "Not only in fashion itself, but change in what a department store is, and what a specialty store is.

"The department store is becoming a new kind of marketplace, based on style of living rather than category. The good department store can offer leisure clothes, table settings, wine glasses, bottle openers, and linens. Or, it can offer swimsuits, sandals, sunglasses, beach umbrellas, and patio furniture.

"While the department store goes after this rather wide range of customers, the specialty store is more likely to zero in on a particular customer group identified by price points or attitude; perhaps the upper middle class, or the middle middle class. It will offer interpretations of traditional, designer and contemporary looks for its particular customer group.

"We now have four different levels of fashion, each with its own image—traditional, update, contemporary and junior.

"To be more specific; we can project a storm coat 'through' those four levels, and we can see that each level will create a different fashion image aimed at a different customer group.

"A traditional storm coat might be a twill jacket.

"The updated version would be longer, if longer lengths are fashionable, with a notched collar or some new fashion detail.

"The contemporary storm coat might be a poplin cape, hooded and lined in a blanket plaid.

"The junior storm coat could be an ankle-length poplin coat, hooded, belted and toggle-buttoned."

A retailer with a strong background in mass merchandising puts together an image made up of component parts. Each part represents a customer group. Mass merchandise chains must make a wide appeal that will draw many customer groups.

But a specialty store can do what its name describes—it can specialize. It can sharpen its fashion image as it pinpoints its customer.

Geraldine Stutz, president of Henri Bendel, describes her store as "either the largest boutique or the smallest specialty store in the world." Ms. Stutz focuses on one customer group, the affluent, fashion-conscious woman. She foresees a time when fashion image will split sharply into two very different parts.

"There will be special stores, like Bendel's, with very highly selected, individual, up-to-date merchandise," predicts Ms. Stutz, "And then there will be great supermarkets."

"In between there is a broad area of medium-priced clothes that are actually getting very expensive—they're nowhere. The middle area is where both department and specialty stores are losing ground.

40

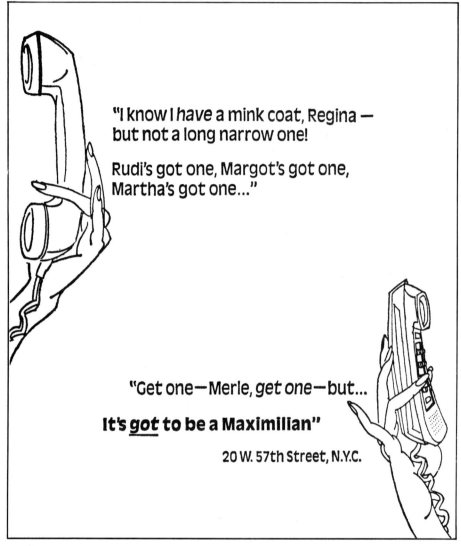

Small space ads (appearing throughout this chapter) build image for four very different New York City retailers. In this ad, Maximilian, prestigious furrier, relies on witty dialogue and simple line drawing to reinforce image of exclusivity. (Actual size of ad.)

Come! Eat! Enjoy!
It's Italian Week at Bonwit's and all along Fifth Avenue.

Bonwit's is treating you to a taste of Italy.
The place? The Kitchen on our Seventh Floor.

Thursday, April 14th from 12:00 to 2:00
SIGNOR BUGIALLI, author of "Master of the
Fine Art of Italian Cooking," puts together
a Renaissance meal with his contemporary
adaptations of classical recipes.
5:00 to 7:00 Italian Wine Tastings.

Friday, April 15th from 12:00 to 2:00
ANDRE DODI demonstrates the art of making
espresso Zabaglione with Medaglia d'Oro
espresso coffee—the espresso that can
be made in any coffee pot.

Saturday, April 16th from 1:00 to 3:00
LARRY GOLDBERG of Goldberg's Pizzeria shows
you how to make a pizza anything but ordinary!

Monday, April 18th from 12:00 to 2:00
FERRARA's pastry chef tells all about
the fine art of Italian pastry.

Tuesday, April 19th from 12:00 to 2:00
SHERRI ZITRON of the School of Contemporary
Cooking prepares a variety of antipasto.

Wednesday, April 20th from 12:00 to 2:00
ARMANDO ORSINI, in his first public appearance,
shares some of his secret pasta recipes.

BONWIT TELLER

The Kitchen, Seventh Floor, Fifth Avenue at 56th Street, New York.

Gourmet food is fashion. Bonwit Teller invites famous food experts to appear in its store. High fashion food adds luster to the store's high fashion image. (Actual size of ad.)

42

"Bendel's customer is special; clothes are part of her life but she doesn't want to be worn by her clothes; she is also interested in her home, her work, her causes . . . she doesn't wear conventional clothes. We don't have a coat department or a suit department. Our customer wears separates, furs, layers, capes, anoraks; she wears dresses mostly in the evening.

"She relies on us to bring her components that she can put together for her own individual look. We are ready to help her, to guide her, but never to dictate to her. That is our image, and I see only one other possible image for the future.

"Picture a marvelous, clean supermarket of fashion. You drive up, exchange your money for scrip or slugs, walk down an aisle, see a pair of corduroy jeans, maybe behind glass. There is a glass panel where you see a color range of 12 shades, there's a card that tells you sizes and prices. It's all done by computer. You drop your slugs in a slot and out come the jeans.

"You put them in your shopping bag and walk out of the store. You don't even have to go through a check-out.

"All the merchandise is classic; jeans, shirts, leotards . . . whatever is accepted.

"This eliminates the problem of service and salespeople.

"This kind of packaged classic is what Americans do best. It will be the way most people shop. Even people who can afford special and individual clothing at high prices will buy some basics in a fashion supermarket, just as people who buy food in the finest small gourmet shops also shop in food chains for staples."

Ms. Stutz sees fashion retailing in the future as highly specialized—a sort of two-lane highway in which the third, middle lane is absorbed. Other retailers see more of a future for middle-of-the road approaches, and stores that maintain a clear image while appealing to a variety of customer groups.

"It is possible to maintain a quality fashion image while broadening customer appeal," comments Allan R. Johnson, chairman of the board, Saks Fifth Avenue. Mr. Johnson counted 31 Saks stores in 14 states as of 1977, mostly in the East.

"We have had to broaden our customer base," notes Mr. Johnson, "The carriage trade is still important, but we are appealing to a wider group of upper-middle class people, in the $25,000 to $50,000 income brackets.

"Our image is based on service and selection. We are determined to remain a full-service store. We are also determined that our branches must carry stock in depth.

"We are projecting a strong designer image; designer image has eclipsed overall store image.

"Adolfo, Bill Blass, Calvin Klein—these are just a few of our top designer names. A high fashion store must showcase its designers so that customers constantly associate these prestigious names with the store.

"The appearance of the designer is vital. Women want to meet the person behind the clothes. In many communities, a designer's appearance is an important social event.

The store that can be a meeting place for customer and designer will keep its fashion image fresh and clear."

We noted at the beginning of this chapter that image is the sum of impressions, the way people see a store.

But do customers see what retailers want them to see?

Alfred Eisenpreis, vice president-retail marketing of the Newspaper Advertising Bureau and a former retailing executive, is critical of retailers who think image is the solution to all their problems. Mr. Eisenpreis urges retailers to look below the surface. "Beware of confusion between image and identity," he warns.

"Image is what you show. In fashion, image may be the high fashion styles a store buys a few of just to show them. But that is not what the store sells. Image is all very well if you want to show and not to sell.

"But you must have identity if you want to sell.

"Image is a mask, and a form of make-believe. A store's identity must be real. It can focus on service, assortment, avant-garde styles, youth-oriented styles. It can aim at an age group or an economic group. It can be self-service or self-selection—those are perfectly good identities if they work."

A store's identity must run parallel to the taste of its customers. But what is taste? How will it change in the future? Mr. Eisenpreis measures possibilities for the future by taking a long view of the past.

"Taste is the totality of a society and cannot be separated from it," says Mr. Eisenpreis. "Most people have tried to isolate a single reason for changes in taste and have always been unsuccessful. Sometimes they say Paris alone has shaped taste. That was never true."

"Taste was and is action and reaction, the combined reaction of total pressures.

"Taste is a way of living with today, the 'today' being any era.

"The new exposure to influences has changed everything. No longer is a woman exposed merely to a Penney's or a Sears catalogue. There are personalities, movies, magazines—probably magazine influence has declined somewhat.

"Today, a designer brings the totality of the whole art world to clothes. Museum art has been adapted to the consumer and there is a proliferation of artistic experimentation, a readiness to experiment that is reflected in fashion.

"This readiness to experiment really started towards the end of World War I and was speeded up by the advent of the nuclear age and other modern inventions.

"Take the electric light. Colors looked different under candlelight and gaslight. A lot of things went unnoticed. But the stronger light of electricity brings color out into the open, makes it a more important element of fashion.

"People didn't use to work in offices—they worked in sweat shops, or they were

44

Loehmann's

A great many
important women
will be appearing
at Loehmann's
this week.

*(All of them our customers
shopping for Spring fashions)*

BRONX, BROOKLYN, QUEENS, N.Y. • HEWLETT, HUNTINGTON, BAY SHORE, L.I.
WHITE PLAINS, MT. VERNON, MT. KISCO, HOWARD BEACH, N.Y.
PARAMUS, E. BRUNSWICK, FLORHAM PARK, N.J. • NORWALK, CONN.

Bronx Store Open To 9:30 Monday Through Saturday Evenings;
All Other Stores Open To 9:30 Wednesday Evenings.

Loehmann's, known for its markdown bargains and hectic atmosphere, pulls a switch. The low-key, tongue-in-cheek invitation is a bid for dignity and more of a fashion image. (Actual size of ad.)

farmers. Women didn't work outside the home at all. What do you need to wear when you milk a cow, or sit over a sewing machine?"

Women no longer need clothes for milking cows—it is done by machine. But such questions have implications for the future. What will women wear as their activities change? As they work in more diversified jobs? Cope with an energy shortage? Travel in outer space? Stores will change as customers' needs change; image will have to keep up with identity.

45

One traditional road to clear image—and identity—has always been open to giant retail chains. With their large customer audience, and their buying power, they have been able to create and sell private label merchandise. (In upper price brackets, the exclusive designer merchandise is parallel to the private label, but exclusivity became a thing of the past in the 1970's.)

Private label merchandise carries a label belonging to one store or a chain of stores. The three great national chains—Sears, Ward's and Penney's—have been distributing staple fashions under their own private labels for many years. Because they have been so scrupulously careful about the specifications they give to manufacturers who produce the merchandise, they have acquired reputations for excellent quality.

Private label fashion merchandise is usually limited to staple fashions for two reasons.

1. Staple fashion merchandise has the broad appeal that will satisfy a mass market.
2. The other reason has to do with the nature of fashion itself. Fashion is of the moment. Private label merchandise must be planned and ordered months ahead of the season. If a retailer were to order a dress six months ahead of the season, a fashion change in the interim might make that dress obsolete before it ever reached the store. The store would lose thousands of dollars.

Branded merchandise is advertised by the manufacturer who produces it. Private label merchandise is not advertised by the manufacturer, therefore he can sell it to the store for less, and the store can sell it to the customer at a higher profit per unit.

Private label merchandise enables large department stores to meet competition from three sources:

1. Discounters, who are active in staple merchandise aimed at the mass market;
2. The national chains, who are old hands in the field of private labels;
3. National brands of manufacturers, which are carried in the department stores.

It would seem that the department stores are competing against themselves by carrying both national brands and private labels, but this is not so. The private label merchandise becomes another brand and increases the assortment the store has to offer its customers. Since customers like a wide choice, this diversity becomes a positive factor.

In this chapter, we have discussed image as it pertains to the department or specialty store. But there are many small stores that sell fashion merchandise; they, too, need image and identity if they are to survive. In our next chapter, we shall examine different kinds of small fashion retailing operations, and the problems they face.

46

Rendering of store front, reference to "bi-lingual" clothes is aimed at Henri Bendel's very special customers, who know that "bi-lingual" means imported fashions.

Small Stores: Survival of the Fittest

6

The small store is an endangered species, struggling to adapt to a hostile environment. Rising costs, labor shortages, competition from giant retailers, and losses due to burglary and robbery combine to put many small stores out of business every year.

Yet new owners appear, hopeful that they will make good, attracted by the idea of independence, and a pride in creating something that they can shape and control with their own decisions.

The small store with one or two owners is difficult to manage. Traditionally, small retail operations were owned by families, and were called *mom 'n pop stores*. Sometimes they specialized in shoes or children's clothing. Often, they supplied the clothing needs for the whole family. They were not high fashion stores, nor did they pretend to be. They provided necessities—underwear, socks, dresses, blouses and coats. Mostly, they offered low- to medium-priced merchandise.

The fashion shop was quite different from the mom 'n pop store. It might specialize in dresses, or coats and suits, or lingerie, corsets and bras. In the days when all women wore hats, there were many millinery shops. They catered to different price ranges; the millinery shop with one hat in its window, and no price tag, said, "expensive."

Shops and mom 'n pop stores were an integral part of commercial communities, especially in downtown shopping areas. They provided variety and a change of pace. The customer could move from a large department store to a small store and see different merchandise.

Shops and mom 'n pop stores sometimes located in residential communities, and became neighborhood stores. Often, they drew and held loyal clienteles. Owners were on a first-name basis with their customers. People depended on these stores for everyday clothing and special-occasion clothing.

Small stores contributed color and warmth and sometimes, excitement, to the life of the neighborhood. It is no exaggeration to say that the small store was part of what people liked to call the American way of life.

During the 1950's, as shopping centers began to grow, the *boutique*, a new kind of small store took root, mostly in urban areas. The name and the idea were French. The idea changed in translation.

In Paris, French couture designers had opened boutiques adjacent to their salons. Designers showed a few styles that were less expensive than their couture designs. The clothes were not custom-made. Ready-to-wear and accessories were displayed together.

Because the boutique was an off-hand experiment, designers could afford to take chances. They produced only two or three pieces of each style. They tried out ideas, some more amusing and daring than the expensive couture clothing. Eventually, these little shops developed a life of their own.

The American boutique also created few-of-a-kind designs. Some were avant-garde and daring. At their best, American boutiques were anti-establishment, ahead of fashion, and inventive.

Some boutique owners had their own workrooms, and did custom or semi-custom work. Others bought from small manufacturers and unknown designers, who were willing to produce in limited quantities.

Smallness kept boutiques flexible. They could drop a bad idea quickly without too much loss, and continue a good idea that caught on. They could move quickly from one style to another.

Fashion-conscious women found that they enjoyed this new way of shopping. It eliminated trudging from department to department, picking up one piece here, another there, being helped by different salespeople, and left to visualize a total look as best they could. Instead, women found everything in one place. In the boutique, dresses, separates and accessories were displayed together; women could visualize a total look instantly, try it on at one time, and buy it from one salesperson. The "salesperson" might well be the owner. Boutique salespeople were friendly and helpful.

Boutiques displayed fashions in their own way. Unlike mass merchandise, where many pieces of the same style hung on a rack, the boutique offered one of each style, and found substitutes for the rack. A dress might hang casually from a screen, an antique table showed off jewelry and other small accessories. The effect was theatrical and amusing.

Even when merchandise was not made to order, the idea of limited quantity was an important aspect of boutique merchandising.

When boutique owners departed from the basic theme of limited quantity, and began to create wholesale collections, and franchised lines, they failed. "Quantity" and "boutique" were like oil and water; they did not mix. Smallness, individuality and service were the keys to true boutique merchandising.

Many stores that called themselves boutiques did not deserve the name; they were trying to cash in on an idea.

Large department and specialty stores added boutique departments. Some of the best specialty stores had invented the boutique on their own, bringing in special merchandise, or culling the best merchandise from different departments and bringing it together in one spot.

Department stores, on the whole, were unsuccessful; the policies of mass merchandising ran counter to boutique merchandising.

Though the boutique movement lost momentum in the 1970's, its philosophy survived. Almost every successful small fashion shop is a boutique in at least one sense of the word: it is special, it represents the owner's point of view.

Its "specialness" may derive from an unusually good assortment. None of the merchandise is exclusive, but the shop owner has hand-picked it. Or, the merchandise may represent a certain fashion mood; contemporary, daring or conservative. It will certainly focus on a price range; middle, middle-high, or high.

The tone of the merchandise will be consistent. It will reach a specific customer group.

The successful fashion shop must also provide good service; helpful, friendly and low-pressure. In this way, it is different from old-fashioned shops, which were often formal and high-pressure.

Informal atmosphere; open, attractive display; friendly, helpful service; merchandise that represents a clear-cut image—these are ingredients of the successful small fashion store.

Many owners with a flair for fashion are doomed to fail before they start because they have not planned properly. Money is important; success does not happen overnight, unless the owner is an experienced merchant with an established clientele.

Most stores must lose money over a period of time before they show a profit. During that time, bills must be paid; it is those bills, and that lean time, that the prospective owner must anticipate.

The small store owner must pay many costs continually once the store is open. Rent, utility bills and maintenance of the store are all important. Advertising may be necessary to attract a clientele. All these costs, and others less obvious, must be planned for; the owner should ask, before opening a new store, "Will I have enough to cover all my costs?"

Among the less obvious costs new owners often overlook are uncollectable bills, damaged and stolen merchandise, theft and fire insurance, taxes, and interest on loans.

Income is another problem; owners who have no outside income may draw too much money from the store for their own personal expenses.

There are many drains on the new store. Even one salary can be a burden. The great advantage of the mom 'n pop store was that there were no salaries to pay. In the

1970's, an owner almost certainly needed some help unless friends were willing to pitch in.

If friends pitched in, then the store was, in effect, a mom 'n pop store, with a substitute family.

But the prospective owner should beware of friends who "promise" to help. Such promises often fade away once the store is open. People mean well, but something else comes up, or they did not realize how taxing and confining the work would be, and since they are not being paid, or they are being paid a very small, token salary, they feel free to drop out.

The loneliness of the small store owner is often underestimated because people assume that customers provide all the "company" an owner needs. It is not so. Customers can be extremely difficult and demanding.

The owner must work long hours. Families of owners of stores who are not involved in the store operation often complain that they are neglected. Owners, under pressure in business, find themselves also under pressure at home.

Owners must divide their time among many tasks: keeping records, dealing with customers, going into the market to buy merchandise, arranging displays and supervising employees. All these activities call for a wide range of skills.

Owners who want to design and create their own merchandise often find that they are so pre-occupied with minding the store that they have insufficient creative energy left for designing.

Often, small store owners become so burdened with work that they are isolated in their stores. Isolation can be harmful. They do not get out to see what their competition is doing. They lose track of what is happening in the world of fashion. This affects their merchandise; they may stay with out-of-date fashions, or adopt very avant-garde fashions. They may use their stores to express their own personal ideas about fashion; making or buying clothes they like, instead of trying to please customers.

Every prospective store owner should ask himself or herself some soul-searching questions, and decide not to make a move until the answers are right.

- Do I have enough money to keep the store going before I show a profit? Do I have enough money to live on during that time?
- Am I choosing a good location? Who will come to such a store? Is the merchandise I have in mind right for that customer?
- Am I going to depend on word-of-mouth and traffic off the street? Is that enough? Or must I advertise to bring in customers? How much will I have to spend on advertising and other forms of promotion?
- Do I have the managerial skills I need to run a store?
- Do I have the physical stamina that I need to work as hard as I will have to work?
- Am I willing to sacrifice my personal life? Friends? Vacations?

Owners of successful small fashion stores have different personalities and tastes, but they share talents and skills. They have made the right choices. They are capable of hard work and sacrifice. They have survived the early, lonely days.

In the long run, survival is the only real proof of success.

Owners of a store that has survived for more than twenty years have obviously made decisions worth studying.

Serendipity 3, a New York City boutique that opened its doors in 1954, was still going strong in 1977, when owners Stephen Bruce and Calvin Holt estimated 1976 volume at "about $1 million." Mr. Bruce and Mr. Holt own the small, five-story building in which Serendipity is located. The store occupies the first two floors. Upper floors house a design studio and offices. The neighborhood is affluent and fashionable.

Serendipity is a combination restaurant-boutique. The restaurant is known for its interesting food and snacks, and draws many celebrities during the day and late at night.

Clothes are produced by small contractors. Merchandise is current and covers a wide price range, from a $10 T-shirt to an $800 gown.

Opening a restaurant and selling novel T-shirts is not a sure-fire formula for success, but Serendipity is worthwhile analyzing, for some elements of its survival are typical of boutique merchandising at its best.

Owner presence is good for business. Customers like to feel that they are in contact with "the boss." From the owner's point of view, it is always worthwhile to hear what customers have to say about merchandise; what they like, what they don't like, and why. At Serendipity, one or both owners are in the store constantly although hours are long. The store is open seven days a week from late morning to late at night. The longest day is Saturday, starting at 11:30 A.M. and ending at 2 A.M.

The shop is a theater. The more theatrical it is, the more often customers will come in to see what is showing. On one St. Patrick's Day, a round table in back of the restaurant displayed interesting Irish cakes, some frosted green. A clothes line was strung across the store. Clothespins held copies of Irish newspapers. Four-leaf clovers of green felt echoed the green felt vests the waiters wore. This kind of ingenious, relatively inexpensive use of props and decor is at the heart of successful boutique merchandising.

Decor and merchandise mix together casually. This is another principle of successful boutique merchandising. Plants, baskets, and clothes hang side by side. Counters are deliberately crowded with a pleasing clutter; their tops are almost hidden by displays of small objects; boxes of soaps, folded T-shirts, scarves and candles. Careful shopping at auctions yielded permanent props, which became fixtures in the restaurant. Tiffany glass shades and a huge clock from an old building are part of the decor of Serendipity's ground floor restaurant.

Other props change from time to time. A cache of old paintings, bought at an auction, will introduce an art deco theme into the upstairs restaurant area—for a while. The paintings can always be removed and stored.

Merchandise is current, yet individual. If caftans are in fashion, the shop will do caftans, but in a special fabric, or with a special trim. If laced corselets are in fashion, the store will slit T-shirts and lace them up the front. Serendipity carries boots, but will not stock a line that is well known because it is offered in major department and specialty stores.

Fashion extends into a source of publicity. When jeans were at the height of their popularity, people brought in their old jeans for remodeling, and asked to have their life stories worked out in patchwork and appliqué. This special service led to a museum of jeans that had been worn by celebrities, which traveled throughout the country, shown under the store name, and found a home as part of the permanent clothing collection of the Costume Institute of the Metropolitan Museum of Art, New York.

Salespeople are low-key; they do not push. They are taught not to make a fuss over visiting celebrities who sometimes want privacy.

Diversification creates flexibility. The combination of restaurant and fashion is unique. Because tables and chairs can be moved, there are no barriers between the restaurant areas and the selling areas. When fashion slows down, restaurant business takes up the slack. The reverse is also true; when the restaurant business slows down, tables and chairs can be removed from the floor to make way for fashion merchandise.

The boutique is one approach to small store merchandising; there are others, less theatrical and more conventional, that can lead to success. But "more conventional" is a relative term, a store that is too conventional has little chance of success. If it carries no more than a standard selection of safe brand names in low or moderate or high price ranges, few women will be attracted to it. Why should they shop in a store that offers them nothing but the same clothes they find in the large department and specialty stores?

A small store can succeed by carrying mass-produced, brand-name lines, but the owner must shop carefully. Brand names must alternate with a few unusual things from smaller manufacturers. Owners must search continually for the small manufacturer who is willing to work with a store that buys in small quantities.

The small fashion store should zero in on a price range, whether it is low to moderate, moderate to high, or high.

It may specialize in a category; sweaters or shirts, pants or dresses, blouses or accessories, or it may specialize in dressy clothes, or casual clothes. Often, a small store's assortment of merchandise gives it a point of view, an individuality, that makes it special. Whatever that point of view is, it must get across to customers, so that they say, "Oh, yes, Store X is a good place to go for . . ."

One point of view mixes young, sophisticated fashion at comparatively moderate price ranges, concentration on separates, and imaginative coordination of separates.

Lonia, a small New York City shop, opened in 1973. Its owner, Linda Friedman, had charted her own fashion territory carefully. She was looking for a smart, fashion-conscious woman who wanted to keep up with the latest styles, who wore a small size, who had some money and would spend it on clothes, but could not afford astronomical prices of designer fashions running into four figures.

The small shop, with about 400 square feet of selling space, drew traffic from the street; it was a busy, midtown block bustling with hotels and good restaurants, frequented by New Yorkers and visitors to the city.

For more than a year, Ms. Friedman worked alone; buying and selling, keeping records, arranging displays for the interior and the two windows, and scrubbing the floor. In 1977, she had a staff of three. To an observer, her annual volume seemed to fall into the under-$500,000 category.

Because Lonia represents one point of view, owners and prospective owners of small fashion shops may find it worthwhile to study the philosophy behind the store. The following points emerged in conversations with Ms. Friedman:

Pick your customer and sell to her. A fashion-conscious, figure-conscious woman with some money to spend will buy skirts, sweaters, blouses, and dresses that reflect current trends. She will want culottes, or skirts, or envelope bags, or shawls when they are in fashion. She will like separates because she can combine and "play with" colors, fabrics, and textures. Also, she may need a size 10 top and a size 12 skirt; separates help solve some size problems.

If you can give this customer clothes smart enough to satisfy her appetite for fashion, she will come back to you, for she compares your $200 outfit to the much more expensive name designer clothing she sees in prestige specialty stores.

Help your customer put together a wardrobe. Remember that she will be more likely to buy a fall coat if she knows she can wear it over the dark separates she bought last spring.

Help your customer learn how to wear clothes. It is surprising how many well-dressed women are unhappy with their bodies, and unsure of themselves when it comes to picking out and wearing clothes. If you have salespeople, the "how to" of wearing will be part of their training.

Don't abandon the customer in the fitting room. (Lonia has a communal fitting room with a mirrored wall so several women can look at themselves at the same time.) The saleswoman goes into the fitting room, helps the customer adjust clothes, suggests the addition or subtraction of a belt or other accessory, puts a pin in a skirt to show how the length can be changed, talks about how the outfit will look with high-heeled shoes. or low-heeled shoes, different pantyhose, different accessories. Though all the merchandise is not there, the salesperson outlines the total look for the customer, so she can see beyond the merchandise, and through to her complete outfit. This gives her confidence to buy.

Recruit salespeople by word-of-mouth. Talk to friends, manufacturers, suppliers; anyone whose opinion is worth listening to. Selling in a "good" store can be interesting and profitable to women with no previous experience. Part-time hours may attract women looking for a part-time job who do not want to settle into a nine-to-five office routine. It is necessary that salespeople be intelligent and attractive; but they need not be educated, if they are adaptable.

Saleswomen should be attractive. They should be able to wear merchandise and look well in it. A woman entering the store sees the saleswoman before she sees the merchandise. She thinks, "How does this saleswoman look? Would I like to look like that? Yes? Then, I can trust her to give me good advice."

Start training, keep on training. In a small shop, each salesperson can know all the stock all the time—that is not possible in a large store. "Knowing" includes an understanding of what styles will look well on what figure types.

It also includes an ability to mix and match separates. There are no restrictive "departments." One manufacturer's sweater can be combined with another manufacturer's pants; this makes the most of all stock.

Let customers know you care what happens after they buy. At Lonia, customers sometimes phone the store at seven in the evening. They have bought several outfits, but have forgotten which part they meant to wear with which. Salespeople remember and remind them; sometimes a chart helps.

Special instructions about care of merchandise are part of post-selling concern. For example, a white silk blouse may be labeled, "dry clean only." But salespeople know that the blouse can be carefully hand-washed; if it is dry-cleaned many times, it may turn yellow. Customers are always grateful for helpful information.

Flexibility—Communicate with manufacturers. The small store owner is in a position to judge response to a style quickly, and to pass such information along to the manufacturer. Is the yoke on a blouse too low? Perhaps the manufacturer can correct it; this kind of information is invaluable. Many large stores wind up with racks of one style at the end of a season precisely because there was something wrong with it—and that something wrong was never corrected.

If a small store owner can communicate with manufacturers and designers, the result is merchandise that pleases everybody in the three-way communication line: manufacturer, retailer and customer.

Flexibility—Shop the market creatively. A neglected number in a long line that big stores overlooked can turn into an exclusive best seller. Brought into the small store, properly displayed and combined with other merchandise, it takes on new appeal.

Flexibility—Ride the crest of the fashion wave. The small store that aims to "keep up" is sensitive to shifts in emphasis from one fashion category to another. If pants are in the background because there has been no major change in styling for a few seasons, skirts will be more important. Just before a new pants silhouette comes in, customers will buy skirts and ignore pants; they sense that it is time for something new.

The small store that keeps up with fashion reflects this rhythm of stop and go, pause and change. It will emphasize skirts, while the owner keeps an eye out for the next new pants silhouette. Then pants are in, the new silhouette is presented to customers and skirts recede from the spotlight or, at least, share it with the new fashion. The same is true of accessories.

A small store that was first with envelope bags will find its customers tiring of envelope bags while large stores that move more slowly are still promoting them. At that point, the small store will de-emphasize bags, waiting for the next new style, and will offer it as soon as it is available; will even get in on the new shape before the big stores have a chance to promote it heavily. Again, smallness is an advantage, inasmuch as it offers flexibility.

Summing up our discussion of two small stores, we find that Serendipity, the boutique, and Lonia, the fashion shop, are alike in some ways and different in others.

Both stress helpful, low-key service.

One initiates its own merchandise; the other goes to market, but shops the market creatively and creates an unusual assortment.

The boutique presents merchandise against a theatrical background, mixing props and fashion, as well as fashion and a restaurant area. The fashion shop presents merchandise against a simple, unobtrusive background.

Neither the boutique nor the fashion shop advertise; they depend on traffic and word-of-mouth. The boutique has been successful in attracting publicity because of its theatrical approach. Both stores are ideally located in neighborhoods that are busy and prosperous—neighborhoods which draw traffic from the street easily.

TIPS ON DISPLAY AND DECOR

Small store owners who cannot afford expensive props and fixtures often find that a little ingenuity goes a long way. Taste, the will to make do, and some skill with hammer, scissors and other simple tools can create appealing, eye-catching displays. Owners can check off the following list of ideas and add their own:

Keep racks against the wall if possible, and leave the central area of the selling floor open. This makes the store more inviting, easier to move around in, and it is good for security. Central racks set up a barrier behind which thieves can operate; the more cluttered the store, the easier it is for thieves to steal without being noticed.

Better a small window that is changed frequently than a large window that is changed once a month. Try to show accessories with ready-to-wear. Borrow, if necessary, from local merchants on a cooperative basis. Borrow from giftware stores, too, and place a card in the window giving them credit.

Use oversize paper dolls, flat and pinned to the wall, for interior display. Or pin merchandise to the wall. Hang bags from upright poles. Fasten down everything securely so that customers can look, but cannot remove a bag from its anchor.

Accumulate a collection of permanent props by shopping auctions and sales. An old glass bowl can hold belts, combs, purses, or other small accessories. Stools, small chests of drawers and odd pieces of fabric can make good display fixtures, in the store interior, or in the window. Baskets, real plants, and wooden packing crates can become interesting props.

Keep a folding screen handy; you can open it up to form an instant dressing room when the store is crowded. It can also be used as a backdrop in a window display.

Sweep, vacuum, empty waste baskets. Nothing is more unfashionable then lint on the carpet and dirty cleaning tissues in the waste paper basket.

Unless you are appealing to a teenage customer group, be firm about eating in the store; one ice-cream cone can ruin a dress. Keep an eye on small children, and ask their parents to restrain them. Keep an eye on pets. Try to be tactful if you must ask an adult to restrain a pet or a child; you must protect your store, but people take offense easily.

If you are doubtful about decor, start off with a light color of paint on your walls. It is much easier to cover light tones with a darker shade than it is to cover dark or bright colors with a light shade. If you use wallpaper, be sure to use paper that peels off; avoid any wall covering that must be steamed off. Steaming is an expensive process.

If you are fixing up your own store, keep it simple. You do not have to have fancy rugs or expensive wall coverings. That can come later. If you want color, consider inexpensive posters.

Keep a guest book. Ask everyone who comes in the store to sign it. This will help you build a direct-mail list. It is a nice personal touch. It can help you with security, too—if you spot suspicious characters, you can ask them, politely, to sign the guest book. Their response will clue you in to their real intentions—thieves do not like to sign anything, even with a false name.

Take a style out of the window if you do not have it in stock. Nothing annoys a customer more than an attractive piece of merchandise in the window that is unavailable in the store.

In our next chapter, we will move on to the point of view of the large store. Selling fashion and sales training in a large store are very different from selling in a small store. Though a saleswoman in a large store must be well informed, she cannot possibly know everything about all the fashion merchandise in a large store; it is all she can do to keep up with her own department.

Store size changes the way fashion is sold, and the way management trains people to sell. The small store owner, training a handful of employees, behaves quite differently from the large store, with a personnel department and a sales training division.

As we conclude this chapter, we may well ask if the small store has a future. The question is easier to raise than to answer.

It would be a pity if small stores did not survive, for they provide excitement, a change of pace, and a sense of personal contact that seems to be disappearing from our daily lives.

What Salespeople Should Know: Techniques of Selling

What is so special about fashion merchandise? Why is it different from oranges or cereal? Why can't a customer pick a skirt as easily as she picks a box of cereal off the supermarket shelf?

There is such a thing as the supermarket approach to selling fashion. It applies to basic, mass merchandise, which can sell off the rack or the shelf with almost no sales help—the customer helps herself.

But the store that offers up-to-date fashion merchandise needs salespeople. This year's skirt is not a box of cereal. Style, color, and fabric are different. These differences raise questions in the customer's mind.

How does this new style look on me? How does it fit into my wardrobe? Will it wrinkle easily? Wash? Should I shorten or lengthen it? These are just a few typical questions that women ask themselves before they buy.

The more special or up-to-date merchandise is, the more it needs a person to present it and sell it.

In this chapter, we will examine the role of the fashion salesperson and the most important characteristics of good selling performance. Those characteristics include knowledgeability, confidence, patience, the ability to improvise, and a good fashion sense.

Knowledgeability. The saleswoman should know what is in stock and how it fits into the overall fashion picture—how it fits into her department, and how it relates to merchandise in other fashion departments.

New synthetic fibers and new fabrics appear each year. The customer wants to know about them. What is this dress made of? How should it be cared for? What does this label really mean when it says "hand wash"? Is the fabric durable or perishable? Is it cool? Warm? Such questions, and others like them, are part of the factual side of knowledgeability.

There is, in addition, the whole area of taste, judgment, and fashion sense. What is becoming? What is smart? Is this pair of pants right or wrong for the woman's figure? Is it an all-purpose style? Is it suitable for specific occasions only? What shoe styles would go well with these pants?

Confidence. The knowledgeable salesperson has every reason to be confident. Not overly confident—an attitude that can annoy the customer—but quietly confident, so that the customer herself is assured and reassured.

Patience. The customer may be right, but she can be rude, annoying, and indecisive. She may ask the same question over and over again. She may insist on trying on every piece of merchandise in stock. Patience has a special meaning, and calls for special endurance, in fashion departments.

Appearance. The way a salesperson looks strikes a customer one way or another—favorably or unfavorably. Since men's clothes are more conventional, and less variable than women's clothes, it is the saleswoman who frequently comes under fire for wearing improper or unattractive clothing.

Cleanliness and good grooming are always proper and attractive. Beyond those two points, what is "proper" depends on the store, and on the attitude of management. We will go more deeply into clothing as part of sales training in our next chapter. Here, we will limit ourselves to a warning: overly restrictive management attitudes toward clothing will lower morale.

Young people selling to young people wear jeans and a great deal of makeup or none at all. Like salesperson, like customer is the rule of these situations, where the relationship is informal, and there is no question of authority or guidance passing from salesperson to customer.

Improvisation. This is still another quality of good salesmanship, one that grows from *knowledgeability* and *confidence.* What does the customer need and want? How does she react to a suggestion? Is she expressing her real needs and wants? How can the salesperson sense all this and put it together in a winning combination—a combination that results in a sale to a satisfied customer?

Detachment. While the saleswoman is often advised to get "involved" with her customer, she needs to learn detachment, too. The art of not reacting emotionally to an emotionally overwrought customer can save energy and prevent humiliation.

Of course, that is easier said than done. When a customer behaves badly, it is difficult to restrain anger and even more difficult not to feel anger. But the minute a salesperson answers angrily, she is involving herself in a situation that will defeat her. The customer can always appeal to a higher authority. On the other hand, a neutral, quiet response may calm a customer and evoke a friendly attitude at the most unexpected times. Some customers are rude because they are demanding friendliness; when they get it, they are so grateful, they buy.

A salesperson should not be required to put up with abuse—abusive language, a loud voice, or insulting manners.

If the situation is hopelessly out of control, it is the salesperson who should appeal to a higher authority, such as a service manager. Sometimes a new face cools off the customer. The aim of salesperson, service manager, buyer, floor manager, and anyone else on the scene is to cut off a bad scene as quickly as possible, before other customers are aware of it.

Interest in fashion. This is not as obvious as it seems. There are salespeople who have little or no interest in clothes. They might as well be selling lamps or potatoes. In a specialty store, they should be shifted to linens and domestics, or taken off the selling floor. Sometimes appearance is a clue to a salesperson's anti-fashion attitude. People who are interested in clothes put themselves together attractively, and show a flair for fashion; even if they do not spend a great deal of money on their clothing.

Selling situations fall into patterns that saleswomen learn to recognize as typical. Following are some examples of classic selling situations. We have set them up as dialogues between a customer, not always reasonable, and a saleswoman, who is the ideal. We have used "S" to indicate saleswoman and "C" to indicate customer. These discussions can be used for sales training.

Experienced saleswomen will recognize themselves and their customers in each situation.

S. May I help you?

C. I'm looking for a white blouse, something like this one on the counter.

S. Do you want to try this one on?

C. Well, I don't know . . . I'm looking for something a little different.

S. (looking at the customer and noting that she is wearing a classic tailored suit with a turtleneck sweater) Perhaps you'd like this one. The cowl neckline would look well with the suit you're wearing.

C. Oh no! I don't like that at *all.*

S. Perhaps this tunic . . . the sleeves are set low . . . it's an interesting new look.

C. Oh no, that wasn't exactly what I had in mind . . . you don't have much in stock, do you?

S. (repressing a desire to say fiercely, 'Well, what *did* you have in your so-called mind, lady?') Why yes, we have lots of new things for fall. Maybe if you tell me what you plan to wear the blouse with, I can help you decide.

C. Oh, skirts, suits, pants . . . I don't really know.

S. Here's a shirt with a convertible mandarin neckline. You can wear it two or three ways, like this (demonstrating)."

C. I don't like it. What else do you have?

At this point, the saleswoman might reasonably conclude that there is not much more she can do. She should now withdraw, leaving the customer with two or three blouses to look at. Two or three are enough; a larger selection will only confuse her.

It is important that the saleswoman withdraw *physically* even if she moves only a few feet away. If another customer is waiting, the saleswoman should approach her immediately.

The first woman is now isolated. If she is not serious, or if she is hopelessly confused or distracted, she will soon leave. If she wants to buy, she has a chance to clarify her thinking. She may decide that she likes something she has already seen. She may decide to go to another department or another store. She may have to wait while the saleswoman is engaged with customer number two.

If customer number one expresses anger because she has to wait, the saleswoman should make every effort not to match anger with anger. Silence is golden, and silence is unanswerable.

Let us change departments and focus on that indecisive customer at another time. Now she is looking for a dress. She needs one, in fact—needs it desperately, for a wedding that is only days away. She has put off shopping till the last possible moment.

S. May I help you?

C. Yes, I'm looking for something dressy to wear to a wedding, size 14 and floor length. (The customer is now much more specific, because she is shopping with a particular occasion in mind.)

S. Our 14's are over here . . . (leading the customer to a rack while looking at her to judge size, weight, height). This silk crepe would look well on you . . . why don't you try it on, for a start?

C. No, it's too bright. I want a pastel or beige.

S. (picking up pale blue crepe pajamas) This is a two-piece pajama with wide pants, very flattering and comfortable.

C. Pants? For a wedding?

S. They're cut so full they look like a skirt. You can wear the right kind of pants almost anywhere. But let's keep looking . . .
(After a while, customer and saleswoman go into the fitting room. The saleswoman will not abandon the customer, but will return from time to time, to remove unwanted clothes and bring in others.)

C. (in fitting room) I didn't realize the pajama outfit was so expensive. It's pretty, but I can't spend that much money. And this outfit makes me look fat. (If the customer *is* fat, there is nothing the saleswoman can do except try to change the subject.)

S. (re-entering with still another dress) Now, let's try this one . . . (she stays with the customer, who is becoming frantic). The waistline needs a little releasing (better than 'letting out') but you can see that there's plenty of seam. The color is good for you. That vertical stripe print makes you look tall (not 'slim'). (Words like 'youthful,' 'slimming,' and 'sexy' often offend the customer, and should be avoided or used very sparingly and carefully.)

C. I don't know . . . I really liked the blue one best, but I just can't spend that much money.

S. How about charging it? If you don't have a charge, we can open one right away.

C. Well, I do have a charge, but . . .

S. That blue dress will be fine for the wedding, and for parties. It won't date and it isn't seasonal . . . you can wear it all year-round. You'll really enjoy wearing it. (Not 'you'll get lots of wear from it' because the dress in question is expensive fashion merchandise, not staple merchandise. If it were, wear would be an important sales point.)

The sale is now in a delicate position. If the customer is obviously distraught and pressured, it is wise to suggest that she go have a cup of coffee, or attend to some other shopping, and then come back to make her final decision. There is always the chance that the customer will not return. But it is a calculated risk.

A distraught, pressured customer probably will not buy, or will buy something that will make her unhappy after she has bought it. She will turn her mistake into negative feelings towards the store. Perhaps she will return the merchandise for credit or refund after she has worn it. Either way, the result is a loss to the store, in terms of cash and goodwill.

There are times when the sale seems to come to a full stop. The saleswoman may decide to let the customer "escape." Or she may be able to get the sale moving again in a positive way by expressing an opinion herself.

Will it be the black or the green sweater, or both? The saleswoman can express a preference. "If you really can't take both, take the green because it's a good color for you," she might say. The customer may be stimulated to agree or disagree. If the customer says, "Oh, no, black is a more basic color," at least she has expressed an opinion herself, and the sale is moving again.

Sometimes conscientious salespeople will show a customer style after style, ignoring restlessness, indifference, and other signs that the customer wants to escape.

On the other hand, multiple sale opportunities are often lost because the salesperson overlooks an opportunity.

A customer who is delighted with a dress, a sweater, or a pair of shoes may be sold several of the same styles in different colors or fabrics.

"Wardrobe" multiple sales fall into different categories. A customer may decide to stock up on sweaters while she can and buy several different styles to go with other separates she already owns.

The designer multiple sale occurs when a customer who buys by label finds a good selection of her favorite designer's clothes.

The duplicate multiple sale may stem from need, as when a young woman going away to college buys panties and T-shirts by the dozen or half-dozen.

The complementary multiple sale results from suggestion selling. Suggestion selling depends on the creativity and taste of the saleswoman. When her customer buys a skirt, the saleswoman shows her an attractive blouse that goes with the skirt, or a jacket, or accessories. This kind of selling is always desirable, and always difficult in a large store, where department divisions and sheer physical distance create obstacles.

The saleswoman in the coat department of a large specialty or department store has no contact with the handbag department, which is probably on the main floor, two floors away. She cannot sell a bag even if she wants to. There is no one who will bring the bag to her. *She* cannot write up the sale. Only someone in the handbag department can write up a handbag sale.

This lack of flexibility, while necessary to an orderly retail organization, or so retailers say, hinders multiple sales and often discourages customers. Nobody likes to plod from one department to the other, assembling an outfit piece by piece. Women do it because they have to, but they do not really enjoy shopping this way. Each transaction seems like a repetition—waiting for the salesperson, showing of credit card or handing over of cash, waiting for the package, moving to the next department.

In a situation where a saleswoman can follow through with merchandise that complements the original unit sold, the customer is more likely to be receptive to new ideas. Often, women have fixed ideas about what they can wear. The knowledgeable, skilled saleswoman who has sold her customer a coat has an opportunity to influence the customer's taste when she can follow through with a recommendation for a scarf, bag, gloves, sweater, skirt, or hat.

The following conversation might take place in a small, well-laid out specialty store.

S. I see you're looking at our dresses. That purple is really attractive. (She did not say that everyone likes purple; that would make it sound too common.) Would you like to try one on?

C. Well, I don't think so . . . it *is* a pretty color, but I couldn't possibly wear it . . . I'm too pale for purple. Besides, it reminds me of funerals.

S. (ignoring the reference to funerals) Why don't you try it and see? You might be pleasantly surprised. I see you're wearing a pale lipstick. With a little brighter makeup you could carry it very nicely.

C. Well, all right, but does it come in brown?

S. I'll bring it in both colors and you can decide for yourself . . . size 14 (being careful to err on the small side if she is not sure which size) is right for you, isn't it?

C. Oh no, I need 16.

S. (in fitting room) You see? It's really quite becoming.

C. It's not as bad as I thought it would be . . . but I'm afraid I'll get tired of it. I don't have very many clothes and I have to wear all my things quite often.

S. No more than any other color you wear . . . it's just that you're used to brown and black and you don't ever expect them to look new. This will be a nice change for you.

C. But what does it go with?

S. You can wear it with brown or black or beige. Or with pale blue or olive or even white. Bright colors really aren't hard to fit into your wardrobe.

C. Well, let me try on the brown now.

S. Yes, I can see why you like to wear brown. It *is* a good color for you. But if you're buying something new, why not try a new color?
(There is now a long pause during which the customer thoughtfully regards herself in the mirror, tries on the purple again, and thinks. During this time, the saleswoman, having other customers to attend to, has left her alone . . . and so much the better in this instance. There is a difference between helping and hovering.)

S. (coming back to fitting room) Let me show you some other things that would work with this dress . . . these shoes won't be your size but just slip your feet into them halfway to get the idea. And here's a plum bag . . . see how it blends with the purple? I know you're not looking for a coat, but I brought in this brown one because I wanted you to see how well the purple goes with your favorite color.

C. I really shouldn't think of spending this much money.

S. (sensing a weakening of resistance) Well, you might as well put yourself together completely while you're buying the dress; if you come back for accessories later, you'll have to match the color from memory, and that's always dangerous. Besides, these things are new now, and we may not have them in your size by the time you get back.

C. Oh, I work right across the street and I come in here every day just to look around. I'll be here all right.

S. (retreating gracefully) In that case you can take your time.

C. You know, I think I'll take the purple. I'm not sure, but maybe it's a good idea. And where are the shoes?

S. Why don't you get dressed while I look for your right shoe size and write up the sales slip?

Endings to selling stories are certainly not always this happy. But with a less assertive saleswoman, the customer might have bought the brown dress and stopped there.

We assume that the saleswoman took a close look at her customer and decided that purple really *was* a perfectly good color for her. That being the case, she has broadened her customer's fashion horizon, and won her confidence. The customer will think favorably not only of the saleswoman, but also of the store.

How and when the saleswoman should express an opinion, and how strongly she should express it, are difficult questions. The answers depend on the fashion authority of the store, the quality of the merchandise, and other intangible factors.

If an indifferent, garishly dressed, loud-voiced saleswoman says "Sure, purple looks fine on you, honey," it is one thing. If a well-dressed, well-mannered, interested saleswoman in a quality store or department says "I think purple is a good color for you" the effect is quite different. Even in a budget department or store, there are times when the saleswoman can be the voice of authority and clinch a sale. And there are times when the customer just does not want to be pushed, even if purple is an absolutely splendid color for her. The only thing that can be said with certainty is—try; stop when there's a danger sign, but always try.

And when a saleswoman tries, she should never, never sound patronizing. "Everybody's wearing purple this year" sounds like a sneer and is a lazy way to sell. Maybe purple *is* a bad color for the customer. Maybe she did not know that purple was fashionable, and now she feels more out of it than ever. The saleswoman should limit herself to general, neutral observations, such as, "Purple seems to be very popular this year," or, "Some of our customers who thought they couldn't wear purple are finding out that they really can." Such statements do not reflect on the customer's taste or knowledge of fashion.

The sale of the purple dress called for special skill because the customer was prejudiced against the color. Here is another example of a multiple sale that calls for skill in tactfully breaking down customer prejudice.

    S. (to customer who appears to be entranced with a coat) Isn't that tweed beautiful?

    C. Oh . . . uh . . . I was just looking. Yes, very nice. But I'd look like a teddy bear in anything that bulky. It's not for me.

    S. Why not just slip it on and see? It's not as overpowering as you think. And you're not that small. (Note word 'small' rather than 'petite' or 'tiny.' Note judicious use of personal remark.)

    C. There, you see . . . I look like a pinhead.

    S. Just a moment . . . (she moves away and comes back quickly with a wide-brimmed hat) See how the hat brings everything into proportion. It's just a matter of some width at the top.

The hat may sell the coat. If it does, it will be because the saleswoman has helped the customer discover a new point of view about what she can wear.

Although the ideal sale involves interaction between a person and a person, the ideal is not always possible. Stores that have found it difficult to recruit, train, and keep salespeople have turned to self-selection and self-service as alternatives.

Packaged pantyhose and bras can be displayed on fixtures. Ready-to-wear is often displayed on racks. The customer makes her choice with little or no assistance from store personnel. A cashier rings up the sale and hands the customer her package. But the need for human hands and human intelligence persists.

Stock displayed on a rack is out of place. Where is the size and color a customer is looking for?

A store brand and a name brand are on display. What is the difference between them besides price? And what does the price difference mean?

A long line forms at the cash register. Customers become fretful and unhappy because they must wait.

While many women would rather help themselves than be subjected to rudeness or indifference of incompetent salespeople, the need for competent salespeople to sell merchandise continues.

The more sophisticated the fashion merchandise, the newer, the more expensive it is, the more human selling skills are required.

That ultimate selling skill, the sensing of real customer needs and desires, as we have described it above, cannot be done by a machine. The best salespeople function like psychologists. Using insight and intelligence, they please customers and make fashion merchandise move.

Trading up is one example of a selling function that only people can perform. Trading up is the selling of merchandise at a price point higher than the price point the customer originally asked for. Expressed more bluntly, it is a way of persuading the customer to spend more money than she intended to spend. A good salesperson "trades up" by convincing the customer that more expensive merchandise will give her more satisfaction.

While more expensive merchandise should be offered, the customer should not be pressured to buy it if she rejects it clearly and strongly. Nor should any customer be snubbed by a salesperson because she cannot afford high-priced merchandise. Trading up is an experiment, a trial balloon—not a way of sledge-hammering the customer.

All salespeople can benefit from asking themselves questions and evaluating their customers as they pass through the selling process. Following are some examples of what customers say, followed by a few examples of what they might mean. Sometimes the saleswoman can deal with the problem, sometime she cannot.

- *I don't like that dress, it's too new and extreme . . .* I'm afraid of wearing something new. My friends may make fun of me. It may not be becoming to me. Maybe I'll be ready for it in another year, but not now. Maybe it's just a fad and I won't be able to wear it next year.

- *I don't like that dress, it's too much like what I have at home* . . . I'm really tired of all my clothes but I don't know what to do about it. I'm scared to try anything too new. Maybe if I saw something with a new detail I'd buy it. Maybe if I weren't so afraid of looking silly I'd try a new silhouette, but if I don't, and it looks awful, I'm going to be depressed.

- *That dress reminds me of a style I wore 20 years ago* . . . Yes, and I was younger and slimmer and prettier and happier then. Why should I remind myself of all that?

- *I really like this outfit, but I'm not sure I have a place to wear it* . . . It's a lot of money to spend, and I'm ashamed to say I can't really afford it. I could afford it, but my husband might be angry if I spent that much money.

- *I want something dressy, but not too showy* . . . I want to look nice but I don't want anyone to think I'm overdressing.

- *I don't like this dress. It has an old-lady look* . . . I can't afford the price. I wish I didn't have to buy an evening dress, but I have to. I'd rather be wearing jeans. If I have to wear an evening dress I want something snappy and I may cut off the hem and shorten it afterwards, so it better be two-piece or have a simple hemline.

- *Do you think this style is too young for me?* . . . I know it's too young for me but I wish it weren't. (The saleswoman is in trouble no matter what she says. If she says "no" and the woman buys the dress, all will be well until someone tells the woman that her dress is not becoming. If the saleswoman says "yes" she is insulting the customer. Best response: Show another more suitable dress and praise it so that the customer can accept it without embarrassment.)

- *I like this dress and I'd take it in a minute, but it's a little too tight, the collar isn't quite right, and the sleeves are too full for my arms* . . . I'm really not ready to buy anything and I want out, so please let me get dressed and leave quietly. I don't know what made me try on the dress in the first place.

- *I think all the styles this year are ugly* . . . I don't like the way I look in clothes. I can't afford to buy anything new, I can't make up my mind.

- *I could buy this dress and be happy with it, but I don't have the right accessories for it* . . . I'm afraid of a new look but I'm ashamed to say so. I've worn the same kind of clothes for years and if I buy one new thing it will throw my whole wardrobe out of focus. Then I'll have to buy more new things. (Best response: Explaining how a new style can be worn with things the customer already owns.)

Flattery as a selling technique is a double-edged sword. One edge is useful, the other is dangerous. The woman who seems to demand flattery is a particularly difficult customer. She may be talking to herself, and she may respond badly to the flattery she seems to seek out.

A sophisticated customer will know when flattery is being used as sales pressure. She will resent it. A sophisticated customer may also feel that she wants to make up her own mind, without any prompting from the saleswoman. Flattery will antagonize her and lose the sale.

Many older women do not like being told that a dress makes them look younger —the statement itself is an admission that they have passed their youth, and need clothes that make them look younger.

There is a certain type of wealthy customer who seems to eat up flattery. She will walk into a salon, expect to be recognized immediately, catered to continuously, and complimented on her looks, her clothes, her achievements, the pictures of her children or grandchildren that she passes around, her dog (which is probably yapping and snapping at everyone's ankles), her new diamond watch, and anything else she has, is, or does.

She spends a lot of money. She is worth all the flattery she wants.

Occasionally a situation arises in which a customer is absolutely determined to buy a fashion that is all wrong for her. After the saleswoman has done her best to steer the customer towards something more suitable, all she can do is sell the horizontally striped dress to the fat lady and hope that no one will tell her it makes her look fatter.

It takes special intelligence and intuitiveness, as well as experience, to guess at hidden customer feelings, as we have explained them above. But it takes only common sense and good motivation to create future sales by following through. The saleswoman who cannot produce exactly what the customer wants will try to get it.

If the saleswoman does not have precisely the style the customer wants, she offers something similar.

If she does not know the answer to a question, she tries to find someone who does.

If she works for a large store, and the merchandise the customer wants is carried in another department, she finds out exactly where that department is and sends the customer there.

If there is a possibility that the merchandise the customer wants will be in stock shortly, the saleswoman takes an order and makes sure that it is sent out.

If the customer does not have enough money to buy a piece of merchandise, she suggests opening a charge account or a lay-away plan.

Dresses, sportswear, separates, formal wear, coats and suits are all part of that larger category known as ready-to-wear. Accessories are merchandised separately and often call for special knowledge and different kinds of selling skills. Shoes, jewelry, and furs are all special. While these departments are often leased, standards should be set for their salespeople, whether the staff is controlled by the store or the lessor.

Fitting shoes is a very special skill. A good salesperson can usually determine whether or not a shoe fits. But the ultimate decision must be made by the woman who wears it after she has bought and worn the shoes.

Sometimes a shoe that is comfortable when it is tried on is uncomfortable when it has been worn for a few hours. Sometimes a salesperson, in his eagerness to complete the sale, will tell a customer that the shoe will "ease onto her foot" after she has worn it. It may, or it may not. If it remains uncomfortable, the customer will probably return it.

Because a health factor is involved, salespeople in a shoe department have a greater responsibility than salespeople in any other department. Shoes that are not a good fit are more than uncomfortable; they may injure the customer's feet. Also, a shoe that has been worn cannot be resold like a dress. A return is a loss to the store.

There is always the customer who will take advantage of this situation and return a pair of shoes, using fit as an excuse, when, in fact, she has simply decided that she does not like the shoes and does not want to keep them.

The service manager can check fit when a customer appears to be returning a pair of shoes under false pretenses. Sometimes, the team of service manager plus salesperson can shame the customer out of her pretense. If they cannot, the store will probably have to take back the shoes and suffer the loss, to keep the customer's goodwill. The best way to avoid such losses is to avoid selling shoes that clearly do not fit the customer. If she insists on buying, she should be warned that she is buying at her own risk, and that the store will *not* take the shoes back.

There is one factor that has made fitting a little easier for the salesperson. Each generation of girls is growing up with larger feet. This trend is so universal that small feet are no longer prized as a sign of beauty. As women have accepted the fact of large feet, they have stopped trying to squeeze their feet into shoes that are too small. So a salesperson can fit most of his customers without worrying about this silly vanity.

The growing practice of displaying all shoe styles that the department or store carries is also a help to the salesperson. When the customer asks for a type of shoe, he can refer her to the display, instead of bringing out box after box of shoes for her approval or rejection.

Shoes come in so many sizes that they are difficult to sell. A woman must find the right combination of width and length; she must also look for a last that conforms to her foot. This involves trying on many shoes.

For the salesperson, it means time spent bringing out boxes and putting them away again, while the customer tries yet another combination.

Another problem is accumulation of inventory—boxes of shoes take up a great deal of storage space.

During the 1970's, some widths were eliminated, and many shoes were shown only in narrow and medium. This simplified stockkeeping and saved storage space in the shoe department. But customers complained that the smaller choice of sizes led to poor fit. The salesperson who does succeed in fitting his customer correctly and in pleasing her, finds himself in an especially good position to make a multiple sale and to build repeat business. Because of the fit factor, a customer will have confidence in a salesperson who has sold her one pair of shoes that are satisfactory. She may be so glad to find a last that fits that she may buy it in several different colors or leathers on the spot. Or she may order the same style again by phone, asking for the salesperson by name.

Shoe salespeople have a tendency to lose contact with ready-to-wear and ready-to-wear fashion trends. This deprives them of important selling ammunition. Women buy shoes after they have bought ready-to-wear. Shoes must relate to their dresses, coats, and suits. Ready-to-wear is the focal point; shoes and other accessories must complement it, they must "go with" ready-to-wear.

Of course it sometimes happens that a woman will buy a striking pair of shoes and build an ensemble around them, but this is the exception, not the rule.

Perhaps salespeople might be a little more patient with indecisive customers if they realized that, as the woman is looking at the shoes on her feet, a kind of moving picture is passing before her eyes. She is mentally going through her wardrobe and thinking of what the shoes will go with; not just other accessories, but coats, suits, and dresses. Perhaps she is even trying to recall a certain shade of beige or blue and wondering how close the shoe she is contemplating comes to the shade she is trying to recall. When a woman gets a dreamy look in her eyes, she may be doing just this. The best thing the salesman can do is leave her alone until the "moving picture" has finished.

Drastic changes in shoe silhouette sometimes make a customer "freeze" in a similar way. After years of seeing her feet in shoes with rounded toes, she must learn to like the way they look in shoes with pointed toes. It takes time for her to adjust to the new silhouette and to accept it as attractive. Reassurance from the salesperson is helpful, but overselling is dangerous. The customer must make the decision herself.

This is another time when "everybody's wearing it" may evoke a negative response. Better to ask the customer what kind of clothes she is now wearing or buying, to relate the new shoes to these other clothes, and to bring the customer around gradually to a point at which she realizes the shoes are part of an overall look she will like and find becoming.

Many department and specialty stores still sell handbags, and a few other accessories in shoe departments. This used to be an excellent way of creating multiple sales, because women wore shoes and bags that matched exactly. A navy shoe called for a navy bag, most of the time. And the two shades of navy had to be the same; the concept of blending light and dark shades of the same color did not exist.

Now coordination of accessories is freer and more creative. Women easily mix shades of one color, two or three colors, fabrics, and leathers. Because it is no longer necessary to match accessories precisely, it is no longer necessary to buy them at the same time in the same place. The customer may buy brown shoes, go into another department, and casually coordinate them with a natural canvas bag. This is a good example of the way changing fashions create new merchandising trends.

Furs offer another example of fashion change linked with merchandising change. When all furs were formal, elegant and expensive, they were sold in a formal, elegant, and expensive salon. The salon was, and is, a separate room or area of the store with little merchandise on display and furniture that suggests a European parlor, which is one meaning of the word, "salon."

During the 1960's and into the 1970's, less formal fur fashions were introduced. Gradually, they moved out of the salon and into more informal store settings. They mixed with ready-to-wear. It seemed appropriate to show a fur poncho or a fur-lined raincoat with sweaters, skirts, and pants. While the salon persists, especially as atmosphere for the most expensive minks and sables, the trend is definitely towards more informal handling and selling of the newer kind of fur merchandise.

Fur buyers found that formality could discourage customer browsing and, therefore, sales. Many women hesitate to enter an area where there is little merchandise on display, and where, rightly or wrongly, they feel salespeople are waiting to "pounce" on them. This holds true for the independent fur store, as well as the fur department in a department or specialty store.

The four- and five-figure fur sale is still usually made in a salon. A woman must enter the fur salon before a sale begins. Fur buyers have learned to instruct their staff to avoid behavior that drives the browsing customer away. Since few customers impulsively pay thousands of dollars for a coat, most big-ticket fur sales start off with browsing.

The shopper is allowed to enter the salon, catch her breath, and look around for a few seconds before anyone approaches her. (This is in contrast to pouncing.)

A salesperson offers help, and may ask if the customer wants to see something specific, or if she would rather look around by herself. The option of looking around is a point clearly made to remove any pressure the customer feels upon entering the salon.

In a little while, a salesperson may approach the customer with one piece of merchandise and invite her to try it on. If showing merchandise evokes a negative response, the customer is left alone, again.

If the customer examines a piece of merchandise herself, and tries it on, a salesperson offers help. The salesperson may point out advantages of the garment without pressuring the customer.

If the salesperson can find a fur that the customer enjoys trying on, the beginning of a selling situation exists, although the sale may not be completed immediately.

Something happens when a woman tries on a fur. It is appealing to the touch and becoming in a way that even the most luxurious fabric is not. It is luxury. It makes a woman feel good just to have it on.

The merchandise should be handled with great respect. The salesperson should not fling a coat over a chair (unless he is trying to be dramatic and prove a point in a very special situation) and he should be careful to adjust the fur on the woman as she tries it on. This may be her first venture into the world of fur—she may not know how to drape a stole, or settle a coat on her shoulders.

The salesperson should remember at all times that this may be a major event in the woman's life. And also, that the spending of a large sum of money is a serious matter for most women, one that is planned well in advance, discussed with family and friends, and decided over a period of time.

When a customer comes in with a friend or relative, the shrewd fur salesperson will try to determine just how much influence that second party has and will sell to the decision-maker.

All questions, even the silliest ones, should be answered carefully. If a woman remarks that she saw the same coat in a store down the street for fifty dollars less, the salesperson should talk about differences in quality without saying negative things about the competing store. Downgrading another store does not soothe the customer; rather, it arouses her suspicions.

The fur salesperson needs knowledge to work with; knowledge about each fur; where it comes from; how warm it is; how well it wears; what will happen to the curl, the luster, the color; what will happen to it in the rain; how much it will shed; what kind of care it requires.

Salespeople should never exaggerate claims. A customer who buys on the basis of exaggerated claims will surely be disappointed. There is the risk of a return. Since a large sum of money is involved, the woman who is unhappy with a fur purchase may well decide that she does not like the entire store and may avoid shopping there in the future.

Sometimes, when a woman cannot make a choice, a third party, usually the buyer in a fur department or the manager of an independent fur store, can help. He will come over and introduce himself politely. He will listen to what has transpired so far. Then he will give his opinion and add his own comments. Even if he says nothing new, his authority, added to the authority of the salesperson, may help the woman decide. This selling technique is called a "takeover."

Whatever the selling strategy, the approach should be friendly. Many fur salon managers and fur buyers, given a choice between the expert technician and the salesperson with less technical knowledge and a good attitude, would choose the latter. Technical knowledge can be acquired; deeply ingrained, negative attitudes are difficult to change.

When a woman who is looking at fur starts to talk, the salesperson may wind up listening to her whole life story before she even tries on the coat. At this point, the merchandise is secondary; what is important is the establishment of a relationship between salesperson and customer.

The new, less expensive "young" or "fun" furs, as they are called, call for selling techniques different from those used to sell traditional, more expensive furs. (The dividing line between the two categories is hazy—it is usually placed at about $750.) Young furs are best sold in informal departments more like ready-to-wear departments than fur salons. Salespeople must be prepared to accept the fact that customers may treat these furs casually, trying them on as if they were dresses or cloth coats.

There are some things, however, that even the casual customer will want to know, especially if she is making her first fur purchase. "Will it wear well?" is a question that most fur customers ask. Explaining durability by comparison is a good way to give a specific yet positive answer. Showing a rabbit coat, the salesperson might say, "It won't wear like raccoon or mink, but it will last for several years, just as a good cloth coat would. And if it sheds, don't worry, there's plenty of fur there."

What has *not* been said is that the coat will not shed at all, under any circumstances. The young customer who is not buying fur to last a "lifetime" as her mother did will find such explanations satisfactory and reassuring. And if she should mistreat her coat and damage it, she cannot accuse the salesperson of having said that the coat would "never" shed or "never" wear out.

Comparisons can be used at all price levels. If the customer who is buying a mink coat asks, "Will it shed?" a good answer is: "Yes, the coat will shed a little when you first wear it, just like a fine carpet." This answer is positive, rather than defensive. It is also definite and frank. And it links the fur with another big-ticket, long-term, quality product with which the customer is probably familiar.

Jewelry, like fur, requires special skill and knowledge. Like fur, it is a big-ticket item, and is, therefore, usually a planned purchase. The customer must have confidence in the jewelry salesperson, for she, the customer, is no more fit to judge the quality of a diamond than she is to judge the quality of a mink coat. She buys on the assumption that the merchandise is what the store says it is.

A department that handles fine jewelry will have its share of wedding ring customers. They require great patience. They are often compulsive comparison shoppers, going from store to store, unable to make a decision because of emotional factors. Often the amount of the purchase will be as little as $30. But these customers represent an opportunity to build a following; where there is a wedding, there will be an anniversary and a birthday, and they may return.

Then there is the woman who is out to buy a ring, but hates her hands because they are red, or short, or have thick knuckles, or because she bites her nails. She cannot be flattered into believing her hands are beautiful, but she can, perhaps, be convinced that they are not ugly, that hands are a reflection of character and personality, and that all women wish they had slender tapering fingers even though very few do. Once such a customer is freed from her own unhappiness and preoccupation with her faults, real or imagined, she will then also feel free to spend money to ornament her hands.

We are not now discussing the very few, very rich women who acquire a diamond necklace as casually as they would a pair of shoes. We are discussing the customer who sees her choice of a piece of jewelry as a revelation of her own taste and personality, and fears such a revelation. We are also considering the male shopper in search of a gift, whether it is for Aunt Betty, his fiancée, or his wife. He is one of the most anxious of all customers, and he needs to be questioned very carefully and reassured very strongly.

Once in a while a male gift shopper with the opposite characteristic turns up. He is extremely confident and opinionated. He knows everything. This customer is relatively easy to deal with. As long as the salesperson does not contradict him, he will be content.

It often happens that a woman, or worse yet, a man, will wander into a jewelry store or department without realizing that he is looking at real jewelry. Often, such a customer is horrified when a price for "the pin with the red stones" is quoted. Salespeople should speak very kindly to this customer. "Tell me about how much you want to spend, so I won't take you out of your price range" is a good opening line.

The customer can then whisper that costume jewelry was really what he had in mind, and the salesperson will send him on to the right department or to another store.

A man shopping for a gift often suffers severe humiliation when forced to admit that he cannot spend hundreds or thousands of dollars. He may feel bitterly resentful towards the salesperson who gives him the bad news. A woman may also become resentful when she finds she cannot afford what she wants. Often, such customers will not settle for a simple piece of real jewelry that they can afford. They have their vision of a large pin and they do not want a small one.

It is useless to show them merchandise when they are in a bitter or resentful frame of mind. The best thing to do is to suggest that they finish their other shopping and consider the matter. This ploy allows them to leave the department or store without embarrassment.

The jewelry salesperson should be quick to pick up customer tastes, preferences, and prejudices. (Many people still believe that opals are bad luck.) If two customers are involved, the salesperson must be able to spot the decision-maker. And, of course, he must be ready to step back at any moment and end the contact on a pleasant note.

Returns on jewelry present a ticklish problem. A woman may come in with a ring she says she has never worn, yet an examination of the stone will show surface scratches that could only come from wear, if the stone was perfect when it was sold. The woman may not be lying—for some reason, women forget how often they slip rings on and off their fingers.

A damaged stone should not be accepted for return. The customer can look at it through a jeweler's glass and see the scratches for herself. Return and exchange policies should be made very clear at the time of the sale.

In spite of all these difficulties, the jewelry salesperson can build a loyal following. The husband who buys a gift for his wife will be back again if the gift is well received. The woman who gets compliments on her ring will almost certainly want more jewelry; jewelry, like furs, can become an addiction.

Men's jewelry is a new profit area that should grow steadily as acceptance becomes more general, even among conservative men. As acceptance grows, the traditional gift-buying pattern is reversed. The woman shops for the man.

The anti-fashion salesman who dislikes the idea of masculine jewelry is as great a danger as the anti-fashion saleswoman.

Accessories—scarves, hats, costume jewelry—become more important as clothing simplifies.

They are a woman's way of creating an individual look for herself. She adds them to shirts, pants, jeans, skirts, sweaters, and dresses.

Some women are frightened of accessories. They shun costume jewelry, not realizing how effectively and inexpensively it can complement their clothes.

Women who think of themselves as clumsy avoid scarves, and envy their friends who always seem to learn the newest ways of tying and wearing scarves.

Scarf buyers comment that women have special difficulties with scarves, stoles, and shawls. Unlike a hat, which must be properly placed on the head, a scarf must be manipulated—tied, draped, folded, and arranged. Many women give up the battle before they start, yet a few simple rules can turn a wary customer into an enthusiastic one.

Scarves must be clean and pressed.

Women must allow themselves a little time, while they are dressing, to arrange a scarf—it cannot be tossed on, unless the wearer has a great deal of dexterity and skill.

Silk is softer and drapes more easily, but some experts say cotton scarfs are better for beginners because they do not slide.

Simple hats and caps, summer straws and winter knits, are accepted more easily, but still call for some special selling techniques.

Get the customer to try on an accessory.

Show her how to wear it—without patronizing her, without making her feel like a fool.

In-store demonstrations and clinics can improve accessory sales enormously and create customer goodwill. Often manufacturers will cooperate, sending in their representatives to demonstrate "how to."

Accessory displays are difficult to maintain because they are constantly in danger of being pulled apart. Yet an inviting display can create an impulse sale, if the salesperson is quick to sense the customer's sudden curiosity and whim.

It helps if saleswomen wear their own merchandise. Unfortunately, winter knit hats appear in stores in June, so that salespeople cannot be expected to wear them, even with air-conditioning. But jewelry and scarves can be worn all year-round.

This kind of selling is often called "suggestion selling" (and sometimes mistakenly called "suggestive selling").

Suggestion selling is a way of increasing the total amount of a sales check, and, at the same time, guiding the customer towards what best suits her needs. Nowhere is guidance more necessary than in the merchandise category known as piece goods.

Piece goods is not ready-to-wear, or accessories, yet it is fashion merchandise. The home sewer, shopping for fabrics is a fashion customer. She may be sewing to save money, to get fit she cannot find in ready-to-wear, to create a special fashion look, or for a combination of those reasons.

But even the most economy-minded home sewer wants to create a finished garment that looks fashionable and professionally made. The term, "home made" is a compliment when applied to food; applied to clothing, it becomes a deadly insult.

Unless the home sewer is expert, she needs help. A salesperson who "waits" is not enough. The salesperson must be able to talk knowledgeably about fabric in relation to patterns, about construction, yardage, and fashion.

Many department stores have lost piece goods business because they could not find and hold adequate staff. While customers browse in fabric departments and give considerable thought to choice of fabric, they often need help. At the very least, someone must pull out the bolt, mark it, and cut it—self-selection and self-service do not work in the piece goods department.

Experienced salespeople working in reputable piece goods stores are alert to customers' needs. The customer may be browsing, and she may be undecided, but what is she looking for? Wool for a coat? Satin for a bridal gown? Such purchases add up to big sales tickets. The salesperson will give the customer a swatch when the swatch will help bring her back to the store after she has made her decision and is ready to buy.

The fabric freak is another customer that the piece goods salesperson learns to recognize. This is the customer who loves to sew, loves fabric and loves clothes. When she sees fabric she likes, she must have it—she is addicted. She may take it home and stow it away for months before she gets around to making it up, but no matter. The fabric freak can be tempted at any time, regardless of how much unused fabric she already owns. At the very worst, they have not really wasted their money; the fabric can be made up eventually; it will not spoil, like perishable food.

Another problem that turned home sewers away from department stores was the very concept of departments. A woman had to buy a pattern from one salesperson, then cross departmental lines to buy fabric, and cross again to buy notions—thread, buttons, zippers, and other sewing accessories. Where notions were carried on a self-selection or self-service basis, long lines at check-out counters made shopping difficult.

It is not absolutely necessary that salespeople who work in a fabric store know how to sew, but it helps. They must certainly know enough about sewing to make judgments about what fabrics will make up well in what patterns, what fabrics best lend themselves to certain styles, how fabrics should be handled and what kind of fabrics beginners should avoid.

It is important to maintain a *continuing* relationship with a fabric customer. If she has a problem, she should feel that she can come back to the store, and that someone will help her solve it.

Sewing classes help build and retain clientele. Women who become discouraged easily need tender loving care as well as instruction; if they feel clumsy and guilty they will not be repeat customers.

Beginning sewers have a fatal tendency to admire elaborate patterns and plaid or flowered fabrics that require the most painstaking matching. The wrong choice of fabric or pattern can lead to early and unnecessary discouragement.

The most successful fabric shops guide and teach. They are also careful about the way they sell the idea of sewing as an economy.

It is better to tell customers that they can make a $300 dress for $50 then to talk about "saving money."

Displays of finished garments, properly accessorized, are more important in home sewing stores. Visualizing the finished garment is always difficult.

Such displays should be clearly labeled with fabric price, pattern label and number, and any other pertinent information.

Deciding whether or not to give swatches is a problem; it is a quick way to ruin a good bolt of fabric. When customers are known in the store, some sacrifice must be made. Professional swatch-collectors who never buy can be refused. One compromise solution is a swatchboard on display, where coordinated fabrics are shown.

The store that sells fabrics, patterns, and notions can put together a complete package for the home sewer.

Sewing machine sales are another aspect of the piece goods business; the store that sells machines must follow up with training immediately. Just as women put away fabric and fail to make it up, women will sometimes buy machines and, after an initial burst of enthusiasm, forget about them. Perhaps the first effort did not turn out well. The customer is discouraged. She will feel guilty. She will resent the store that sold her the machine, even though it is certainly not the store's fault that she has not used it! Direct mail or, in a small community, personal phone calls can encourage the customer, and bring her back to a more hopeful attitude, so that she will buy fabric and a pattern and get to work. Even if she makes something as simple as a pillow cover, that one positive result will help her continue. Home furnishings is another area of home sewing with its own share of fashion interest.

The home sewing customer has changed—this is yet another result of women's liberation. If women can work wood and handle tools, then it follows that men can sew.

Boys, as well as girls, entered sewing classes in high schools in the 1970's. As this expanded customer group develops, old-fashioned sewing may turn into a new-fashioned get-together activity for young people.

Whether a salesperson is selling fabric, notions, coats or shoes, the sale as a transaction is a path with a beginning, a middle and an end. Along that path, there are crucial points that can make or break the sale.

The first contact with the customer, and even the moments before contact, when customer and salesperson approach each other, are important.

Some stores train their salespeople to say "Good morning" or "Good afternoon, may I help you?" as a courtesy. Standardized greetings can become mechanical and impersonal, and are not always necessary. When the voice is too bright, too cheerful, too harsh, or too anything, the customer is repelled, rather than attracted.

The salesperson and customer must establish their relationship. The salesperson will help and guide and show. The customer will react and buy.

The salesperson must begin to form an instant profile of the customer, who she is, what she wants and whether she is browsing or really intent on buying. As the sale begins, the salesperson begins to absorb all this information by looking and thinking, as well as talking.

Once the terms of the salesperson-customer relationship are set, the sale can get under way. Merchandise is shown, compared, questioned, removed, and finally the customer may decide to buy.

All these phases of the transaction are crucial; at any moment the customer may respond positively or negatively. A drift towards the negative calls for a switch of selling tactics. A drift towards positive response calls for encouragement and continued movement so that the pace does not slow down.

The end of the sale is also crucial. Once the customer's decision is made, there are two possibilities. One is another sale. If the salesperson can create a multiple sale, the transaction continues. At some point, the selling process comes to an end.

Then the salesperson should send the customer off as quickly and efficiently as possible.

Wrapping, checking a charge account, giving change and all clerical work should be accomplished quietly without further discussion.

The customer who is forced to stand around and wait for a package becomes irritable and restless, and rightly so. During crowded holiday seasons, this post-sale period can become a major problem. Sometimes, a sale that has been made is lost because the customer refuses to wait while all the red tape is unwound.

At this point, responsibility passes from the salesperson to the service staff. All the good work of the salesperson can be undone if the service staff does not support the salesperson. When the last loose ends are tied up neatly, the customer leaves with a good impression of the store that enhances store image.

CUSTOMER TYPES AND HOW TO DEAL WITH THEM

Each customer is different, but customers with certain behavior patterns turn up frequently.

The Eccentric Shopper. Every store has a few of these—people who shop compulsively but never buy. Sometimes they are polite, and invent excuses for not buying at the very last minute, just when the salesperson is ready to write a sales check or ring up a sale. Eccentrics become known in a department or store. After a while, salespeople learn to go through the motions of showing them a few pieces of merchandise, and then politely moving on to another customer.

The Browser. Browsers may be nuisances and browsers may turn into genuine customers. The non-buying browser may be a woman killing time until she meets her friend for lunch, or the man who cannot make up his mind what to buy, and does not really want to buy. Or, the browser may be a woman who enjoys shopping and spending money. Browsers who are capable of buying are recognized by their interest in merchandise.

The browser who is not interested in buying shows this in a detached, disinterested attitude that an experienced salesperson recognizes quickly.

The Bargain Hunter. Bargain hunters show up for sales, but not only for sales. They want the best quality for the least money. They cannot understand why the dress that costs $50 is not cut as full or finished as carefully as the dress that sells for $100 or $300. They complain a lot. They like to argue, therefore the best way to handle them is to show them the merchandise, give them the facts, and refuse to argue about quality or price or anything else.

They may or may not buy, but because they may buy, it is better to keep them as calm as possible. Some bargain hunters have excitable, even manic personalities that inflict real hardships on salespeople, who should not be asked to put up with the kind of badgering that borders on abuse.

Other bargain hunters are merely thoughtless. Some are quite wealthy. They are "hunters" in the true sense of the word, and they enjoy saving money as a matter of principle, not because they have to.

The Serious Shopper. Serious shoppers need or want a specific kind of merchandise. Deal with them honestly, show what is available and try to help them decide what best meets their needs or wants. Listen to them carefully; what they say provides clues that may steer the sale to a successful conclusion.

The Pressured Shopper. Pressured shoppers are in a hurry, are nervous or irritable, or distracted, or indecisive, or all of these things. Perhaps they postponed shopping until the last possible minute. Now the moment of truth is at hand. It is up to salespeople to help pressured shoppers overcome their difficulties.

Some customers want to talk about their problems. In other cases, the intelligent salesperson will sense a private, emotional problem, and will tactfully refrain from asking unnecessary questions.

Customers buy under pressure when they pick out gifts for birthdays, anniversaries, or other special occasions. Christmas, of course, is the top pressure period.

Women who must have new outfits for specific occasions shop under pressure, especially when the occasion is only a few days away.

Perhaps such a woman is not sure what kind of outfit she needs. Formal? Informal? In this case, the salesperson can help by asking questions. Where and when is the party, if it is a party? What time of day or night? Was there a written invitation, and did it specify "black tie?"

Customers preparing to go on vacation are shopping under pressure, with a sense of having many chores and too little time before the day of departure.

Brides-to-be, their families, and attendants, are all shopping under very special pressure. Emotion often runs high and personality conflicts are intensified.

We have dwelled at great length on the difficulties of selling fashion. There are rewards, as well as difficulties. When a woman's eyes light up with pleasure, and she says, "Thank you so much—this is just what I wanted," the saleswoman can feel that she has done a very real service for another human being that goes beyond the exchange of money. When a customer comes back to report how many compliments she gets every time she wears a certain dress or coat or ring, then the saleswoman has every reason to be pleased with herself for having done her job well.

We have discussed the ingredients of the best sales performance in this chapter. In our next chapter, we will look at some of the ways in which management can improve sales performance, and bring reality closer to the ideals outlined in this chapter.

Summing up our chapter on selling techniques, here are some "do's" and "don'ts" for selling strategy addressed directly to the salesperson.

Do talk quietly.

Don't raise your voice or shout across the floor.

Do try to make a judgment as to whether a garment is truly becoming to a customer or not.

Don't tell her automatically that whatever she is trying on looks great.

Do try to size up the customer quickly—her figure problems, her state of mind, her need for guidance.

Don't fail to express an honest opinion when a customer cannot make a choice.

Do find out for what purpose or occasion the customer is buying a dress, coat, suit, or ensemble.

Do try to find out what kind of clothes the customer already owns.

Do try to trade up a price range.

Don't insist on trading up if the customer responds in a negative way.

Don't snub the customer who says she cannot afford a certain price.

Don't make assumptions about how much money the customer has on the basis of clothes she is wearing.

Don't say anything unfavorable about a competitive store.

Don't try to pressure the customer into buying something she is not sure she likes.

Do offer to put a piece of merchandise aside for a few hours so the customer can make up her mind without pressure.

Don't leave a customer stranded in the fitting room.

Don't try to wait on too many customers at a time in a fitting room situation.

Don't give an indecisive customer too many choices.

Do take away rejected merchandise as quickly as possible.

Don't flatter insincerely.

Don't ignore a customer who has been waiting for some time.

Do tell her, "I'll be with you in a few minutes."

Don't say, "It doesn't look well on you."

Do say, "It doesn't do a thing for you."

Don't address anyone as "sweetie," "dear," or "honey."

Don't tell an older woman a style makes her look young.

Do tell her a style is becoming.

Don't try to pressure a customer into buying by saying, "Everybody's wearing it," or "That's what they're showing this year."

Don't say "Can I help you?" and then leave the customer.

Do invite cash customers to open a charge account.

Do be extremely cautious about words like "slimming," "sexy," and "youthful."

Don't mispronounce "lingerie." The *only* correct pronunciation is, *lin* (rhymes with man), *jer* (rhymes with her), *'ee* (rhymes with me).

Don't say, "We can make it larger."

Do say, "We can release the seams."

Don't say, "You'll get a lot of wear out of this dress," in a fashion store.
Do say, "This dress will give you a great deal of pleasure," or, "This won't be a closet dress—you'll find yourself wearing it very often."
Do say, "You really should buy this dress while we have it; we may not have it in your size when you come back."

How To Increase
Effectiveness
of Salespeople

During the depression of the 1930's, jobs were so scarce that Macy's was able to pick and choose sales help. They hired only women with college degrees—or so the story goes, immortalized by the International Ladies Garment Workers Union in its hit musical, "Pins and Needles." In it, a "salesgirl" sang, "I used to be on the daisy chain, but now I'm a chain store daisy."

8

There have been changes since the day of the chain story daisy. There are many more employment opportunities for women with or without college degrees than there were in the 1930's.

Selling is a job that calls for considerable skill, yet it ranks low in terms of prestige. It is a job associated with serving. In the United States, serving is considered menial work, and menial work is considered inferior to white-collar or office work. Most retail salespeople do not earn good salaries, and many have little hope of advancement. As a result of these factors, there is a shortage of good salespeople.

The truth is that stores cannot afford to avoid trying to solve it. Too much is at stake. The rate of walkouts is phenomenally high. (A walkout is a sale that is lost because the customer has "walked out" without buying anything. Failure of salespeople, in one way or another, is its most important cause.)

The late George Engel, of George C. Engel Co., management consultants, made studies of walkouts in some of the largest stores in the country. Although these studies were compiled some time ago, the situation has not changed, and the material is still valid. It was found that in one department store the median walkout figure was 88 percent and went as high as 96 percent. When store management was informed of these figures, it responded with indifference.

Commenting on that situation, Mr. Engel pointed out that a store with 88 percent walkouts could increase its profits tremendously by cutting down walkouts on 3 percent, to 85 percent. If the store were selling only 12 percent of its shoppers, cutting back the walkout rate 3 percent would mean that it would be selling 15 percent of its shoppers. Those three percentage points would be an increase in volume of 25 percent, a rate of increase that retailers envisage only in their happiest dreams.

Mr. Engel rated store attitudes towards sales personnel as "obsolete." Some stores have convictions about their selling potential that cannot be shaken. One store, for example, is convinced that it cannot sell better merchandise. Another, that it cannot sell older people—and that young people are difficult, too.

"Many personnel departments operate on a very low-morale basis. 'Thank God she took the job' is their general attitude towards a new salesperson. Personnel sees the selling job as a dead end with low pay and long hours. And when it comes to training, the salesperson is lucky to get instruction on how to make out a sales check and when she gets paid."

According to Mr. Engel, the three worst problems facing stores in handling salespeople are:

1. Insufficient personnel when needed;
2. Inadequate supervision;
3. Unimaginative sales training.

"You find some salespeople who are too aggressive, some who actually don't like better merchandise and won't push it, some who try to sell too much, and some who simply don't have enough information for the customer . . . The store should find all these things out . . .

"For example, girls who don't like selling better merchandise but who are very good in moving basics would help the store much more in a fast-turn volume department. Treating them as part of a depersonalized mass staff and not making the most of their special talents is to hurt the store's selling effort . . ."

Mr. Engel's constructive advice calls for one comment: If personnel departments are surprised and relieved when a woman accepts a selling job, it does not necessarily mean that their attitude is bad. It may be that the job *does* pay badly, and the hours *are* long. If these conditions are not corrected, no amount of sales training or morale boosting will help.

In addition to the high rate of walkouts, there is additional proof that stores lose sales because of poor sales staffs. A study published by the Retail Research Institute of the National Retail Merchants Association entitled, "A Study of Consumer Frustrations." It includes the following comments made by customers when asked how they felt about salespeople:

"As cashiers, charming; as help, no help at all."
"I like them to leave me alone."
"Pests."
"Pains in the neck."

"Taboo—don't need people's opinions."

"Handicap."

One solution to the problem is to eliminate salespeople wherever possible, relying on self-selection, self-service, and as much packaged merchandise as possible.

Towards this end, many stores have re-designed their selling floors, eliminating counters. If there is no person to bring out the merchandise and show it, why have a counter?

Instead, racks, rods, and tables display as much merchandise as possible. Some person on the floor may point out a size range or a fashion category, but does not get involved in a one-on-one discussion with the customer.

Many women like to see a lot of merchandise and work their way through it. Others find the amount of merchandise overpowering; they become confused and tire easily.

The absence of a traditional salesperson eliminates dialogues illustrated in Chapter 7. The customer is talking to herself, deciding for herself, and bringing the merchandise to a cashier when she has made up her mind.

In stores that carry fashion merchandise that is new and different, service is the fuel that moves a sale toward a positive conclusion. Selling fashion depends on people who sell as well as customers who buy. Salesperson, merchandise, customer is the trio that creates the sale.

Management needs to re-evaluate selling assignments continually. People with poor skills can be transferred to self-selection areas where they are guides and guards rather than salespeople.

A woman who likes to trade up will do well in a high fashion department. A woman who likes children will do well in children's wear. A man who has a talent for coordination will make use of it by selling shirts, neckwear, and sportswear, if he is allowed to cross departmental lines.

More women are moving into men's wear, and doing well in departments traditionally reserved for *salesmen*. The reverse is not true in large department stores.

Men do sell to women in small stores and boutiques, which are often owned and staffed by men.

Young people sell well to other young people. Sometimes, young people will turn to older salespeople for advice. Many older customers, on the other hand, have little confidence in young salespeople.

By placing people where they perform best, the store will get best results.

It is up to the store to use ingenuity in recruiting. Older women are often excellent part-time saleswomen—they are delighted to have a chance to work outside their homes. They can be reached through mailing lists and senior citizen organizations, as well as through ads in local newspapers.

Young people can be recruited through contacts with teachers and placement services in local high schools and career schools.

Some people are available for a second part-time job. Teachers and government workers may be willing to work Saturdays. Wives of men who work Saturdays are sometimes available for Saturday work. The wife or husband of an evening school student may want evening work.

Management must screen inexperienced applicants carefully. How can you tell if they can sell? You can't for sure. But you can look and ask questions.

How is the applicant dressed? Is unsuitable dress an expression of rebellion? Or is this an older woman who just is not used to dealing with fashion? Or a young person from a minority group with no money to spend on clothes?

Some people are more intelligent than they seem, although they have difficulty expressing themselves with words, especially in an interview.

Questions to ask applicants include:
- What kind of stores do you shop in? Or would if you could?
- Do you like clothes? What kind?
- What do you think of current fashion? Or a particular current fashion such as culottes, jeans, silk flowers? What do you like and dislike?
- Do you think you might like to work with people?
- What has been your experience with salespeople when you shop for yourself?
- Why are you applying to this store for a job?
- Have you ever shopped in this store? What do you like about it?
- Do you know anybody who works here? Did someone advise you to apply here?

Sometimes the quality of the response to these questions will provide the interviewer with valuable information. Perhaps this applicant has some undeveloped ability; a flair for fashion that can be developed.

Setting a standard for appearance. Besides specific rules and regulations, there are ways of giving job applicants an idea of what will be expected from them.

Show them a Sears, Ward or Penney catalogue. Show them a magazine like *Vogue* or *Glamour* with photographs. Point to pictures and say, "This is the way we'd like you to look." Or, "Not this glamorous . . . a little less. . . ." Or, "Not this basic, but simple. . . ."

Giving applicants visual aides can stimulate them to learn. Not everybody learns by reading. Some people learn by looking at pictures, or by listening to sounds.

Once applicants become employees, they face orientation. They must absorb information and become part of the store.

Questions like—Who's my boss? Who's her boss? Where is the cafeteria? When is coffee break?—are all part of orientation. Information about sick leave, fringe benefits, and vacation should also be answered at this time. A good deal of this is general store policy. Written material, if well prepared, is usually handed to the new employee, but the questions should be answered verbally as well.

Store procedures and actual sales training follow orientation or are taught at the same time.

Opening a charge account. The new saleswoman should be invited to open a charge account so that she can participate in the fashion life of the store as a customer, while she is learning how to be an employee. Her charge account tells her she is the equal of customers. Her discount is a privilege for store employees only—part of the benefits that accrue to her because of her job.

Appearance. Appearance is a touchy matter when it implies criticism. Written material with illustrations, films, tapes, and slides with commentary all help get across a personal message.

Illustrations are an important part of written material. Material that says, "Don't wear short skirts" leaves the reader with a question—"What is 'very short'?" But an illustration is precise; it shows exactly what management considers very short.

"Neat" and "attractive" are vague words that every woman identifies in her own way. Better to show visual material that gives specific examples of proper and improper clothing.

Where bad habits persist, the supervisor or personnel manager will have to correct individually. Young women may need toning down. Long hair and high heels are out of place on the selling floor.

Older women may need encouragement to dress more fashionably; to discard droopy dresses and modify old-fashioned hair styles.

The woman who cannot adjust raises a question about herself. Does she belong in a fashion department? Give her some time, a good employee discount, encourage her to shop in the store, and keep trying to raise her fashion consciousness.

Rules about dress change as fashion changes. The old idea that saleswomen in a prestige store must wear black or navy blue, and look almost in uniform, is gone, though some stores still have relatively stringent rules about color and prints.

Although pants are an accepted way of dressing, the saleswoman in pants is, at this writing, still a subject of controversy. Mass stores allow pants. Prestige stores sometimes forbid saleswomen to wear pants. Others compromise, and insist on skirts on the main floor and in designer departments, while permitting pants in upstairs departments.

There is little doubt that this barrier will break down eventually. Well-cut pants are not only comfortable, they are practical and modest. The saleswoman who must reach, bend, and stretch is freer to move in pants than in a skirt.

Rules that have *not* changed include the rules that forbid heavy perfume and makeup, excessive jewelry, and plunging necklines. The saleswoman is not a sexpot.

Continual sales training is essential for fashion salespeople. Unlike other jobs that consist of repeated tasks, the job of the saleswoman changes constantly, because fashion itself changes constantly.

During the initial training period, the saleswoman is confronted with large quantities of information about the store, about her own behavior, and about merchandise. As she moves into the mainstream of the store, she gradually absorbs this information—or as much of it as she needs for her day-to-day work. But the learning process never stops, because the flow of new merchandise never stops.

Anne Saum, of Anne Saum and Associates, training specialists, has spent years helping store management develop effective sales training programs. Here she lists the essential ingredients of sales training in a fashion store.

- Sales training must be continual.
- The training department must work with the buyer or department manager.
- There should be a clear line of authority.
- The buyer or department manager must create a good atmosphere.

Elaborating on the need for continual sales training, Ms. Saum remarks that too many stores feel the initial period is the end of training, when in fact it should be just the beginning. Every sale is different, because every customer is different. Therefore, selling is not something that can be learned by memorizing a formula: It is, rather, a creative process that calls for quick thinking and improvisation, often under pressure.

The department manager is responsible for day-to-day training. She knows the salespeople. She sees them in action. She knows what faults need correcting and what gaps in knowledge need to be filled.

When there is a radical fashion change, the department manager must work with the training department to develop a plan for acclimating saleswomen to the incoming fashions. Special fashion shows should be held, as complete as customer fashion shows but with a different kind of commentary. The accent should be on how to sell; why certain colors are worn together, who can wear short skirts, what kind of stockings should be worn with them—all these and many more details should be explained.

There are certain "places" of change in fashion—the waist, the hips, the hemline, the shoulders. These "places" must be pointed out to saleswomen each time fashion changes. This is the way they learn to look at merchandise.

After a few seasons, saleswomen will begin to remember that the waistline that was sharply indented is now relaxed; the shoulders that were narrow and sloping are now broad and squared-off, and so on. The more a saleswoman develops this kind of fashion memory, the better equipped she is to sell.

Saleswomen tend to resist fashion change, Ms. Saum notes. A saleswoman will remember that she sold a style successfully last year. She would rather sell it again than try to sell something new that might meet with customer resistance. So she must be pre-sold on a new fashion herself, before it reaches the selling floor.

If new merchandise comes into the store and nobody has called it to the saleswoman's attention, it automatically becomes "old stock" as far as she is concerned. That means she will feel no excitement about it, and it certainly follows that she will fail to communicate any excitement to her customers.

Ms. Saum points out that the department manager has three opportunities to flag the saleswoman's attention. The first opportunity comes just after the merchandise has been ordered; the second arises when the first few pieces of merchandise arrive in the store; the third, when the merchandise peaks in the store.

The department manager should make use of all three. She must communicate to her staff the interesting and saleable features of the merchandise. If the buyer functions as department manager, she herself knows why she ordered the merchandise. Unless she gets these points across, the salespeople will not be able to get them across to customers.

The need for a clear line of authority is essential to good morale, Ms. Saum has discovered in her work with store management. The saleswoman is at the bottom of the heap, so to speak. There are many people over her, many people who may give her orders. Some of those orders may conflict. The display manager may tell her to do something that the department manager has told her not to do. So she becomes confused. Even if the orders are consistent, they build up pressure. They also build up resentment. Nobody likes to take orders, but most people can reconcile themselves to obeying one person. When that one "boss" becomes several or many people, there is bound to be resentment.

The department manager can avoid this situation by insisting that all instructions to sales staff channel through her. She then becomes the one person who gives the orders in her department. Just how she gives them is very important. She will set the pattern for her sales staff, for better or worse. If she barks, they will, too. If she gets rattled when someone interrupts her, her saleswomen will get rattled when customers interrupt them. If she is disorganized, her saleswomen will be disorganized.

The department manager should be an expert in human relations. She should give clear, and consistent instructions, treat everybody fairly, recognize and reward good work, and never scold in public. Anger should be controlled and expressed in private. All these factors help create the atmosphere in which saleswomen work, and atmosphere affects their performance.

On the subject of salary, Ms. Saum points out that there are guidelines that management can follow if it so desires. One of these is the use of selling cost as a yardstick for measuring salary.

A saleswoman's selling cost is the ratio of her salary to the amount of merchandise she sells. If she earned $100 a week and sold $2,000 worth of merchandise a week, her selling cost would be 100 divided by 2,000 or, five percent. If she sold more merchandise, and her salary stayed the same, her selling cost would go down.

If management felt a five percent selling cost was satisfactory, then it might well use that yardstick at salary review time, whether such reviews took place at three-month, six-month, or twelve-month intervals.

If, for example, the saleswoman in question should increase her average sales for a six-month period to $2,500 a week, the five percent selling cost yardstick would indicate that management should now consider paying her $125 weekly.

This type of incentive is just one way of rewarding good sales performance; others include giving an end-of-the-year or seasonal bonus or paying a commission. Whatever system is used, regular salary reviews are essential.

Along with these "do's," Ms. Saum also has a list of "don'ts" for retailers:

"*Don't* think that sales training is the cure for all ills."

"*Don't* let supervisors treat salespeople rudely."

"*Don't* be pessimistic—attitudes can be influenced and changed."

One more "don't" to be added to the three above is:

"*Don't* confuse pep talks with sales training."

Pep talks have little or no content and are merely exhortations to "do better." Sales training communicates specific information and enthusiasm.

"I think these new dresses are great, girls, and I just know you're going to love selling them." That's a *pep talk.*

"Look—these dresses have belts. Remember how many of your customers have been asking for dresses with belts? Now you'll have something to show them. Be sure you tell them that the belts are designed to be worn loosely, like this—not cinched tightly." That's *sales training.*

During training sessions, saleswomen should not only see new merchandise, they should examine it and any special feature closely. If the fabric is a new one, they will need to know what it is, how it performs, and how it should be cleaned. Saleswomen should also be told how a particular piece of merchandise fits into the whole fashion picture. If it is a dress, what kind of shoes should be worn with it? What figure faults will it emphasize or disguise? Will it appeal to a particular age group? Is it versatile or for a specific occasion? These are just some of the facts saleswomen should know about merchandise.

When a market becomes more important, or when it takes on new characteristics, saleswomen must be made aware of the trend. A coat buyer will have to tell her staff about the new raincoats, whether or not they are sold in her department. (If they are not, they are competition for her department, and saleswomen should know this.)

Explaining new merchandise is one function of the sales training session; another is instruction in selling techniques.

Members of the staff should be encouraged to report any unusual or difficult situation they encountered on the selling floor. The pattern might run like this: The saleswoman makes her report and gives her own interpretation of the situation. The department manager, who is leading the session, calls on two or three staff members to comment; then she sums up and adds her own interpretation.

93

Two saleswomen can be called on to "act out" a pre-selected situation, one that either of them has experienced. One will play the customer; one will play the role of the saleswoman.

If they can shed their inhibitions and lose themselves in their "parts," such "play acting" can be useful. The saleswomen get a chance to let off steam. The department manager can form some opinions of their personalities and abilities. When the "play" is over, saleswomen in the audience will comment on each "performance," and add their own ideas about the way the situation should have been handled.

The training session should not be allowed to deteriorate into a "gripe" session. But, if there is a special problem that needs attention, the staff may call it to the attention of the department manager.

If the staff, as a group, has been making some mistake, the department manager can correct it, criticizing her saleswomen as a group. It cannot be said too often—individual criticism should be given in private, even if "private" means a buyer's cubbyhole of an office.

Praise, on the other hand, can be bestowed in public, for it is a morale and status-building factor.

There are other ways in which selling skills can be sharpened at a training session.

Films and slides are useful educational tools. If they are shown, there should be a follow-up. What did the staff think of this film and why? Was it realistic? Did they identify with anyone in the film? Were there any situations that reminded them of something they themselves experienced?

Videotape equipment and television are playing an increasingly important role in sales training. Sessions can be recorded and played back for self-criticism, or they can be circulated through other branches of a chain store.

Fashion shows can be taped for showing at all branches of a chain. The savings in dollars are tremendous. While a film or taped show is not the same thing as a live performance, it is a workable substitute. The speed with which a tape can be sent to branch units is a plus. Within days after a new fashion has been bought, its image can be transmitted to branch stores hundreds of miles away, and sales training can begin.

Young people, especially, seem to enjoy films on television in a store as much as they do at home. The use of film and tape as a training tool for staff will probably increase in the future.

Like all education, sales training does not exist in a vacuum. If a saleswoman cannot relate to information, if she cannot link it somehow with some experience of her own, then it will be useless. Since everyone's experiences are different, good training material must have a wide appeal.

Vendors sometimes address a sales staff and convey useful information about their merchandise. What they have *to say* should be evaluated beforehand to make sure that it is not just self-serving.

Any favorable mention of the store in a newspaper or magazine should be called to the staff's attention. If a piece of merchandise is going to receive editorial credit in a publication, that publication should be shown to the sales staff. Storewide events should also be called to the staff's attention in the training session.

Store executives may address departmental meetings from time to time. This makes the staff feel that they "belong," and that management cares about them. They will also acquire a better understanding of the total store picture if the display manager, the fashion coordinator, and other important executives make it clear that they want to share their ideas with rank-and-file sales staff.

The buyer who does her own on-the-job training will find that her natural assertiveness and outgoing personality stand her in good stead. These same qualities should be required of the department manager who undertakes training responsibilities.

The service manager or buyer may supervise the filling out of want slips, those simple forms that salespeople use to tell management that a customer has asked for something the store did not have. The want slip is an invaluable source of information to buyers; it is their link to the vital selling action on the floor.

Some salespeople will be quick to report the lack of merchandise they could have sold if they had it; others will need urging. Many salespeople will be reluctant to discuss merchandise that is not selling well, for fear of offending their superiors.

Salespeople should be encouraged to express themselves freely, whether the news is good or bad. If a coat hangs badly, the saleswoman will be the first to notice it on her customer, and management should spot the defect quickly. Perhaps a second order can be stopped until the correction is made.

In high fashion departments, salespeople may keep records of individual customers, though this practice is fading fast. It is still an excellent way to build sales and bring the customer back to the store.

One famous specialty store chain trains its saleswomen to keep records of their best customers. Each one makes notes on customer tastes, preferences, hair and eye color, height, weight, birthday, age, and any other important facts. These records are checked by supervisors and spot-checked by floor managers, buyers, and the personnel department. Each saleswoman is expected to increase her "book" over a period of time; five new customers a month is the goal.

A spokesman for this chain notes that special problems exist in the departments that sell the most expensive fashions. Saleswomen in those departments are accustomed to making big-ticket sales. Dress prices run way up in the hundreds. The saleswomen work on commission. Some of them earn more than $25,000 a year. Because each sale is so big, and because each saleswoman has her own customer following, the saleswomen are sometimes intolerant of women whom they do not know as customers.

When an unknown woman enters the department, the saleswomen size her up quickly. If they decide that she is not "serious," that is, that she is just shopping and has no intention of buying, she gets a fast brush-off. A saleswoman shows her one or two dresses and says, "That's all we have."

While the saleswoman's judgment may be correct in some cases, this pattern often discourages and antagonizes women who really want to buy.

Store management has found a partial solution to this problem.

The buyer or the assistant buyer "patrols" the floor from time to time, to see if such a situation is developing. When it does occur, the buyer or her assistant will move in and try to reopen the sale. "I see you are looking at dresses," she will say "Have you seen our new Italian imports?" Then she will wait on the customer herself. This is an example of a situation that requires the presence of a supervisor on the selling floor.

Management presence on the selling floor can be a positive factor. If a supervisor "helps out" and the salesperson completes the transaction, all is well. If a supervisor is watching a particular person who is performing badly, everybody on the floor will know it.

If a supervisor is on the floor to learn, to inform herself, to keep up with her customers, salespeople will know that, too. They will appreciate that kind of presence. Salespeople will also appreciate the buyer or manager who asks them what *they* think —on the floor, as well as in the training session.

The late Nathan Ohrbach, founder of Ohrbach's and president of the store for many years, did not hesitate to walk the floors of his store. He had started out in the coat-and-suit business, and coats and suits were his favorite category. Often, he would spot a woman trying on a coat, walk up to her quietly, and say, "That's your coat, take it" or, "The red one looked better on you." His judgment was always sound.

Today, stores are often owned by conglomerates that own many different kinds of businesses. The personal touch is lacking in such organizations. The president who walks the floor because he wants to keep in touch with his customers is more likely to exist in a family-owned store.

Some stores are trying to replace personal supervision with impersonal systems of employee evaluation. Sometimes these systems are developed in the store, sometimes they are developed by retail consultants.

Some of these systems seek to motivate performance by grading or ranking the salesperson according to dollars produced. A good "producer" of dollars will earn more money or be promoted to a more profitable department, or both. A poor producer will be ranked in a low category and will not proceed up the ladder from low to higher rank, and low to higher salary.

People tend to dislike being categorized and classified. Sometimes, it turns out that the chief value of a system is the reassurance it provides for management, rather than the motivation it provides for salespeople. The system may become a substitute for judgment. No system can really substitute for human management. When management does not manage, in the end, salespeople do not sell.

The impersonality of systems is a problem of big stores. Small stores face different problems. The very small store offers little possibility of advancement to its few employees.

The absence of one saleswoman in a department of a large store may not be felt. If necessary, someone from another department can be brought in as a temporary replacement. But the absence of one saleswoman in a small store may be a real hardship if the staff consists of the owner and two or three other saleswomen. Someone may have to give up her day off, or the owner may have to delay important work to help out.

If the sales staff is small, they will be spending a great deal of time together. Personality conflicts that might be smoothed over in a large store are intensified when the group is small.

The store owner can lighten his own work load and motivate his sales staff by delegating authority whenever possible. One senior staff member will be in charge in his absence. If a saleswoman shows a talent for display, she should be encouraged to use that talent. If she has especially neat handwriting, she could be the one to write personal notes to customers, in the owner's name or in her own name.

In a small store, there must be an understanding that everyone will pitch in and do everything, including sweeping the floor at night. Without such an understanding, there will be constant squabbling and conflict. The pleasant tasks, as well as the unpleasant ones, should be shared.

Whether a store is large or small, management ought to understand the connection between promotion possibilities for rank and file employees, like salespeople, and motivation.

Is the store family-owned and managed? If members of a family own and control the store, and reserve top, policy-making positions for themselves, promotion possibilities are limited.

Is the store owned by a corporation? Does that corporation make any attempt to help rank and file employees, like salespeople, rise if they show promise? Are they limited to low-grade supervisory positions?

What is the store's record on hiring, training, and promoting women? Blacks? Other minorities?

Women have traditionally been stopped at the buyer or merchandise manager level, though this is changing. However, most top-ranking retail executives are still white males.

How does all this relate to selling?

If management hopes to recruit quality salespeople, there must be a real promise of advancement. Hourly rates of $2, $2.25 and $2.50 compare unfavorably with many factory as well as office jobs.

The psychological hazards of selling increase when economically disadvantaged salespeople are handling merchandise far beyond what they themselves can afford to buy. The saleswoman must show a customer a cashmere sweater and say, "How lovely, wouldn't you like to try it on?" At the same time, she knows she cannot own that cashmere sweater. In her heart, she hates the customer because she envies her, yet her job calls for her to suppress her hate and envy.

This kind of relationship would tax a skilled, emotionally secure person; it is extremely hard on an unskilled person who may also be emotionally insecure.

Enlightened retailers understand the importance of good physical working conditions. Employees need clean rest rooms, a lounge, a cafeteria, and public phones.

In a small store, where a cafeteria would be impractical, management can provide a comfortable room for lounging and eating, and a small refrigerator for lunches brought from home.

Lockers for personal possessions are necessary in a large store.

Heat and air-conditioning are essential.

Many salespeople complain that they are never allowed to sit down, even when they are not waiting on a customer. This practice goes back to the old days of retailing, and should be abandoned.

The executive who insists on "no sitting" should try a day or two on the selling floor to see what it is really like. Fears of loafing and personal conversation are unfounded; salespeople can, and do, loaf and talk among themselves just as easily when they are on their feet, as many shoppers know.

More stores go beyond minimal physical conditions every year as management realizes how much comfort and convenience raise performance on the job.

Above and beyond salary, there are small ways in which management can reward good performance. A gift certificate to the store for a small amount of money, extra time off during the slow season, lunch with the department manager or buyer, a birthday card—these are just a few ways in which management can show its appreciation of employees. Contests with prizes often improve performance and morale at the same time.

Whether a store is large or small, personal attention will be appreciated by the sales staff and will contribute to improvement of selling performance by building loyalty.

Sam Feinberg, columnist for *Women's Wear Daily (WWD)*, specializing in retail personnel problems, puts it this way:

"A worker's loyalty may be bought neither by browbeating nor raises. It can be won only by constant proof from all executives in day-by-day actions that leadership is equated with service, not domination, that volume and profits are at the mercy of the 'whole' man and woman, not of faceless, bloodless creatures . . ."

Too often, top management, seated in the executive suite, is far removed from the day-to-day problems of salespeople. Because there are so few opportunities for communication between top executive and rank and file, we offer, as a case history, the experience of a young woman who sold sportswear for a prestigious New York store during the Christmas holiday season. After Christmas, she was offered a permanent job, but refused it, and took a job as a waitress.

"We had three days of training. It was so busy . . . there was supposed to be someone I could go to, to ask a question. But she was busy, too. I couldn't interrupt her when she was writing up a sale. And I couldn't wait. The customers were in a hurry. Sometimes I just had to guess what was the right thing to do.

"Some of the permanent saleswomen gave me orders . . . I didn't know what to do about that. When a customer came in who was known, someone difficult, the permanents didn't want to be bothered with her, so they passed her along to me or one of the other temporaries.

"There seemed to be a lot of people giving me orders. There was one woman who said, 'keep moving, keep moving.' The customers came in waves. Sometimes I would just stop to catch my breath and they would be after me. 'If you don't have a customer, you can arrange stock,' they said. That wasn't my job.

"Customers were angry because I couldn't do gift wrapping. They were in a hurry and they didn't want to wait. I just couldn't believe how rude some of those women were, even the rich ones. They fought over me. It was funny, sometimes. They would argue with each other. One would say, 'I was here first.' Sometimes I thought I was in a bargain basement, not a good store.

"I didn't have any place to leave my coat or my bag.

"I didn't know what to do when customers gave me their credit cards that lit up the wrong buttons and meant they weren't supposed to charge any more. I tried to be tactful, but when the customers insisted, I was embarrassed. Finally I said, 'Well, you just can't use your card,' and they were furious and made scenes.

"They changed my hours two days after I started work. I had nothing to say about it. They just told me. I had to work half an hour later to make up my tally book. They didn't tell me that before I started work. If I started to make up my book early, they stopped me.

"They told me to push certain styles, sometimes the styles that weren't selling well. They told me to say everything was beautiful. Customers just don't believe you when you say that.

"There were some things I know were little, but they bothered me. Like the signs stuck up everywhere that said, 'sell.' They were supposed to inspire us, but I thought they were a turn-off. And we had to sign in and out, even for breaks. And in the cafeteria, mayonnaise on a sandwich was five cents extra, and extra hot water was five cents more. It was really chintzy. And we could never sit down, not for a minute.

"But the worst thing was the security talks. They didn't just warn us, they raised their voices and harangued us and threatened us. They told us case histories; stories about how people who had stolen were punished, all the details.

"I would never steal. I don't think all that scolding stopped anyone who was a thief. It just humiliated the good people."

Every retailer could answer this list of grievances with a comparable list of grievances. Salespeople are irresponsible—they say they will work until Christmas and then quit two weeks before Christmas. They are lazy, sloppy, dishonest, rude to customers, indifferent to merchandise, and uninterested in learning. There is truth in all these complaints, just as there is truth in the saleswoman's complaints.

Where does equity lie? The saleswoman's reactions suggest some guidelines for sensible, decent, productive policies—policies that are obviously easier to state than to carry out.

- Start holiday training before the heart of the busy season.
- Explain store policy. There is a reason for signing in and out, or there should be. If there is no good reason, change the policy.
- Make certain allowances for temporary help.
- Consider procedures that can be curtailed during busy periods.
- Be realistic about supervision. A "buddy" system is not going to work when the "buddy" is too occupied with her own work to help out someone else.
- Make sure every employee knows exactly what is expected of her. This applies to hours and duties.
- Changing an employee's hours arbitrarily is bad policy.
- A supervisor should be on hand to mediate disputes between salesperson and customer. The case of the two customers fighting for one saleswoman's attention also calls for intervention of a supervisor.
- *Pushing* merchandise is not *selling* merchandise. Few customers are taken in by hard sell tactics. Telling a saleswoman to say everything is beautiful is poor training, and reflects contempt for customers, as well as for salespeople.
- Sitting down for a moment is no crime. A saleswoman might well sit down when she is writing up a sale. (Curiously, this complaint evokes a customer complaint about lack of seating.)
- Lectures about security and theft can be delivered with dignity and without abuse. Management should remember that the highest percentage of theft is executive theft. Permanent salespeople are often aware of this situation, and are sometimes forced to participate in it.

These guidelines call for constant study and re-evaluation, if training for salespeople is to be effective.

Advertising: The Written Word—Print

9

Advertising is a message sent from store to customer. The store pays for the message, hoping customers will come in and buy its merchandise, and that they will think of the store as a good place to shop.

Small stores often depend on traffic off the street and word-of-mouth. Word-of-mouth refers to the message that one customer passes to another, recommending a store as a good place to shop. It is valuable, but informal and undependable. Most stores that sell fashion in any substantial volume cannot depend on word-of-mouth; they must get their message to customers regularly and in a more concrete way.

Fashion is a special product; it is timely. Fashion advertising helps move merchandise out of the store to make way for new merchandise. What is not sold winds up on the markdown rack.

Before going into the specifics of fashion advertising, we will examine some of the ways in which advertising in general is described and defined.

National advertising and *retail* advertising are two typical classifications.

Most national advertising is run by *manufacturers* who want to sell a product. The product may be soap, or food, or a chain of restaurants, or a headache remedy, or it may be fashion. Shirt and shoe manufacturers are examples of fashion products that are advertised nationally. The manufacturer pays for the advertising. The manufacturer does not care where the customer buys the product, as long as it sells.

While all manufacturers of products like a quick response, the ad may pull over a long period of time, especially if the product is not seasonal. (Aspirin is an example of a product that is not seasonal.) National advertising is beamed at customers all over the country, or it may be aimed at a region—the Midwest, the Far West or the Northeast.

Retail advertising is quite different. It is prepared and paid for by a *store,* and it aims to sell the store as well as the merchandise. The retailer cares very much where the customer shops. Store X wants women to buy clothing in store X, and it must sell its store's reputation along with its merchandise.

A good deal of retail advertising is seasonal and timely—this is especially true of fashion advertising. Seasons change, holidays come and go, styles change. The response must be quick; the customer must come in tomorrow, not next month.

Retail advertising, when run by a local store, aims at a local audience within the shopping radius of the store.

While most fashion retailers advertise locally, the giant retail chains, like Sears, J.C. Penney and Ward, advertise nationally. (These general merchandise chains sell hard goods as well as soft goods, including fashion.)

Giant retail chains advertise nationally because they have a network of stores stretching across the country; stores that draw a national audience.

Such national chain retailers, like other national advertisers, usually depend on agencies to prepare their advertising.

Advertising agencies are a relatively new element in fashion advertising. Traditionally, it was prepared in the store, where most fashion advertising is still prepared. This has its advantages. An in-store staff will always be more closely in touch with what is happening in the store than an outside agency.

When advertising is prepared by an in-store department, some work is often farmed out. For instance, the advertising department's art director may hire a photographer or an artist to handle illustrations. Photographers and artists are hired on a free-lance basis and work outside the store, but the art director will give them instructions and control their work.

Most retail fashion advertising runs in a newspaper or magazine. Of the two, the newspaper is most important.

The relationship between fashion retailing and newspapers is historic. The newspaper, of all advertising media, is the oldest "home" of fashion advertising.

We often refer to newspapers as one of the media, or, we may call it an advertising medium. Newspapers and magazines are print media. Radio and television are broadcast media. There are others—for instance, billboards are an outdoor medium.

All advertising media, from billboards to television, are used to sell, to transmit that message to someone, or some group of people who will buy a product. But not all advertising sells a product directly. Some ads sell an idea. This difference is the basis for another way in which advertising is described.

Retail advertising is usually described in this way. Ads can be item or merchandise ads, or they can be institutional.

The *item* ad sells a dress, a skirt, a small appliance, a large piece of furniture— it sells *merchandise*.

The *institutional* ad sells the *idea* of the store as a good place to shop. There are many different kinds of institutional ads. An institutional ad may announce the opening of a new department or a store. It may announce that the store has been remodeled. It may invite customers to come in and meet a designer, to see a demonstration or some special exhibit. It may offer a special service like gift-wrapping or personal shopping. It may wish its customers a happy holiday season.

Institutional ads of a general nature may greet a celebrity who is visiting the community, or note the opening of a theater season, or opera or ballet.

Why should a store spend money to mention things so far removed from merchandise? The store is selling itself. It is showing that it "has a heart," that it sees itself as part of the community, not as a cold, isolated institution. Large stores, especially, need to "warm up" their images with this kind of institutional advertising.

At the same time, the store is demonstrating that it is aware of what is happening in the community, aware of its customers needs, feelings and desires, and up-to-date on community events. The image of awareness has a direct bearing on fashion. Customers feel that an up-to-date, aware store is more likely to carry up-to-date fashions.

In a sense, every ad a store runs is institutional, even its merchandise ads, for every ad says something about the store by the way it presents merchandise.

The dividing line between institutional and item advertising is not always clear. An ad that invites the customer to see a new line of bras and bodywear, adding that expert salespeople will help her choose the style that is best for her is an example of an ad combining item and institutional qualities. The ad is selling specific merchandise, but it is also selling its own fashion expertise, which is a service, which is institutional.

Some merchants think that institutional advertising is wasteful because it does not produce direct sales. But it helps create the atmosphere in which customers buy; an atmosphere of confidence and authority.

When a woman is hesitating about a fashion purchase, her confidence in the fashion authority of the store may influence her decision. A store that announces designer appearances, offers special services, and brings in experts to demonstrate the "how to" of fashion is establishing itself as a fashion authority and building customer confidence.

We have discussed institutional advertising in terms of store or retail advertising, but we should note that manufacturers, as well as stores, can and do run institutional ads. The phone company tells us it has a heart, and cares about us. Oil producers tell us they want to keep costs down. These are examples of national advertisers trying to improve their image through institutional advertising.

With these definitions of institutional or item, national or retail advertisements in mind, we now proceed to fashion advertising. We have mentioned the advertising department as the source of fashion ads, but advertising "departments" come in all sizes. A large store, or a chain, will have a large staff. A medium-sized store may have a department of two or three people, who may also handle publicity and other tasks.

104

```
5/3    ny times   1200 li.   M-5-20   d. 40 sir james blouses

carol cooper garey    ext. 7447
```

set rule per style

May 8th is Mother's Day. Make it count with over-easy shirts, ~~with a~~

the coolest shapes this side of summer. ⌠From Sir James, the white

12/13. *Optima Italic rag left*

collared and cuffed pullover in taffy,⌠red or black polyester and

cotton, 6 to 16 sizes, $18. The drawstring⌠blouson with rolled cuffs,

trimmed in white with red or black⌠polyester and cotton, 6 to 14 sizes, $22.

Blouse Collections,⌠Street Floor. — *insert* *broadcloth*

15 pi. from right

Some steps in preparing a print ad. Layout is created (not shown here) with space allowed for copy and illustration. Decision for art or photography is made. Copywriter writes copy to fit space. Copy is marked for printer.

Copy set in type, as shown. It will be pasted up with photos on a cardboard, with store logo. Finished layout is known as "mechanical," and must be approved by advertising department and buyer.

May 8th is Mother's Day. Make it count with over-easy shirts. The coolest shapes this side of summer. From Sir James, the white collared and cuffed pullover in taffy, red or black polyester and cotton, 6 to 16 sizes, $18. The drawstring blouson with rolled cuffs, trimmed in white with red or black polyester and cotton broadcloth, 6 to 14 sizes, $22. Blouse Collections, Street Floor. Saks Fifth Avenue

New York • White Plains • Springfield • Garden City • Bergen

May 8th is Mother's Day. Make it count with over-easy shirts. The coolest shapes this side of summer. From Sir James, the white collared and cuffed pullover in taffy, red or black, 6 to 16 sizes, $18. The drawstring blouson with rolled cuffs, trimmed in white with red or black, 6 to 14 sizes, $22. Both, polyester and cotton broadcloth. Blouse Collections, Street Floor.

Saks Fifth Avenue

New York • White Plains • Springfield • Garden City • Bergen

Proof is a duplicate of the mechanical as it appears in print. At this stage, it is still possible to make vital, last-minute corrections.

In a really small store, the owner functions as advertising manager, and does whatever is necessary to create and place ads. The owner may call upon a local agency or the advertising department of a local newspaper, radio or television station for professional help. When store owners go it alone, with no help, they often produce advertising of poor quality.

Some small stores do not advertise at all, while others advertise occasionally, perhaps at the beginning of a season. Or, they may advertise an end-of-season clearance sale. This kind of announcement advertising runs in newspapers, and on local radio or television stations. (Direct mail, another form of advertising, will be discussed at the end of this chapter.)

The larger the store, the larger the advertising department. A large advertising department is headed by an advertising manager, who may report to a vice president in charge of sales promotion. In some stores, the vice president in charge of sales promotion also functions as advertising manager; this is an example of the flexibility of jobs and job titles.

The advertising manager heads three divisions of the department: art, copy, production.

If we were to describe these divisions in the most elementary way, we would say that the art division is in charge of illustration; the copy division is in charge of copy, or written words; and production is in charge of assembling and preparing the ad for printing.

There may also be a traffic division, or a traffic manager, who keeps the ad moving through all its stages of preparation, making sure that it is completed in time to meet printing deadlines.

In smaller departments, production and traffic functions are combined. In large departments, there will be a fashion coordinator or stylist who keeps track of merchandise and selects accessories for photographs.

Whether the department is large or small, the *elements* of a retail ad are similar.

There is usually a *picture*. In a fashion ad, the picture or illustration may be a drawing or a photograph of the merchandise.

Copy is the written message; the words that tell the story about merchandise.

The *logo*, or store name, is the signature that identifies the ad.

Empty space, or *white space* surrounding the other elements is an important element itself, for it makes the ad readable and attractive. Not enough white space is a common advertising flaw.

Layout refers to the arrangement of all the elements in the space allotted to the ad. The layout of each does not happen spontaneously; it follows a pre-arranged plan or *format*.

Format is the plan for the general appearance or look of the ad. Will the illustration be large or small? Photo or sketch? How will the copy, including headline, be positioned? How much white space will there be? These questions are questions of format. Format precedes and dictates layout.

There is a great deal to be said about advertising planning and strategy, but that is not the subject of this chapter. Suffice it to say that planning happens before—long before the actual ad is prepared.

No matter how well advertising is planned and prepared, there are limits as to how well it will perform.

Thinking in terms of fashion, the question of the timeliness of the merchandise is one of the first questions to be asked when a fashion ad fails to pull.

Stores traditionally receive and advertise merchandise way ahead of the season—fall merchandise is promoted in June; spring fashions are promoted in February.

This out-of-season timing is responsible for the failure of many ads.

There are other questions to be asked when an ad fails. Is the merchandise right for the store's customers? Is it too expensive or inexpensive? Too avant-garde? Too conservative? Too much like what has been offered before? Too much like what other stores are offering?

An "act of God" can ruin the best advertising. A blizzard or an extremely hot day keeps customers at home. During times of severe economic stress or depression, most people cannot afford to buy clothes beyond basic necessities—if that much.

Of course, questions must also be asked about the ad, and about the advertising format. Are they right for the merchandise? Do they talk to the store's customers? Are they too hard sell? Too soft sell?

Hard sell and soft sell are terms that are frequently used to describe fashion presentation.

Hard sell ads are run mostly by promotional stores. Often, they feature sales and special events, always, with the emphasis on price and value. The hard sell ad is like the hard sell television commercial; it tries to grab the customer by hitting her over the head, so to speak, with a strong message.

The hard sell fashion ad is easy to recognize. The letters are heavy and dark. There is little white space in the ad—it is crowded with copy and illustrations.

Illustrations are very basic photographs or simple drawings. There is little or no background or mood. If the merchandise has an important selling feature, that feature will be emphasized in both copy and illustration. Fleece-lined coats will be illustrated with the edge turned back so the fleece lining shows clearly. Pleated skirts will be shown with emphasis on the pleats. Those details accentuate the desirability of merchandise at its price.

Soft sell advertising appeals to women who can spend money for clothing beyond basic necessities, and places more emphasis on fashion than on price. These ads speak to a customer who cares about fashion rightness.

Ads are not cluttered with copy and illustrations. They are well designed, so that

108

Frank Smith, that great sport
from Evan Picone, joins us today
from 12 to 4, with trunks of
smart new things for the casual New York
woman. She'll adore the luxe quality
of his camel-coloured cashmere blazer, $140,
and pants, $90, vest, $78, and dirndl, $60,
so delightful over a stock tied cream-coloured
polyester blouse, $28. For 6 to 16 sizes
in Sport Separates Collections, Third Floor.

Dainty hands will adore the baby-softness
of long cashmere gloves, made for
Milady in the Scottish highlands. Natural,
brown, or black for small, medium and
large sizes, $11. Gloves Collections, Street Floor.

Brimming with possibilities, the
fetching felt cloche is stencilled with
one of the new motifs that is
so popular in Paris. Brick, camel,
off-white, teal, wine, rust, $25.
To warm Madame and the hearts of
those who see her, a six-foot
fling of wool scarfing. Natural, grey rust
or white, $7.50. Hat and
Scarf Collections, 8th Floor.

Stroll down the Avenue deserve
the jaunty tassels and perforations of
a stack-heeled kidskin kiltie.
So practical for Today in grey or
brown, $84. Young Dimensions
in Shoes, Seventh Floor.

Ever punctual, the Busy woman
wears our exclusive 17-jewel
watch, so decorative on her slim wrist
with a gold-toned metal case
striped in black and red enamel and a
black patent band that has a
snakeskin motif, $50. Guaranteed for
1 year against any defect originally in the
movement. Fashion Jewelry
Collections, Street Floor.

Precious things are best kept
in one of the smart new French purses,
so delightful because she can
keep it with her always. Black, brown,
red or bone rawhide with those
new moderne designs in whipsnake, $10.
Small Leather Goods, Street Floor.

SAKS FIFTH AVENUE
CELEBRATING FIFTY YEARS OF FASHION

Saks celebrated its 50th anniversary by reviving its original format with "floating" layout in which merchandise is laid out as separate units. Compare this to carefully planned compositions of modern ads. Copy also "floated" in separate blocks. Logo and art deco motif above logo (bottom of ad) were carried through campaign.

BUCCELLATI

You see diamonds and 18k gold in a bracelet that looks like lace, and you know it's Buccellati $20,500.

703 Fifth Ave., New York, N.Y. 10022, (212) 755-3253. Major credit cards accepted.

Jewelry is especially difficult to illustrate. Here, Buccellati photographs a spectacular diamond bracelet in close-up. No props needed; the merchandise speaks for itself. (Actual size of ad.)

110

Now you can do more
than window-shop!

Saks Fifth Avenue will be

Open Today
from 12 to 5

December 19

New York, White Plains, Garden City

New York will be open
weeknights until 8:30,
White Plains, Springfield
and Garden City will be open
until 9:00 p.m.

The best things come in shiny packages from Saks Fifth Avenue

Announcement ad from Saks Fifth Avenue informs customers of special shopping hours just before Christmas. (Actual size of ad.)

each element stands out clearly. Merchandise is accessorized. There may be props, or a background. The ad sets a mood. Junior clothes look young and perky, evening gowns look romantic, sportswear looks easygoing and casual.

111

Copy also sets a mood, and persuades without shouting.

There are many degrees of hard and soft sell. Just as the human voice can talk in many tones, from a shout to a whisper, so can an ad "talk" in a variety of tones— some loud, some soft. Each store must find a tone that will reach its customers effectively.

It is usual in advertising circles to equate hard sell with bad advertising and soft sell with good advertising. Not all soft sell advertising is good, or perhaps effective would be the better word.

Unfortunately, it is true that hard sell advertising is often poorly executed and ineffective. There is no reason why this need be. The low-income customer to whom hard sell advertising appeals wants plain, unvarnished facts. She wants to see the fleece lining in the coat and the gores in the skirt. She wants to know how much she is going to pay and how much money she will save. Such information can be presented attractively.

It is hard to believe that an attractive, easy-to-read format would not pull in more customers than a crowded, tacky format, with unappealing art, shouting copy, and cluttered, unorganized layout.

Of course, white space costs money—all advertising space costs money, and some advertisers feel that the more they crowd into a given space, the more merchandise the ad will sell. They are wrong—sometimes less is more.

Whether an ad is hard sell or soft sell, whether it appeals to the rich, the middle-class or the low-income customer, it must meet certain standards if it is to be effective.

Clarity. The ad must be easy to look at and read. The reader must grasp the message quickly.

Individuality. The format must be distinctive, so that the reader senses that this is a "store X" ad even before she sees the logo of store X.

Continuity. A format is established. The merchandise in each ad is different, but each ad relates to other ads, because of shared ingredients that are part of format—layout, copy, art.

Large stores with a heavy volume of advertising sometimes use more that one format. In such a case, each format has its own continuity; and some elements, like the tone of copy, and the store logo, are the same in both formats.

Credibility. The customer must believe the ad. Copy claims must be justified. The term, "wash-and-wear" has been abused; this has created a lack of credibility among women who have been disappointed in so-called wash-and-wear clothing. Claims like "sturdy" and "one-of-a-kind" should also be justified.

If a store continually offers "fantastic bargains" that turn out to be less than fantastic, the disappointed customers will not believe that store's advertising. There is a loss of credibility. It takes time for a store to destroy its own credibility, and even more time to re-build credibility after it has been destroyed.

Truthfulness and verisimillitude. Verisimillitude is a kind of truthfulness, or likeness to reality. If a skirt is moderately full, the artist illustrating the ad has some license to exaggerate the fullness. That is called "romancing" the merchandise, and it applies to copy as well as art. But beyond a certain point, romance turns into distortion. The customer who comes into the store expecting to see a very full skirt will be disappointed, if there is too much difference between the picture in the ad and the reality of the garment in her hand. When picture and garment match, we can say that the illustration, and the ad, have verisimillitude.

Fashion drawings are exaggerated—no real woman is so tall and slender. Yet they must not be so exaggerated that women cannot identify with them, unless the ad is very special. An ad aimed at a very young audience, or a very high fashion audience, can take liberties. Most ads must create an illusion of reality even while they romance the merchandise.

Sheer fabric must look sheer, the motif of prints must be clear, satin must have shine and glow, and so on.

So there is a certain tension in a fashion ad, especially a high fashion, soft sell ad. It is stylized and glamorized—it "romances" the merchandise. Yet it must be real enough for the reader to identify with. These are conflicting requirements that pull an ad in two directions at the same time.

If the merchandise is too exaggerated, if it has been too "romanced," the ad will not be convincing. Copy that is too hard sell, or overloaded with adjectives, will not work, either. As with a noisy television commercial, at a certain point, the viewer or reader shuts off the noise—and the sell.

The volume of advertising in a large department or specialty store is tremendous. Work must be done quickly, to meet deadlines, yet it must be done carefully, for a mistake in a detail can destroy the effectiveness of the ad. Many ads are being prepared at the same time. The pace of the advertising department usually ranges from hectic to frantic.

Some decisions are made before work on an actual ad. For example, the ad has been scheduled for a specific space. A shoe or other accessory may be scheduled for small space, though a group of shoes may be scheduled for a full page, especially if they were created by a famous designer. A single garment on a single figure may be shown in a one-column ad in a magazine or newspaper.

Sometimes two pages facing each other are used; this is called a *double truck*. Sometimes two horizontal half pages facing each other are used. Double truck ads can do many things—for instance, they can show a wide assortment of merchandise in a single category: eight pairs of shorts, or eight T-shirts. Besides full pages and half pages, ads may run in different sizes and shapes, all of which relate to the total size and shape of the newspaper page, and the total number of columns on the page.

Advertising space is paid for on the basis of the number of lines per column inch.

Henri Bendel issues its own fashionable scrip money just before Christmas, for gift giving, and calls it, "bendel bills."

tunics...going over big, going over everything, and ours exclusively

Tumbling. Billowing. Spilling with sensational over-sizing. Over...the key word! Over narrow pants. Over great big puffs of skirt. Over shorts. Over nothing else but you. The tunic...having one is not enough. And, as you know, one can never have too much of a good thing. Left to right: Smock-front tunic dress in khaki, wine or yellow. 100% cotton. By M.J.M. S-M. $40. Roll-sleeve tunic in grape, slate blue, brick red or rose. Polyester/cotton voile. By Mi Bru San. S-M-L. $28. Tucked front, belted tunic in khaki, wine, teal or rust. 100% cotton. By M.J.M. S-M-L. $29.

Left to right: Shirred tunic in berry, rust, olive or sand. Polyester/cotton gauze. S-M-L. $34. Scoop neck, button tunic in brown, dusty green, sand or lilac. Polyester/cotton gauze. S-M-L. $30. Placket-front tunic in lilac, peach, white or beige. Polyester/cotton voile. S-M-L. $34. Smock tunic in lilac, peach, yellow or natural. Polyester/cotton gauze. S-M-L. $28. All by Mi Bru San. **Shop Macy's Sunday 12 to 5.** Young Collector Sportswear (D.662/168). Third Floor, Herald Square and your Macy's. Sorry, no mail, phone or COD's.

macy's
loosen up...it's spring

Photography has immediacy, reality and mood. Macy's shows an assortment of tunics in a double-page ad. Photography catches a happy, easy-going mood as a drawing could not, and also conveys a feeling of the size and the shape of the clothes. The headline, "Tunics . . . going over big . . ." is an example of a play on words that gets across the fashion message.

An ad might run on two columns by eight inches, on three columns by six inches, or in many other combinations of width and depth.

The art director must know the exact size and shape of the ad in order to plan the layout.

If the ad is going to show merchandise, as most fashion ads do, it will be photographed or sketched. The photographer or artist will probably be retained on a free-lance basis. The merchandise must be sent to the artist or photographer.

Meanwhile, back in the store, the copywriter must also see the merchandise in order to write copy. It sometimes happens that the photographer or artist whisks away the merchandise before the copywriter has a chance to see it. In that case, the copywriter must rely on the information on the buyer's fact sheet. If she is lucky, she will have a tissue layout with a rough sketch.

If there is a stylist or fashion coordinator in the advertising department, she will have a say in choosing models for a photograph, and picking out accessories.

The role of different members of the advertising department staff varies from store to store. A strong art director may have a great deal to say about layout. In another situation, the advertising manager may virtually dictate layout.

An advertising department may have a number of copywriters; traditionally, men write men's wear copy and women write women's wear copy, though this is beginning to change.

There is plenty of room for conflict. For instance, the buyer may want to feature a conservative, safe style, while the art director, and other members of the advertising staff, maintain that a more interesting style should be featured. The buyer wants to feature the safe style because it will sell best—or so the buyer thinks. There will be a discussion, not always quiet or friendly. Eventually, a decision will be reached, and the ad will be completed.

There are many advertising experts who claim that illustration is the most important element of any fashion merchandise ad. It is certainly the element that the newspaper or magazine reader sees first.

The decision to use art (as in sketching or drawing) or photography is vital. There are advantages and disadvantages to both.

Photography is at its best on the heavy, slick paper of a good magazine. It is harder to show merchandise effectively in a photograph printed in a newspaper because the quality of the paper itself is poorer; newsprint tends to absorb the photograph.

There are other disadvantages to photography—costs. There is the photographer's fee, and the fees for the fashion models who pose in the clothes. Unless the photographer can build props or settings in the studio, the work is done outside the studio, or "on location." Location may be as simple as a city street, yet it is not simple. Again, there is a question of cost and also convenience. The house and the stairs belong to someone who must give permission. The owner of the house will also be paid a fee. Outdoor light is undependable. If the photos come out badly, there may be no time for a re-take.

Still, there are advantages to photography that sometimes outweigh the disadvantages. There is nothing like a good fashion photograph for verisimillitude. A photograph of a woman in a bathing suit on a beach says "swimming" with strength and immediacy. If the photograph is a close-up, showing swimsuit fabric, skin, hair, and sunlight, the impact on the reader is forceful.

Photography can also show fabric and style with this same strength. The crispness of eyelet, the sheen of satin, the nub of a tweed, register quickly in a good fashion photograph.

Fashion art (a drawing or sketch as opposed to a photograph) has its own advantages and disadvantages. It lacks the verisimillitude and immediacy of a photograph. A sketch does not look like a real person because it is not a real person.

Each technique is capable of dramatizing and enhancing different kinds of merchandise in different ways. An artist can render fabric beautifully, and can sometimes show details that blur and disappear in a photograph. The twill weave of a gabardine may disappear in a photograph, but it can be expressed clearly in a drawing.

An advantage of a fashion illustration is the structure of the fashion figure. Even the slimmest model tends to look chunky in a photograph. But the fashion figure, as drawn, is tall and slim. Drawings are measured by the length of a head. A fashion figure is nine and a half to ten heads tall. (A real-life figure is about eight and a half heads tall.) The extra length of the fashion figure is in the legs, and sometimes in the torso between shoulder and waist. Clothes always look better on tall women with long legs.

Stores have traditionally switched from art to photography and back to art again. There are fashions in advertising, just as there are fashions in everything else. Some retailers use combinations of art and photography effectively.

There were a great many changes in fashion advertising during the 1970's, reflecting many changes in retail management at the very highest levels.

While sudden change has always been characteristic of retailing management as an industry, it did seem that the pace of change speeded up in the 1970's. Presidents and vice presidents, as well as lesser executives, moved around from store to store in a game of musical chairs. Often, when a new team took over a store, or a chain, it felt obliged to change the advertising format completely. One campaign succeeded another as one management group succeeded another, creating complete breaks in continuity that often left customers wondering whose advertising belonged to whom.

When a new management team takes over, and decides to change advertising format, one of the first elements considered is illustration.

Illustration reveals a good deal about the store's thinking. Who does the store think its customer is? What does she look like? How does she live? Most important of all: *how does she want to look?* Wholesome and freckle-faced? Snobbishly elegant? Spiritual? Kooky and young? Pert and junior-ish? These are just a few shades of meaning that are revealed in the artist's rendering of face, figure, movement, and gesture of the figure wearing the clothing that the store wants to sell.

The store had better make a good choice, for if it fails to pinpoint its image and match that image to its customer, the customer will look at a drawing, and think, "that's not me." She turns the page, and the impact of the ad is lost.

Here are some examples of artists with distinctive styles who worked for New York City-based department and specialty chains during the turbulent 1970's. Each artist was chosen because he or she projected a certain look that the store saw as representative of the customer it was trying to reach.

Michael Vollbracht, who worked for Bloomingdale's for a while, enjoyed filling

The best fashion artists have individual, recognizable styles that create an impression of the store, as well as the clothes shown in the ad. The ads shown here are just a sampling; there are more artists, more styles and more ways to show clothes at their best.

The long, lean look that was meant for a city slicker like me. It's the pantsuit that's more tunic than pants. Shirting, carried to an extreme over sleek trousers is the perfect way to do the town this spring! Long-sleeved, side-slit tunic with back pockets, over pants. In toast-colored cotton, 6 to 14 sizes, $43.

Spring in the city, new ground to cover. Lucky me with pant-suiting that's pure inspiration. A crisp butcher's coat that wraps over slacks expresses my adventurous attitude, shares my limitless potential. Black cotton butcher's coat and pants, 6 to 14 sizes, $50. Sport Separates Collections, Third Floor. Call (212) PL 3-4000. Add sales tax on mail and phone, 1.25 handling charge beyond our regular delivery area.

Welcome spring! Welcome the dash of pantsuiting that explores all possibilities! And it's from *Saks Fifth Avenue*

Red Cross. The Good Neighbor.

Antonio pioneered in pop art techniques. Here, his two figures in an ad for Saks Fifth Avenue are posed simply. Luscious curves, contrast of deep tone and white in swirling patterns, create exciting rhythm and movement. There is a strong feeling of the bodies beneath the clothes, which makes this ad sensuous and appealing.

a whole page with figures. His drawings had a molded look, based on planes mapped out in lush black and gray areas. His figures had an almost poster-like quality. His faces had a deliberately hard, old-time movie star glamour. When he was working for Bloomingdale's, Vollbracht used space almost as if he were illustrating a book, surrounding the page with fanciful borders. For instance, long locks of hair with an art nouveau quality would trail off into a frame for the page. Or the store logo itself was changed and worked into the overall design of the ad.

Pedro Barrios worked for Bloomingdale's and Saks Fifth Avenue, among others. His drawings seemed influenced strongly by the fashion art of the 1920's. His thin, fine lines would start curving at the top of a small head and continue, seemingly without a break, to the toe. His arrangements of figures sometimes suggested Japanese prints, and influence filtered through the 1920's. His faces were of little importance, yet the whole figure was graceful, and the merchandise always came through clearly.

Kenneth Paul Block was chosen to represent Bergdorf Goodman, the specialty store, when they finally abandoned a very old-fashioned format of clusters of tiny ads, each one showing one piece of merchandise. The change was a real improvement; full- or seven-column newspaper pages were used to show one or two figures.

Block has always been noted for his sinuous line. His style was ideal for the expensive, high-fashion image Bergdorf needed. His figures were supple; the line always curved continually, varying from light to dark, and creating a subtle perspective, so that even the figure at rest moved, with a shoulder thrown back, a leg thrust forward. The heads and features were sensitive; a bit snobbish; a bit wistful.

Fred Greenhill, one of Lord & Taylor's artists, had yet another style. His all-American women somehow missed being dull, even though they looked so wholesome. Greenhill used wash and line masterfully to show fabric and silhouette; some of his "drawings" seemed not to have any outlines at all, and not one non-essential detail. His simplicity was deceptive. He projected an image of fashion without the slightest hint of arrogance, and he could transform a simple dress into an eye-catching ad.

Not all first-rate artists work for large stores. *Sandra Leichman* was an example of a fine artist who worked for a smaller retailer, Martha, a three-unit chain of shops in New York and Florida. These shops carry the most expensive designer clothes and cater to an extremely affluent clientele who appreciate established name designers. The Martha customer does not go in for rolled jeans; she wears Galanos, Trigère and Blass.

Martha advertised in small space and showed one figure in an ad. Leichman drew figures with appropriate low-key elegance, using soft tones and unexaggerated poses. It is a good trick to draw a fashion figure that looks natural, for a fashion figure never is natural. Leichman's drawings showed a young woman, as all fashion drawings must, but there was never a feeling of extreme youth that would alienate the mature clientele of the store. Her women were of no age, and achieved fashion "snap" without a drop-dead effect that would have been all wrong for the store's image.

along the straight and narrow

Lean, vertical lines...covered by weightless shells. The Missoni coats. That draw the eye up, down...stopping only to notice the precise details that mark every piece. And a bit of braided rope fastened at the waist by the tiniest crystal balls: Missoni. The prophets. The striped coat, 155.00. The striped turtleneck, 60.00. The ribbed-striped skirt, 90.00. The belt, 16.00 The black sleeveless tunic, 130.00. The striped dress, 155.00. With the belt...and the Missoni visored hat, 32.00. Everything for sizes 4-12... in black and bark brown with white. The Shop for Missoni, Third Floor, New York. Also available in White Plains.

bloomingdale's

Michael Vollbracht maps out planes in lush blacks and grays. In this ad for Bloomingdale's, he turned fabric into a decorative element. His figures have a molded, poster-like look. His faces have a movie-star glamour.

quiet fire...

One long, lean column of smoky black...flickering molten gold. Just enough
to shimmer, suggest a glimmer of something quite beautiful beneath.
Causing the kind of quiet sensation he does best...Scott Barrie. Place Elegante, Third Floor.
The black matte jersey dress, outlined in gold Lurex® , for sizes 4 to 12. 220.00.

bloomingdale's/scott barrie

1000 Third Avenue, New York. 355-5900. Open late Monday and Thursday evenings.

Pedro Barrios works with thin lines that curve without breaking. His work is flat, in the manner of the
1920's, and in the manner of Japanese prints. This ad for Bloomingdale's creates a strong contrast
between the rather mysterious, isolated figure and the starkly simple linear background.

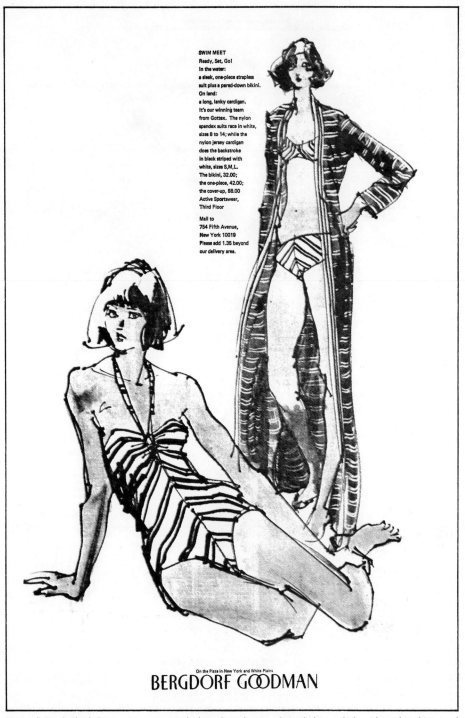

121

Kenneth Paul Block has a sinuous, supple line that changes from light to dark without breaking, and creates its own subtle perspective. Even figures at rest have movement; a shoulder is thrown back, a leg casually bent. His drawings project elegance in a natural, spontaneous way.

Woman to woman: an exploration inward.
And this three-week life-study begins tomorrow with The Body Workshop at Bonwit Teller.

The female form has been celebrated
in art and science and song.
But how does that relate to you?
How does that bring you
closer to your feelings, and needs?

How much better to find honesty,
understanding and privacy. To meet
the designers and expert fitters
who can put you back
in touch with your body.

For some, the tender underpinnings
of John Kloss are perfection.
For others, nothing can match
the almost custom feeling
of Edith Lances. And for all the
women somewhere in between:
just how much is enough control?
Or how little?

That's why we know our Body Workshop
is for everybody. With trained
fitters who know subtle differences
in shape, control and contour. And
with a collection so encompassing
it can only be called definitive.

Warners. Olga. Smoothie.
Bill Blass. John Kloss. Emilio Pucci.
Kaiser-Roth. Edith Lances.
Christian Dior. Poirette.
Formfit Rogers. Lily of France.
Hollywood Vassarette. Jantzen.
Character. Huit. LeJaby.
Vanity Fair. And this,
just to name a few.

Inner awareness. That's really
the theme of The Body Workshop.
To understand what you are, and
can be. For the next three weeks,
we'll bring it all together:
the designers and the fitters
and the collections. And all you
have to do is bring yourself.

The Body Workshop,
on our intimate Fifth Floor
Fifth Avenue at 56th Street, New York.

BONWIT TELLER

DRAWINGS BY JIM HOWARD

"Woman to woman: an exploration inward . . ." kicks off an intimate apparel promotion at Bonwit Teller. Jim Howard's drawing is an attention-getting poster. Copy lists designers whose merchandise will be featured. The artist uses light and dark tones as if he were a photographer playing with lighting and shadow. This ad has an institutional quality, though it is very much a fashion ad.

MARY MC FADDEN: SEEING LIFE AS ART,
WOMAN AS INSPIRATION.

When you are ready to pursue beauty as you would knowledge or success, you are ready to enter the aesthetic realm of Mary McFadden. Part iconoclast, complete artist, she has created a world of infinite and intricate paths to beauty. This is one. A butterfly tunic alight with molten thread, held in suspension over floor length skirting.

MARY MC FADDEN MAKES A RARE APPEARANCE AT OUR FORMAL FASHION SHOWING OF HER COLLECTION MONDAY, MARCH 13TH AT 11:30 A.M. OR SPEND A FEW QUIET MOMENTS WITH MARY WHEN WE PRESENT INFORMAL MODELING ON MONDAY AND TUESDAY TILL 4:00 IN THE DESIGNER SALON, SIXTH FLOOR

BONWIT TELLER

NEW YORK   MANHASSET   SCARSDALE   SHORT HILLS   PHILADELPHIA ·   WYNNEWOOD   JENKINTOWN   CHICAGO   OAK BROOK   BOSTON   TROY   PALM BEACH   BEVERLY HILLS

In another ad for Bonwit Teller, Howard features one figure against a dark ground. The prestige of the designer, Mary McFadden, is the theme. This ad, too, has a photographic quality.

Victor Joris' boxer pants—total knockouts in every new length

Starting left: 25.00, 30.00, 55.00, 55.00 in cotton sailcloth; the tanks, T's and other tops in cotton

knit from a collection at 25.00 and 30.00 Everything, Lord & Taylor

ours alone, in Designer Sportswear, Third Floor, Lord & Taylor,

Fifth Avenue at 39th Street. And Manhasset, Westchester, Garden City, Millburn, Ridgewood-Paramus and Stamford

Fred Greenhill, one of Lord & Taylor's artists, uses areas of wash rather than sharp outlines to block in his figures. His drawings suggest an all-American chic, just beyond wholesomeness. These figures are grouped simply yet skillfully on the page; the space is well-used.

Follow the leg at Lord&Taylor

All the fashion watchers do—
we have the most fabulous legs in town,
in our new collection of sensational Lortay pantystockings.
Sweater ribs. Sheer stripes. Chalk stripes. Opaques.
Mosaic opaques. Classic sheers, unclassic colors.
Everything to make your own look, to make
the eyes follow you! From 2.50 to 6.00 the pair.
Knee highs in chalk stripes, 2.00 Street Floor, Lord & Taylor—
call 391-3300 (24 hours a day). And
at all Lord & Taylor stores.

Another Greenhill ad for shoes demonstrates one way to show accessories on the body, in this case, the leg. One large leg dominates the layout and gives a center of interest to the ad. Note use of white space. Placement of headline is unconventional, but readable.

126

Oscar de la Renta for Martha

A sweep of shawl, a flare of skirt in a dramatic print of wool and cotton challis. Crisp counterpoint: the curving jacket in cotton and viscose rayon. Under it, the pure luxe of a pure silk shirt. Oscar de la Renta's newest statement for fall. Part of the excitement at Martha's now. $450. The shawl, $60.

Martha

475 Park Avenue
We honor the American Express Card

Not all first-rate artists work for large stores. Sandra Leichman's small space ad for Martha is drawn with low-key elegance, but avoids exaggeration and hard chic, which would be wrong for the store's image. (Actual size of ad.)

The artists mentioned are, of course, only a sampling; many fine ones have been omitted. In the 1970's, more fashion artists began to sign their work; a credit long overdue.

Another overdue change was the use of black models. Fashion magazines had featured black women editorially from the late 1960's on. Advertising usually follows, rather than leads, in breaking new ground. By the mid-1970's, retail stores were showing black women. Curiously, some of the stores carrying expensive merchandise showed black women in their catalogues, but did not feature them in daily newspaper ads. This conservative attitude would seem, at the very least, to be bad business, for black women had increased spending power. Yet some retailers continued to expect black women to respond to advertising showing only white faces.

We have dwelt on illustration because it plays so vital a role in fashion advertising. However, there are fashion ads without illustrations, usually, institutional ads.

But there is no such thing as an ad without copy. Copy is the written message, the words that inform, set a mood and persuade. Without information, there can be no sell. Illustration shows. Copy tells. They work together to sell.

The store logo itself is part of the copy—it is the word that tells customers where to shop.

Copy is usually broken down into the *headline*, which makes an announcement or sets a theme, and the *body copy*, which contains more detailed information.

There are many styles of copy, ranging from the direct, simple hard sell approach, stressing only essential information and price, to the soft sell copy that creates a situation or suggests an occasion. Copy may be light and witty. Many writers are fond of puns and other word play. The light touch is not easy to achieve, and nothing is worse than copy that tries to sound light-hearted and fails. In copy as in illustration, it takes a great deal of effort to produce work that looks effortless!

High fashion copy may take a cool, reserved tone. There was a time when the snobbish approach was the only approach a high-fashion store could take; this has changed. Copy, like art, reflects its era. Brief, informal copy that does not sound pretentious is the best copy, whatever its tone. Pretentious advertising is always bad advertising—no customer wants a store to talk to her heavily, or with condescension.

Copy may be personal or impersonal. It may tell a story to intrigue the customer and help her identify with the merchandise. Copy often finishes with a "call to action," or line urging or inviting customers to come in and buy. Whether the call to action urges strongly or invites casually depends on whether the ad is hard sell or soft sell.

All fashion copy must include specific information about the merchandise. There is a school of thought that believes copy should be brief, and include little else but price, sizes, colors, fabric, and some specific detail that the illustration does not show. For example, a reversible coat, a removable capelet, an underskirt, a back zipper in a turtleneck sweater.

128

There are high-fashion ads for very expensive designer clothing that do not include price. Perhaps the store thinks that reference to price is vulgar. Or it may be that women who buy such clothes know that their price runs to four figures, and do not care. This attitude recalls a remark of a multi-millionaire, who was asked the price of his yacht. He replied, "If you have to ask the price, you can't afford it." So it may be with expensive designer clothes that are advertised without price.

In a successful ad, illustration and copy work together, supplementing each other. The copy should not echo the illustration. An illustration showing a polka-dotted dress need not be reinforced by copy that says, "This dress is polka-dotted. . . ." Surely there is something more interesting to say about the dress that the illustration does not show.

Some customers might need to be told that brown-and-white perforated pumps are spectator pumps, but the customers of a store that prides itself on its fashion sophistication should not make the mistake of over-informing its equally sophisticated customers, who know what a spectator pump looks like. They would rather be told that tapered toes are new, or that heels are getting higher or lower, or that the instep is cut in a new way for comfort.

To inform is to persuade; it is hard to separate the two functions. To repeat needlessly is to bore the customer into turning the newspaper page.

Sometimes needless repetition and reinforcement reflects the fears and insecurities of top management executives, who may be more knowledgeable about operations and finances than they are about fashion.

What is good copy? What is bad copy? We can go back to our elements of good advertising—clarity, credibility, and so on—but we will still find disagreement about what is good, mediocre, and bad. What is good for one store may be bad for another.

"Terrific buy in warm sweaters just when you need them most" is a first-rate line of advertising copy for a promotional store, but not for a store that wants to create an image of fashion selection or assortment.

Because standards of what is good and what is bad are so uncertain, we offer some specific examples of good fashion ads—they are good from one observer's point of view. These ads were culled from New York City ads, and ran in New York newspapers.

The reader who disagrees with these choices should test himself or herself by making other choices, and then analyzing them. Why are they better?

Some copy is quoted only in part. The store name follows the initial quote.

"Woman to woman: an exploration inward. See Warner's new brief subjects, now showing at The Body Workshop." Bonwit Teller. This is part of an innerwear promotion launched with a full-page ad and followed up with a series of small space ads. "Woman to woman" is a good phrase, honest and straightforward, yet suggestive of intimacy.

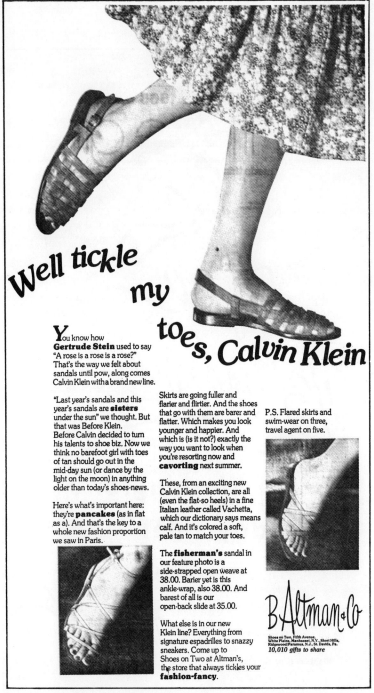

Well tickle my toes, Calvin Klein

You know how **Gertrude Stein** used to say "A rose is a rose is a rose?" That's the way we felt about sandals until pow, along comes Calvin Klein with a brand new line.

"Last year's sandals and this year's sandals are **sisters** under the sun" we thought. But that was Before Klein. Before Calvin decided to turn his talents to shoe biz. Now we think no barefoot girl with toes of tan should go out in the mid-day sun (or dance by the light on the moon) in anything older than today's shoes-news.

Here's what's important here: they're **pancakes** (as in flat as a). And that's the key to a whole new fashion proportion we saw in Paris.

Skirts are going fuller and flarier and flirtier. And the shoes that go with them are barer and flatter. Which makes you look younger and happier. And which is (is it not?) exactly the way you want to look when you're resorting now and **cavorting** next summer.

These, from an exciting new Calvin Klein collection, are all (even the flat-so heels) in a fine Italian leather called Vachetta, which our dictionary says means calf. And it's colored a soft, pale tan to match your toes.

The **fisherman's** sandal in our feature photo is a side-strapped open weave at 38.00. Barier yet is this ankle-wrap, also 38.00. And barest of all is our open-back slide at 35.00.

What else is in our new Klein line? Everything from signature espadrilles to snazzy sneakers. Come up to Shoes on Two at Altman's, the store that always tickles your **fashion-fancy.**

P.S. Flared skirts and swim-wear on three, travel agent on five.

B. Altman & Co

Shoes on Two, Fifth Avenue
White Plains, Manhasset, N.Y., Short Hills,
Ridgewood/Paramus, N.J., St. Davids, Pa.
10,010 gifts to share

B. Altman uses long copy as an element of its ads, telling a story and talking to its readers in a chatty, intimate way. Here, the headline is arranged irregularly around the largest illustration. Words in the copy are "bumped up" (set in dark type).

Sale ads need not be dull. Lord & Taylor's Washington's Birthday Sale ad avoids showing merchandise, creates a light-hearted effect by tossing a hat and powdered wig up in the air, and inviting customers to ". . . join in the savings . . ." The mood is festive.

It also implies liberation, which takes on a nice double meaning when applied to innerwear or bodywear. Liberation implies women's liberation as a philosophy and liberation in the sense that the garments allow freedom of movement, and are comfortable to wear. "Brief subjects" is a pun based on the name for short films. In inner wear, the word "brief" refers to panties or pantie girdles.

Another ad in the same series repeated the theme line. "Woman to woman: an exploration inward. Go strapless but not breathless with Poirette at The Body Workshop . . ." This theme line, and its repetition, is conceptual advertising, closer to national product advertising than conventional retail advertising.

A concept is an idea or a theme from which ads are pulled, as opposed to a format, which is a physical look that identifies ads.

The Bonwit campaign was linked to in-store designer appearances, announced as invitations to customers to come in and be fitted with bodywear, "Strapless but not breathless" is an excellent way of saying that these garments will fit comfortably, and function. The sound of the words has a ring or a lilt that is characteristic of the best copy.

"Diane's second skin dressing" (headline) . . . Diane von Furstenberg's body tee. Supple. Slinked. Basic to your nature and moving in on a soft shape. . . ." Bloomingdale's. Notice that the headline uses the designer's first name only. This is an example of a personal, intimate tone. Also, this store's sophisticated customers will know immediately who "Diane" is. Even so, body copy starts off immediately with the designer's full name.

Sometimes a copywriter will invent a name for a style with one or two descriptive words, or a short phrase that catches the essence of its most important features. Such copy can be very effective; it can also include a pun or a rhyme, for a touch of fun. "Body tee" is a copywriter's name for a dress based on a T-shirt design.

Some other names for T-shirt tops from a Bonwit Teller ad: "World on a string one-shoulder tee. . . . peppier peplum tee . . . the tee, squared . . . the soft shoulder tee . . . the unruffable ruffled tee. . . ."

"Snake charmers" describes snakeskin handbags in an ad run by Bloomingdale's. From the same store, "the one shoulder smolder" aptly describes an alluring dress by naming it with a description of its neckline.

"Isn't it romantic. Pastel eyelet dressing" is the headline on an ad from A & S (Abraham & Straus) that takes personal, narrative approach to copy. "I'm a true romantic! I like my movies melancholy, my clothing feminine and my most favorite colors are pastels. No wonder I fell in love with Wildfire's (brand name) antique cotton dressing in soft colors. . . ." This is an ad for eyelet cotton separates in junior sizes. Illustration is a moody photograph. The same ad, addressed to an older customer group, might have been written with a completely different approach.

Another junior ad run by Macy's, New York, starts off with a headline, "Juniors!

**BERGDORF'S
SPECIAL SALE**
Miss Bergdorf
Contemporary Dresses
30.00 and 34.00
originally 44.00 and 46.00
To wear right now . . .
T-shirt dresses, sundresses,
striped and plaid cottons
from Craig and Evelyn de Jonge.
Come and see!
PLUS
Pre-Summer Clearance
of more marvelous dresses
for Miss Bergdorf
from P.J. Walsh,
Ellen Tracy, Leslie J
1/3 to 1/2 off
original prices
Miss Bergdorf,
Fifth Floor

On the Plaza in New York and White Plains
**BERGDORF
GOODMAN**

**BERGDORF'S
PRIVATE LABEL
HOSIERY SALE**
Demi-toe Pantyhose or
Sandalfoot Pantyhose, 2.00
regularly 2.50
Control-top Pantyhose
Demi-toe or Sandalfoot, 2.50
regularly 3.00
Girdle-top Pantyhose
Demi-toe or Sandalfoot, 4.00
regularly 5.00
Knee highs, 1.00
regularly 1.25
All of nylon in Classic Beige,
Tawny, Bisque, Navy,
Morning Mist, Espresso
Brown or Black.
Hosiery, Street Floor

Mail to
754 Fifth Avenue,
New York 10019.
(212) PL3-7300
Please add 1.10
beyond our
delivery area and
on all orders
under 10.01.

On the Plaza in New York and White Plains
**BERGDORF
GOODMAN**

**BERGDORF'S
SPECIAL SALE**
Better Separates
1/3 to 1/2 off
original prices
A very special group of
skirts and T-shirts
to stock up for summer.
Do come!
PLUS
Pre-Summer Clearance
Designer Sportswear
from Anne Klein,
Calvin Klein, Beene Bag,
Blassport, Kasper,
Fredricks, even some
golf clothes from
Active Sportswear
1/3 to 1/2 off
original prices
Country & Casual,
Third Floor

On the Plaza in New York and White Plains
**BERGDORF
GOODMAN**

Bergdorf Goodman uses Kenneth Paul Block's silhouettes effectively in a series of sale ads. The dark tone and outlining frame are attention-getting. Plenty of white space helps.

Make Macy's your short stop for summer." The punning headline introduces an ad for shorts showing six styles in an action photograph. Copy reads, "Reveal those legs. Let the sun shine on them. Watch admirers take a second glance. Don't be surprised if a fellow jogger asks to run alongside you. In short . . . we've got 'em all, for all the good times you'll be having this summer." Specific copy of each style follows.

"We've got 'em all" stresses the assortment theme that is associated with department stores like Macy's. In that short, informal phrase, the store tells its readers that it is headquarters for shorts, that they will find a wide selection of styles to choose from.

The copy appeals directly to a deep desire; the desire to look attractive and to be noticed by men. The tone is perky, sentences are short, language is informal and conversational. "Reveal . . . Let the sun shine . . ." are commands, but they are not authoritarian commands. Rather, the tone is equal-to-equal, a sort of "Hey, get with it" approach that works for a young audience when it is well done. It must sound natural and unforced, as this copy does. Such an approach would be utterly inappropriate if used by a specialty store to address older women, in an ad selling expensive evening gowns, or designer sportswear.

There are other copy approaches to fashion. One is the establishment of the store as the source of fashion authority. This is a fashion specialty store technique. "Lord & Taylor loves the sundress" is the headline on an interesting ad that takes up almost a full page, yet shows only one dress. The store is putting its fashion know-how on the line, and asking the customers to trust its fashion judgment. Copy reads, "Albert Nipon's deep purple cotton rates rave reviews whether it comes out with the sun or the stars. . . ."

In Spring 1977, B. Altman & Co. ran a series of small space, institutional ads timed to coincide with Paris ready-to-wear openings. The ads were all copy, written in a style suggesting newspaper bulletins transmitted by a reporter.

"Florence, March 27th", one ad read, "At the European fashion openings. Beautiful city. Beautiful clothes. Bought some great knits. Coats, sweaters, skirts. . . ." Copy continued in this style, signing off with a logo. These ads are institutional because they create a fashion image for the store. Here is Altman's, keeping up with the latest fashion news, and letting its customers in on what is happening in Europe. The ads are like little previews of fashions to come.

A designer sportswear ad that appeals to a sophisticated audience runs headline into copy. "Calvin. He's gone soft. On linen. Tailored, but ready to be rumpled. Right to be tied with feminine scallops. All, parts of a summer's day . . ." Saks Fifth Avenue. At the end of the copy, there is mention of the Calvin Klein boutique.

The copy uses short phrases that are not complete sentences to create a clipped effect. It is deliberately ungrammatical. Such devices are very tricky. They succeed only when done in the most skillful way. It is easy for highly stylized copy to fail, and when it fails, it is awful, for it sounds forced and affected.

PARIS, MARCH 24

HERE TO PREVIEW FALL FASHIONS.
SPOKE WITH JEAN CACHAREL THIS
A.M. HIS COLLECTION CHARMING:
BOXY PLEATED SKIRT, HIGH-RISE
TROUSERS, SMALL JACKETS. MISTY
TARTANS. SILK PRINT DRESSES
WITH MATCHING PANTS.
MORE LATER.
ALTMAN'S FASHION GROUP

B Altman & Co

Fifth Avenue

MILAN, MARCH 31

GEOFFREY BEENE SHOW RATED ONE OF
YEAR'S TOP COLLECTION. COAT DRESSES,
VEST DRESSES, SLIMMER SHAPES.
NEW: GOOSE-DOWN SLICKER OVER CLOQUE
FOR EVENING. NEW: BIAS-CUT VIOLET
SATIN. NEW: MIXED PARTS IN FUZZY
WOOLS AND QUILTS.
MORE LATER.
ALTMAN'S FASHION GROUP

B Altman & Co

Fifth Avenue

"News flash" ad run by B. Altman, one of a series, is like a reporter's story on European openings. Closing line, "More later," is a sign-off line that keeps up reader interest. Good all-copy ads like this are rare.

Just as the artist who exaggerates and stylizes a fashion drawing, the copywriter may distort the "rules" of writing English. The good artist has learned to draw without distortion before distorting. The good writer has learned to write correctly before writing incorrectly.

Rules must be learned before they can be broken.

While we would rather avoid strict rules, here are some guidelines that may help writers and copy chiefs.

New fashion terms should be used only when the copywriter is talking to a sophisticated audience; women who know all about the latest fashions. "Our pirate separates" would have meaning for women who knew that French designer Kenzo had shown a pirate look. But a mass audience would need more explicit details; hats and scarves, belted tunics, bold stripes and so on.

Mass stores and true fashion stores that sell expensive apparel need different words to describe the same idea. When the high fashion store says opportunity, the mass store says sale; when the high fashion store says value, the mass store says bargain. Some other examples: holiday, two weeks with pay; luncheon, lunch.

Foreign words should be used with restraint, as they are likely to be misused and misunderstood. They are not a sign of elegance; English can be as elegant as any language if it is written correctly and imaginatively.

Copywriters should avoid picking up words from publications and other copy. There are exceptions to this rule, but picking up a word is like patching a dress. The patch shows, and there is a bumpiness or unevenness in the finished copy. The freshest, most effective copy comes out of the copywriter's head. This does not mean that writers should avoid influences and impressions; it means that they should not imitate what has already been done.

Anything that sounds snobbish should be examined very, very carefully. Attitudes toward snobbishness are changing. A little bit goes a long way.

Even high fashion stores that used to emphasize exclusivity and strike a snobbish tone are adopting a more informative approach. (This is sometimes called an "editorial" approach, as opposed to a strong selling approach with more adjectives than information.)

The best fashion advertising is informative in one way or another. Even the hard sell ad that announces, "Great bargain in sweaters, $5 off" is telling the customer something she wants to know. Fashion-oriented ads are more informative. The B. Altman institutional campaign we described was purely editorial; it was a super-newsy approach to fashion.

Lord & Taylor is giving its customers information when it advises its readers that a sundress can be worn day or night.

Macy's offers shorts as a new kind of sportswear.

Readers will absorb and store away this information; it becomes part of their total fashion knowledge. That is why so many women "take a look at the ads" to find out what is happening in fashion.

While most fashion ads run in newspapers, many ads appear in national magazines. Some magazine ads are hard to classify as retail or national, institutional or item. As an example, we can consider an ad run by Marshall Field & Co., Chicago, in *The New Yorker*, the prestige national weekly magazine. Field's full-page ad showed a photograph of a woman in a caftan. Price, colors, and sizes were included, along with descriptive copy. The tone of the ad was distinctly high fashion, and suggested the caftan as a Mother's Day gift.

Was this a national or a retail ad? The store does not have branches all over the country, but *The New Yorker* is a national magazine. The ad was both.

Was this an institutional or an item ad? It was both. Merchandise was shown, but the ad was selling the store as a prestige place to shop *through* the merchandise.

We cite this last example to show that advertising is difficult to classify by rules. There are always exceptions.

DIRECT MAIL

Direct mail is another kind of print advertising that works well for small and large stores. Direct mail is a print medium, though it does not appear in newspapers or magazines. It is material mailed directly to the customer; it can be anything from a simple postcard announcing a sale to an elaborate catalogue of more than a hundred pages, with full-color illustrations.

Direct mail has its own set of advantages as compared to other media. It is relatively inexpensive, even though postage and labor costs have risen. It reaches a maximum number of people who are customers, or potential customers, for it is sent to people who have been in the store, bought something from the store, or have charge accounts.

This degree of concentration is high compared to newspapers and television. Many people who read newspapers have absolutely no interest in women's clothing; this is also true of television. (The people reached by a newspaper or magazine ad who are not potential customers are referred to as "waste circulation.")

Direct mail can offer retailers a minimum of waste circulation.

Still another advantage of direct mail has to do with response, which can be recorded and evaluated. When an ad for a dress runs in a newspaper, customers may refer to it, or they may not, when they come into the store and buy the dress. They may just be passing by, they may have been shopping for something else—the response to the ad cannot be precisely recorded.

If the ad ran in several newspapers and magazines, it is hard to tell which publication drew the best response. Not so with direct mail. Envelopes, mailing pieces,

Kay Windsor's fresh stripes in 100% Dupont
Dacron® polyester — two effortless ways to
dress from now on!
8A. Shirt jacket dress with solid-trimmed
striped jacket over a solid, sleeveless dress.
Blue and green or pink and green. 10-20. **44.00**
8B. Tee-shaped striped dress, bateau neck.
Blue and green or pink and green. 8-18. **30.00**
Miss G. Dresses

8C. The three-piece pantsuit by Carol's
Choice Ltd. Division of Lady Carol. Easy-care
dressing in 100% polyester. Blue or green.
12-20, **33.00**   14½-22½, **35.00**
Boulevard Dresses & Women's World

Ribs to spare by Booth Bay. Fresh, easy-care
tops of 100% Dupont Dacron® polyester — all
with their own skinny belts.
9A. Ribbed mock turtle-neck with zip back.
White, red, navy, light blue, pink or chamois.
36-42. **10.00**
9B. Ribbed tank top. Turquoise, red, white,
peach, yellow or mint. 36-42. **10.00**
9C. White-collared rib-knit top. Navy or red
with white. 36-42. **12.00**
Boulevard Sportswear

Rida's muscle-sleeved tee-shirts show off
pretty biceps. Both, washable, easy-care 100%
polyester knit in white, red, navy or blue. S-M-L
9D. With plain jewel neck. **6.00**
9E. With split-neck collar. **9.00**
Street Floor Blouses

Mail-order catalogues are less nuts-and-bolts, more fashionable. In this Gimbels catalogue, professional
models are photographed against backgrounds. Their sportswear is carefully accessorized with belts,
jewelry, hats.

and coupons can be coded so that the advertiser knows exactly which mailing piece drew customer response.

More department and specialty chains sent out mail-order catalogues in the mid-1970's than ever before. Some of these catalogues served a double purpose; they were also slipped into Sunday editions of metropolitan daily newspapers, and used as inserts. Department store catalogues covered hard goods as well as fashion and other soft goods.

Some department stores offered relatively conventional, low-priced merchandise. Prestige specialty chains spent a great deal of care and money putting together their catalogues. Specialty store catalogues were devoted almost entirely to fashion. Models were chosen carefully; top-flight art and photography were used.

Elaborate catalogues are produced with the help of cooperative advertising which is paid for by vendor money. (Vendor is another term for manufacturer.) Acceptance of vendor money raises an inevitable question: to what extent does such acceptance influence buyers' choice of merchandise to be featured in the catalogue? Many reputable retailers state that they would not pick merchandise unsuitable for their catalogue, that the money comes from their major resources, and that they would choose merchandise for the catalogue from those resources regardless of the money.

Some observers of the retail scene comment that acceptance of vendor money locks retailers into featuring standard, basic merchandise in catalogues. They add that, from store to store, one can see the same brand names and the same merchandise.

As with print advertising, look-alike catalogues can be perilous; if the customer receives several catalogues, she may be bored with them all.

In spite of these dangers, many catalogues have been extremely successful. This success is puzzling from at least one point of view.

As shopping centers increase, bringing more stores to more customers in different parts of the country, why would anybody need to shop from a catalogue?

This does seem like a paradox, but the answer is inherent in the nature of the shopping center itself. As we pointed out in Chapter 4, selling space in stores located in shopping centers is limited. Merchandise assortments must be edited down to meet the needs of limited space. It may well be that the woman looking through a catalogue will see fashion merchandise that is not available in a store in a shopping center. For that customer, the catalogue is an expanded store, and an additional source of fashion merchandise.

Direct mail communicates with customers in other ways.

It is useful in announcing special events to customers. It supports print advertising; each reinforces the other. The customer gets a message by mail and sees an ad in her daily newspaper at the same time.

Charge customers are often sent mailings a day or two ahead of a general announcement; because they have charge accounts in the store they are given first choice of sale merchandise, or perhaps they get invited to the first of a series of designer appearances.

Small "stuffers" or single sheets showing a piece of merchandise are often enclosed with charge account bills.

Many of these mailings are paid for with vendor money, and they ride piggy-back, so to speak, on the charge account statement, which would have to be mailed out in any case. So any business that comes in is a plus—the store has little or nothing to lose.

While every store has different needs, we can make some general observations about direct mail that can serve as a guide to fashion retailers. (We discussed ways in which small stores can best use direct mail in Chapter 6.)

- Keep it simple. Remember the customer is bombarded with promotional mail. She does not have time to read lots of copy. The message should be brief and to the point.
- Include vital information. Fabric, sizes, color, and price are the most important facts, but other special fashion features are also essential. The customer is ordering from a picture and copy, and makes her decision to buy *without seeing merchandise.* She should know exactly what she will receive, and receive what she expects.
- Be specific about delivery, return, credit, exchanges, and the specification of second choices, if necessary.
- Be sure you can keep your promises about delivery! There is such a thing as an act of God that prevents delivery, or fulfillment, as it is called, but if you have promised delivery by Christmas, you had better be able to keep that promise! Mother's Day is another holiday that calls for precise delivery dates.
- When planning an order blank, leave enough space for the customer to write in the style number, or name, or whatever other information you have specified. A customer cannot write a five-digit number in a space that is one-eighth of an inch wide. If possible, avoid five-digit numbers altogether.
- Plan layouts in catalogues so that copy is as close to the picture as possible. *Don't* confuse the customer.
- Do not assume that catalogue merchandise photographed against exotic background will sell better. Often a simple studio set-up will sell just as effectively as a tropical island in the background. Tropical island backgrounds can enhance merchandise, but there are limits to how much enhancement is needed.
- Try to create movement and pace in a fashion catalogue, so that one layout leads naturally into another, just as one department in a well-planned store leads into another. From simple daytime sportswear, to dressier sportswear and dresses, to evening wear is an example of a natural flow of merchandise. Tell a story in headlines if you can.
- *Accessorize, accessorize, accessorize.* Show the accessories in blown-up inserts.

Saks ties in direct mail with its 50th anniversary promotion. Invitation to fashion show, a self-mailer, carries out look of campaign. So does silver mini-portfolio with brown type. Inside, separate thin sheets of paper announce a series of designer appearances, each one, with a different art deco motif.

This is a good chance for multiple sales.

- Do not overcrowd charge envelopes. Do not use the flaps for coupons. It is distracting and confusing to the customer. Less is more—we cannot say it too many times.
- Pay attention to postcards, especially sale announcements. They can be attractive without being expensive; they need not look tacky.
- When sending out invitations to a fashion show, try to personalize them by addressing the customer directly, for instance, "Won't you come and see . . ."
- Send out announcements a week or two in advance, so that customers will have time to plan to attend your store event.
- Remember that direct mail is one part of your total advertising program. Coordinate it; make it work with ads and all your other promotional efforts.

Advertising: The Spoken Word— Television and Radio

10

Television came of age as an advertising medium for retailers during the 1960's and 1970's. In the mid-70's, retailers were spending at the rate of $1.5 billion annually, a 300 percent increase over a decade earlier.

There are many examples of the sharp increase, and perhaps more important, the *rate* of increase. May Co., one of the giants in the department store field, increased its TV outlay from $4 million to $9 million between 1974 and 1975. During that same period, two other major department store chains, Federated Department Stores and R. H. Macy & Co., just about doubled their television advertising.

The figures cited above are for all categories of merchandise, but there is no question that a solid chunk of this money helped advertise fashion merchandise.

The increase in television advertising for fashion merchandise is spelled out dramatically at Famous-Barr, the St. Louis-based department store chain. From somewhat over $20,000 in 1974, the chain jumped to more than $200,000 in 1975 for fashion goods specifically!

As might be expected, the three largest dollar expenditures came from the three national chains—Sears, Montgomery Ward, and J.C. Penney. Sears' early and heavy use of television gives a clue to the reason why other retailers substantially increased their television spending in the mid-70's.

Sears, the largest of the national chains, has stores virtually everywhere, therefore Sears has potential customers virtually everywhere. It follows that a Sears investment in television is worthwhile; the Sears message will reach a maximum potential customer audience.

From 1960 on, regional store divisions developed, saturating a single- or multi-state area with stores. More stores meant more potential customers in a given area; this increased customer audience made television a more practical advertising medium, for television covered precisely the audience retailers wanted to reach.

For example, in the 1950's, it would have been foolish for the Macy's New York division to pay for a television audience that extended throughout New York State and part of Connecticut, when there were only a few Macy's stores huddled together in New York City.

In the mid-70's, Macy's has sixteen units in the New York-Connecticut area, and is in a position to consider television advertising more seriously.

Of course, television costs were affected by inflation in the 1970's, along with everything else; time costs and production costs rose. Time costs for national television rose astronomically.

In spite of increased costs, many retailers who saturated areas with stores found television advertising a sound investment, for they increased the number of potential customers they could reach.

The retail situation as we have discussed it so far applies to all retailers; those who sell autos and appliances as well as fashion.

Now, we turn to fashion as a special category of retail advertising. It has its own characteristics and needs. And there is no doubt that fashion represents a substantial share of the total retail investment in television advertising.

Television as an advertising medium offers fashion retailers advantages that stem from the nature of fashion. Clothes come in *colors,* and television can show them in color, while newspaper advertising appears in black and white. The newspaper ad that lists the color "blue" cannot equal the impact of the blue dress as it appears on the TV screen. To understand the importance of color, we need only close our eyes and imagine ourselves in a store in which all the merchandise is black and white!

Movement is an important advantage of television. It has special significance for fashion, as compared to other merchandise categories. We do not need to see a piece of furniture move to appreciate it—unless it is a convertible sofa-bed. But when we see a woman modeling a dress on the television screen, we see it more clearly because we see it move on the body.

A gathered skirt falls softly or stands out. The gathers may lie flat at the hips or bunch up, like a traditional dirndl skirt. This makes a difference in the silhouette, and in the way the skirt swings as the model walks.

A slinky matte jersey clings to the body as it moves. If the skirt is narrow at the hem, that narrowness affects the way the model moves.

A crisp broadcloth shirt appears with a perky stand-up collar and rolled sleeves. Perhaps the model rolls the sleeves to show how they can be worn at different lengths.

A coat or cape reverses to another color and fabric. In print advertising, the coat could be shown on two figures, but rarely is. It remains for the copy to describe the style as reversible; certainly much less effective than showing a woman wearing the garment first one way, then another.

A loose tent dress or a blouson falls softly away from the body, but the body shows against the fabric as the model moves.

A tight stretch bathing suit, body suit or T-shirt clings to the torso, creating a sexy, come-hither look. Narrow trousers or jeans create a long-legged look. Full, satin trousers flow from the body.

A softly ruffled neckline frames the face in a flattering way. The look is quite different from the stand-up shirt collar.

A pleated skirt swirls out in fullness. A cape swirls out from the shoulders as the model moves.

The model need not limit herself to walking; she can show the fashion in motion as she sits, bends, stretches, runs, and turns. Print advertising can show any one of these motions—but only one.

Movement makes a stunning contribution to the presentation of fashion merchandise. Even though it is shown on a beautiful model, the woman who sees the commercial is far closer to an answer to her question, "How will it look on me?" than she is as a newspaper reader.

Immediacy or reality is another important advantage of television. This is related to verisimillitude—the verisimillitude of the photograph as opposed to the drawing. A photograph looks "realer" than a drawing; more like a living person. A moving photograph, which is what television is, goes a step further.

Is the model at a party, wearing an evening gown? The viewer pictures herself at the party; she becomes that woman on the screen.

Is the model playing tennis on an outdoor court in the sunshine? Her dress or shorts flash across the background, in action. The woman watching the TV screen identifies—if she plays tennis—and feels the skirt move against her legs, feels the sun on her back, the racket in her hand. This is immediacy, and it can sell fashion.

Sound is another advantage of television (and radio). A voice is talking about the clothes. (Not all fashion commentators speak well; not all commentary is well written; that is another matter.) A voice at its best and commentary at its best can be more persuasive than written words that must be read.

Music and other sound effects can set a mood.

With all these advantages—*color, movement,* and *sound*—we might wonder why fashion retailers have not completely abandoned print. Most stores still devote a major portion of their advertising budget to print. Some of the reasons why relate to economics; others are psychological; still others have to do with the comparative newness of television as an advertising medium.

Fashion retailers have lived with print advertising for many years; it is difficult for them to adjust to a new medium calling for new skills. Television commercials are usually produced outside the store. (Although, paradoxically, some of the best ones are produced in the store.)

"Going outside" represents a loss of control. It is quite different from the in-store situation, in which the store's advertising department creates and controls ads for newspapers and magazines.

The difficulties of zeroing in on a specific fashion customer have made some fashion retailers wary of television. Who is the customer? What programming does she watch? When does she watch? Working status, marital status, family composition, age, education, and income are all important factors in selecting the right audience of potential customers.

A store would not advertise an expensive, high fashion dress to an audience of low-income housewives. Juniors and teenagers would be a good audience for commercials on jeans, but not high-income matrons over the age of 50.

A good deal of sophisticated information about television audiences is available, but most of it relates to cars, soap, toothpaste, cosmetics, and other nationally advertised products.

Many fashion retailers are confident that a woman will pick up a newspaper and leaf through it some time during the day. They are less confident that a woman in a certain age and income group will be watching television at a specific time.

This difficulty underscores the tangibility of print versus television; the commercial not watched is a lost commercial. A newspaper or magazine is a "thing" that does not vanish in 20 or 30 seconds.

A woman may read and re-read an ad in a newspaper. A *magazine* has an even longer life. A newspaper or magazine ad can be torn out and saved for future reference even after the publication is discarded.

Television has immediacy, but it does not have the lasting impact of print. The commercial cannot be "torn out and saved."

Newspapers are the traditional medium of retail advertising, and fashion advertising in particular. In a sense, fashion retailers "own" the medium. They can buy preferred positions that command reader attention. Fashion ads can dominate a newspaper.

But on television, the fashion commercial faces intense competition from manufacturers' products, all vying for viewers' attention. Fashion cannot dominate other product commercials.

Fashion newspaper ads appear in an editorial environment as well as an environment of other ads. That is, they are surrounded by news stories; the editorial content of the newspaper. While editorial material in a newspaper may be shocking or even offensive, the reader may ignore it, skim it lightly, or read the ads first and then come back to the editorial content of the paper.

The television viewer does not have these choices. Everything comes at her at once—program and commercials—unless she switches channels or turns off the set.

If the editorial content of a television program arouses some strong emotion, favorable or unfavorable, that emotion carries over as the program ends or pauses for the commercial.

We must keep the immediacy of television in mind as we consider the impact of the editorial environment of television. It is one thing to read a sensational story in a newspaper. That is a second-hand experience. It is quite another thing to watch a television program with its immediacy, its sound, movement, color, action, news content, or story line. Television makes a much stronger impact on the viewer; puts her in a mood or frame of mind. Does the commercial come in the middle of the program? Perhaps she will be distracted, thinking only of what will happen next on the program.

These ideas are of concern to fashion retailers, some of whom feel that the impact of television editorial environment is just too strong—they fear it will smother their fashion message.

Flexibility is another factor that influences the fashion retailer's choice of advertising media. Television is becoming much more flexible, thanks to improvements in equipment. It is possible to produce commercials more quickly than it was ten or even five years ago. Still, a metropolitan daily newspaper seems more suited to the needs of a mass fashion retailer.

Every day, there is new merchandise to be presented. It is timely. It is seasonal. It must move in and out of the store quickly. Ads can be scheduled to run every day; schedules can be changed when needed. As yet, some retailers say, television cannot equal the day-to-day flexibility—and continuity—offered by a daily newspaper.

For many retailers, television versus print is not the question. They depend on print and use television to supplement it, or, in a few cases, they depend on television and use print as a supplement. Radio, direct mail, catalogues and in-store promotions all work with television. Any advertising medium works better when it is *one part* of a well-coordinated program.

The retailer who wants to learn how to use television will find expert help within reach. There are advertising agencies and small production companies in many parts of the country. They exist in small cities as well as large cities. Local television networks offer useful advice, too, as well as production facilities. Vendor material, when properly used, can also be helpful.

Though there are so many differences between print and television, they can be compared in some ways, for they are both advertising media.

The newspaper fills space.

The television commercial fills time.

Rising costs compel advertisers to use less space in print, fewer seconds on TV.

Some print ads look cluttered and crowded in the smaller space; there is too much message, and it gets lost in the shuffle.

The same thing happens on TV. Images flashing quickly on and off the screen, and a rush of words clutter television commercials, so that the impact of the total message is lost.

Clarity is as important in television advertising as it is in print. As is continuity.

Individuality is perhaps more important on television, where each message competes with many others for the viewer's attention—and memory.

The positioning of a television commercial in a certain time slot can be compared to the positioning of an ad in a magazine or newspaper. In both cases, there are preferred positions which gain more attention and cost more. "Prime time" on television may be compared to the second page of the first section of a Sunday metropolitan newspaper.

A television commercial may appear regularly on a specific program, which means it will appear at a certain time every day or every week.

There is another kind of commercial fashion retailers often use; the "spot." The *spot* is inserted into a television schedule at a certain time, and is not linked with a specific program. Sometimes stores use a series of spots within a short period of time to pull in customers for a sale or other special event. When many spots appear within one day, or two days, or a week, this is called a "saturation campaign." Saturation campaigns usually work in conjunction with radio and print advertising.

A store may substantially increase its business with a saturation campaign advertising special bargains in dresses.

Credibility plays an even more important role in such a campaign than it does in a print ad, because of the intensity of the advertising push. When a woman is bombarded with messages day after day, hour after hour, there is a good chance that she will respond and visit the store.

If she sees a picture of attractive merchandise on the television screen, the merchandise in the store had better measure up to its promise. If reality falls short of the promise of the picture or the verbal message accompanying it, the customer will be disappointed. Somehow, because television seems alive, disillusion with television commercials strikes the customers even harder than disillusion with print ads.

The result of such disillusion is a loss of credibility. That may not be a one-time loss; it can be permanent, long-range, and very damaging to the store. If the actual merchandise is so unattractive that it cannot be shown on television, then it had better not be shown at all.

Sometimes there is a fine line between changing the merchandise and enhancing it for television. Certainly a dress or shirt should be pressed so that it looks neat. It should fit the model properly, so the silhouette can be seen. Little details like loose buttons and hanging threads should be repaired. This is *enhancement*.

Making a skirt fuller, adding different fabric or substituting a copy of the dress goes beyond enhancement. Few advertisers resort to such trickery, for it does not pay off in the long run.

We could not possibly, in one chapter, give a full explanation of how television commercials are made. Still, the fashion retailer can benefit from a brief discussion of some of the ingredients of different kinds of commercials, always keeping in mind that there is much more to be said on the subject.*

Fashion advertising goes back to the early days of television, in the 1950's, when the medium was brand new.

In the early days of television, programs and commercials were "live." Real people appeared on the screen. Sometimes they made mistakes. In the case of fashion, a model slipped, a dress tore, or became disarranged, so that it was not shown to advantage. The commentator might read the wrong description for the dress on camera, so that viewers were confused. They were also amused—mistakes always amuse the television audience —but amusement does not sell merchandise.

By the 1970's, live television was a thing of the past. Most programs and all commercials, with very few exceptions, were made on film or tape.

Slides. The most inexpensive, basic commercial is a series of *slides,* each showing merchandise, with a store name superimposed ("super" is the television term) on the slide at the beginning and end. Even this simple form has many variations; more or less attention can be focused on the store as opposed to the merchandise.

Sometimes the opening and closing slides are used alone for a briefer message with an institutional flavor. The merchandise changes from time to time, while the opening and closing slides are retained. This is called a "sandwich." The opening and closing are the "bread" and the merchandise inside is the "filling."

Another variation combines a filmed or taped opening and closing with slides.

Some motion can be introduced into the slide commercial by moving the camera in close on the slide, or by moving it from side to side, so that details of the merchandise show more clearly. The camera can move in close on a collar or sleeve detail, or a belt, or could move horizontally across the slide from one figure to another.

Film and Tape. The 1970's brought many technical advances in taping and filming equipment. It became lighter, smaller, and more portable. Such improvements increased flexibility of production and cut production costs. Television became practical for fashion retailers who could not consider it in the days when recording equipment looked like the inside of a space ship, and weighed about as much.

For example, portable equipment can move into a department or specialty store and tape several commercials in one day, focusing on different merchandise in different departments. This brings down the cost of each commercial. Using the store as a setting creates an intimate, institutional feeling that helps build store image.

Equipment changes so rapidly that today's new wonder is obsolete tomorrow. Still, in a general way, we can note some advantages of film and tape as of the 1970's.

Tape costs less. It can be replayed instantly and edited quickly.

*A good source of information for all retailers interested in television is the book, *Making TV Pay Off: A Retailer's Guide to Television,* Howard P. Abrahams, Fairchild Publications.

148

More special effects are possible with film—optical effects, and effects that create very special moods, or fantasy worlds. Mood and fantasy are especially important in selling fashion. Certain fashion commercials call for the advantages of film.

On outdoor location, film offers better control than tape—control of lighting, for example. ("On location" refers to a site outside the studio, chosen as a background and setting for the commercial. It may be a desert or an island, a museum or an elegant home; a garden or a faraway continent.)

Constant changes in equipment and ways of using it promise even more sophisticated techniques for the future.

Whether a commercial is made with slides, tape or film, it begins just as the print ad does; with merchandise and an idea. The idea takes shape in a typed script. The script is a page with two columns. One column is headed, "audio." The audio portion of the commercial includes words, indications for music, and other sound effects.

The other portion is headed, "video." The video portion of the commercial describes the picture that goes with the words and other sound effects.

The script is made up into a *storyboard*. A storyboard looks like a comic strip. Each box is referred to as a "frame." The upper portion of the box shows the picture. Below the picture, the accompanying words, plus instructions for music and sound effects, are written in. The storyboard is the blueprint for the commercial that will guide the production team.

What we have described is standard advertising procedure. In a national agency, or in an agency working with a department store chain that advertises continually and nationally, the preparation of the script and storyboard is a slow process. Ideas are considered and discarded before the "concept" is determined. If the agency comes up with an idea, appropriate store personnel must approve of it.

Then actors or models are chosen. Special music may be written, or a musical arrangement may be bought from companies that specialize in supplying music of all kinds, to create different moods.

Then the commercial goes into production.

That is not the way most fashion commercials are made. The typical fashion retailer works so quickly that there is barely time for a script. An idea is drawn up roughly; sometimes there is no storyboard, a situation that can lead to chaos, even when the commercial is simple and short.

If slides are used, production is even simpler. Film or tape may be made directly from color slides showing merchandise.

An announcer may appear on camera, or the words may be spoken by a voice over. Store name is announced, clothes are shown, the store name, perhaps with a slogan, appears again.

The J. C. Penney storyboard we chose for illustration on page 150 is part of an exceptionally fine campaign. Groups of models form and re-form in interesting ways, always moving in slow motion. This distinctive style gives the viewer a good chance to observe all the details of the fashion merchandise. Music and commentary are properly low-key and in the background; the clothes are the center of interest. The concept is broad and flexible; it can be adapted to any kind of clothing.

Whether a commercial is based on slides, tape or film, it projects store image. Fashion, price, and combinations of the two form the basis for a wide variety of fashion images. The image of fashion at a price can be projected in different ways; some shoutingly loud and hard sell; others, direct but in a lower key.

Target Stores, a midwestern mass merchandise chain based in Minneapolis, with fifty-two units as of the mid-1970's, relies heavily on television to project its own special image of fashion at a price. Price and price reductions on brand names are clearly mentioned in its commercials; yet they are a far cry from typical hard sell commercials associated with this kind of fashion retail operation. The announcers' voices are clear, but there is no shouting. There is no overloading of adjectives—just crisp description. Clothes are shown on models who are attractive, but do not have the theatrical beauty of high fashion models, nor do they move as high fashion models move. They walk naturally. They are more attractive than the average woman, yet the average woman can easily identify with them.

Chuck Miller, Target's senior vice president, advertising and sales promotion, is very image-conscious.

"We are not just advertising merchandise, we are advertising reputation," comments Mr. Miller. "It's impossible to show merchandise without saying something about what your store is. We want to say 'value' to our customer, but we also want to say other things.

"There are all sorts of hidden, implied messages in fashion commercials, as well as visible, stated messages and promises. Our commercials imply that we have stock in depth—not just a few pieces that will go to the first two customers who come in to the store.

"We make it clear that these are current styles—not last year's leftovers, and that they are wanted styles—not 'dogs.'

"The power of these promises is very strong. We want our customer to trust us. We don't want to look too slick to her—we want her to see us as straightforward and direct."

Like the print ad, the television commercial is saying something about the store even when it focuses on specific merchandise.

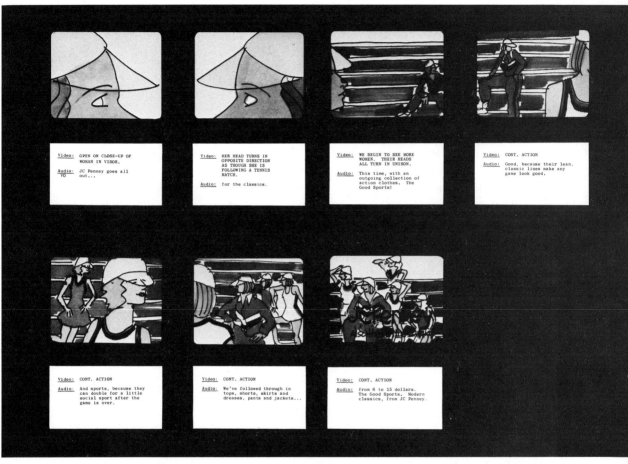

Storyboard for J.C. Penney (above) shows how commercial is prepared, with pictures (video) and words (audio). This commercial was part of a campaign developed by advertising agency McCaffrey and McCall, Inc. Unifying theme was slow, graceful movement of models into group, showing a variety of styles. It's a good example of clean, attractive presentation, without distracting gimmicks. Last frame (facing page, bottom) shows group with store logo. National TV is practical for a chain like Penney's, which has stores across the country.

Though most fashion retailers use television to sell specific merchandise, some have focused on more institutional themes.

As in print, the merchandise message brings immediate results. The institutional message may produce some immediate results, but its real effect is long range and hard to pinpoint.

The Joseph P. Horne Co., Pittsburgh, Pennsylvania, a department store chain with eight units, mostly in the Pittsburgh area, taped an effective institutional commercial in its downtown store, and produced several other commercials at the same time, thus cutting costs.

Though Horne is not known primarily for high-priced merchandise, management decided to draw attention to the store's designer area, known as Peacock Alley.

The thirty-second spot used a man's voice-over and sophisticated music with a touch of guitar.

The commercial opened on a shot of the sculptured peacock that is a prop in the store's designer area; it is the departmental symbol.

The action of the commercial was simple.

An elegant model twines her arm around the peacock and faces the camera. She plays with a feather boa wrapped around her neck.

This is done in close-up. The model looks straight into the camera, then the camera follows her, so that the viewer gets a good look at her evening gown. She turns, and walks away into the distance, always moving slowly and naturally, without any cliché fashion gestures. She looks over her shoulder into the camera—that is, she looks at the viewer.

While the model is moving, the announcer's voice reels off a list of famous designers. "Burrows, Trigère, St. Laurent, Cardin, Ruffin. . . ."

As the model walks away from the camera, the voice continues to list names, ending with the simple announcement, ". . . new plumage from the Joseph Horne Company."

The store name is printed over the final frame.

What does such a commercial do for the store? Perhaps it sells a few dresses, but that is not its most important effect. It tells women that there is a place in this store that offers a certain kind of merchandise.

Then there is the hidden message—the Horne Company is a store with such a strong fashion image that, even though it does not specialize in high fashion, it has a good selection of high fashion for those customers who want it. This creates prestige and increases customer confidence.

The simple device of listing designer names says "wide selection" much more effectively than the words, "wide selection."

The commercial is aimed at a specific audience, and also at a more general audience. Women who cannot afford to buy high fashion designer clothes may recognize some of the designer names. If they do not, the tone of the commercial, with its aura of quality, will make a favorable impression on them. Even women who do not buy designer clothes like to think that they shop in a store that sells designer clothes.

The specific audience for the commercial, those well-to-do, fashion-conscious women who wear designer clothes, recognize the designer names. Those customers know what a Trigère dress looks like, and what a Blass outfit looks like, and so on down the list. Some of them may not know about Peacock Alley; many do, and have shopped there. To this specific audience, the commercial is a reminder. "Here we are," it says, "And we have the kind of clothes you wear."

There are many other messages television can deliver, and there are many creative ways in which fashion television can put across its message.

A commercial for a brand-name raincoat was shot in a store, against a very simple background of racks of raincoats.

A young saleswoman is helping a young man pick out a raincoat. The two young people speak directly to each other; she, advising him; he, asking her questions.

"Do you like the color?" the young man asks casually.

"Oh, yes," the young woman replies, in a low voice, almost a sigh, of approval.

"What about the collar—does it fit?" the man asks.

"It sure does," the young woman answers, in the same tone.

"Do you really like it?" the young man asks.

"And how," the young woman responds.

The entire commercial is short and low-key. It has a real-life feeling; the viewer seems to be in the store, listening to a conversation. Yet, in the course of that conversation, every important selling feature of the raincoat is mentioned!

The traditional way to sell that raincoat would be to have an announcer or voice over list all the selling features while a man modeled the raincoat. "Great new collar! Convertible cape! Wide assortment of colors! Adjustable belt!"

By creating a realistic situation, the advertiser took advantage of the best features television has to offer: its reality, action, sound, and its story-telling possibilities.

To summarize briefly, there are many things a fashion commercial can do.
- It can sell merchandise.
- It can build image.
- Saturation campaigns pull for special store events.
- Image-building commercials affect the customer's attitude towards the store.
- Commercials can be news stories: announcing a storewide promotion, appearance of a designer or other celebrity as guest, or a special demonstration. All of these events take place at specific times.

- A commercial can announce the opening of a new department or a new store.
- It can remind customers that they have only ten days left to finish their Christmas shopping, that Mother's Day is coming, or that children will be going back to school in a few weeks and will need new clothes.

A fashion commercial can do these things with an immediacy that is a powerful call to action.

Any discussion of how and why television is used to sell fashion must be incomplete, for television as a medium is still relatively new. Much has been discovered, more remains to be discovered.

Engineers and scientists discover new techniques. Producers, directors, technicians, editors, writers, artists, and many other skilled people pool their talents to use those techniques most effectively.

There are no hard and fast rules that guarantee a first-rate commercial, but we can list some "do's" and don'ts" that point out directions. Some of these directions are based on material published by the Television Bureau of Advertising, Inc.

- *Do* learn to think visually. The picture *supplements* the words; it does not *repeat* them. If you are showing a full-skirted, polka dot dress, do not say, "Look at this gorgeous full-skirted, polka dot dress." Talk about the silkiness of the fabric, the way the dress lends itself to accessorizing.
- *Do* address yourself to a *specific* customer. You do not have to tell a sophisticated woman that pantsuits are good for traveling. She knows. You do not need to show inexpensive sportswear against an exotic background on a tropical island; you will do better with an informal patio.
- *Do* consider using *your own store* as a *setting* for commercials—you will get an extra institutional message across.
- *Do* consider using *store personnel* in your fashion commercials if they can move and talk in front of the camera—this is great for employee morale and it adds reality to your message.
- No matter how simple your commercial is, plan it out on a storyboard. Even a rough storyboard will be a valuable guide when you go into production. It will save time, money, and prevent bad mistakes that result from hasty decisions made under pressure.
- *Do* try to avoid old-fashioned clichés in movement. The arrogant toss of the head, the bending of elbow and wrist to point a finger at the collar or some other fashion detail—these are not interesting fashion gestures. It is better to let the model move naturally, and show the detail in a close-up. Let the camera do as much work as possible.
- *Do* keep all commentary and sounds to a minimum. Most commercials have too many words.
- *Do* consider special music to help identify your commercials; an unusual

instrument or an unusual arrangement might do more to make your message outstanding than a conventional jingle.

- *Do* make sure that music does not distract from words or picture. Music should enhance, set a mood, or provide a transition.
- *Do* be sure to include essential facts such as price, colors, sizes, brand name, and fabric content. If you cannot include them all, be sure to include price and fabric content; those facts are important to your customer. In some high fashion or institutional commercials, details may not be necessary.
- *Do* describe fabrics clearly, going beyond the letter of the law, especially when they are synthetics or synthetic blends. Synthetic fiber brand names mean very little to the customer; she wants to know how the fabric performs. You must be careful about making comparisons to natural fiber fabrics, but it can be done. Terms like broadcloth, linen, silk, percale and chiffon tell the customer what she wants to know. It is usually necessary to specify whether the fabric is knit or woven.
- *Do* use vendor material cautiously, mixing it with your own material so that the finished commercial says "your store" rather than "manufacturer brand."
- *Do* learn the difference between the written word and the spoken word. Fashion talk that sounds fine in print copy may sound terrible when it is read aloud; it may also be difficult to read. (Peter Piper picked a peck of pickled peppers.)
- *Do* accessorize your models even if you are not selling accessories. The right shoes, scarves, and jewelry can make your ready-to-wear look better.
- *Don't* try too hard to be clever. Tricky camera effects and tricky commentary may make you feel like an expert—but may detract from the selling power of your commercial.
- *Don't* neglect hair and makeup. Both should follow current trends.
- *Don't* forget to plan your props before you go into production. You lose time if you have to run out at the last minute for a tea cup or a radio.
- *Don't* use too many props; they will distract viewers from your merchandise.
- *Don't* be afraid to admit what you do not know. If you are a retailer, you are not a TV expert. Look for good advice, pay for it and follow it. You will learn as you go on.
- *Don't* overlook the possibilities of showing shoes, jewelry, and other small objects in imaginative ways. Cameras can do wonderful things. A ring can be shown on a hand in tight close-up just underneath the chin and mouth, so that the ring really shows. Shoes can be shown on feet dangling over the arm of a chair, walking around casually at a cocktail party, and in other situations.
- *Don't* forget to conclude with a "call to action" that invites or urges the viewer to come into the store.

Our last "don't" comes directly from the Television Bureau experts:

- *Don't* pay any attention to any of the rules if you get a sensational idea that breaks them all and works for you.

There is much more to be said about selling fashion on television. If retailers are willing to open their minds and experiment a little, they will discover a powerful selling tool.

As technical advances bring down costs, it seems safe to predict that the television screen will become a store in the home—a store that will move large quantities of fashion merchandise.

Radio. Radio, the other broadcast medium, tells; it cannot show. It reaches the ears, but not the eyes. This would seem an obstacle to any selling of fashion, but radio can be very important to fashion retailers.

Radio is an ideal medium for announcements. It is relatively cheap, and many spot announcements can be scheduled within a short-term period.

Radio can deliver a call to come in and see a good bargain, a new shipment of seasonal merchandise, a demonstration, a fashion show, a visiting celebrity, a new department, or a newly opened store.

Radio reaches its audience at times that television cannot. In rural and suburban areas where there is no mass transportation. People drive cars to get to wherever they are going. There is always a radio in the car. The working person going to and from work turns on the radio.

Women can watch television while they do certain kinds of housework. There are now mini-TV sets for the kitchen, but it is far easier to listen than watch while doing tasks that require visual concentration; for instance, cooking.

Teenagers are devoted to rock music radio programs, and ads placed on such programs reach this particular audience. The radio goes out of the home; teenagers carry radios with them wherever they go, and seem literally glued to their favorite programs.

Radio can be used creatively; its very limitation can become an asset. Dialogues between two people in conversational form get the message across. Sound effects create the picture in the mind of the audience.

A fashion retailer can create a dialogue between two women in a beauty parlor by simulating typical beauty parlor sounds—a dryer, chatter, the snip of scissors.

Clinking dishes and glasses suggest a restaurant. No props or costumes are needed.

Since sound and voice are the main elements of radio, they are of vital importance. Shouting and hard sell are as wrong on radio as on television. A pleasant, crisp voice that speaks clearly without gushing gets a spot message across effectively.

Where special material is involved, voices can be warm, cool, insinuating, sexy, childish—they can create any mood that the retailer needs to enhance merchandise.

A good script writer can describe fashion merchandise in a way that will arouse the curiosity of the listener.

If a commercial aims at selling specific merchandise, the script should give a feeling of the clothes. An easy-fitting dress; a neatly tailored, fitted jacket; a floating chiffon gown with gathered skirt; a toga-like silhouette; full sleeves; a narrow skirt—these are all examples of "straight" description as opposed to selling adjectives like "beautiful" and "divine" that really tell the listener nothing about the merchandise.

157

The less detail, the better, unless it is an important detail. Every shirt has a collar, and it is of no importance to say that a shirt has a collar. But does the collar have double lapels faced with a contrasting print? That becomes a fashion feature worth mentioning, if there is time, *because the listener cannot see it.*

In radio, as in television, time should not be cluttered or crowded. The listener should not be bombarded with words. A brief description, light music *under* the voice, not over, or sound effects—and finish up with the store name.

Radio advertisers may choose spot announcements or, like television advertisers, may link their message to a specific show that they feel provides a good environment for their store's merchandise and their store image.

All advertising is a form of promotion; it is what a store does to move merchandise. Most promotional activities have one element in common; they are theatrical. They seek to attract and enhance. They play to an audience of potential customers.

In our next two chapters, we will examine some other kinds of promotional tools that retailers use to sell fashion.

Display and Fixturing
Set the Stage

P romotion is show business—it is stage, scenery, props, and sometimes, performers. It is a cluster of things some active, some passive, that enhance merchandise and call it to the attention of shoppers.

11

Advertising is one phase of promotion; there are many others. Store layout and design, window display, interior display, fixturing, lighting, and signage are all examples of promotional tools that can enhance fashion.

The flower a service manager wears in his or her lapel says, "Here I am, ready to help," and indirectly paves the way for selling. No detail is too small: a pair of white satin shoes thoughtfully placed in the dressing room of a bridal department for the customer to use while trying on bridal gowns is promotional.

On the other hand there is the dinner party, held in or outside the store, complete with dancing, a fashion show, and formally invited guests. That, too, is promotional. If part of the proceeds of tickets sold for the dinner is to benefit a charity, the store is cultivating the goodwill of its community. That is promotion on a grand scale.

All these aspects of promotion surround and enhance the merchandise just as a stage setting enhances the actors and actresses in a play. Retailing is a theatrical business, and fashion represents retailing at its most theatrical. Women respond to the mood of clothes; their responses can be cued by the environment in which they see the clothes.

The environment of the store starts with the windows; they are outside the store, and they are the first part of it the customer sees. If she is passing by and is attracted by a window display, she may enter the store impulsively. If she has planned a visit to the store, the windows will make an impression on her, even if she only glances at them briefly.

There was a time when fashion mannequins were rigidly posed in windows at equal distances from each other. There was even a time when mannequins had no

Designer fashions move in a procession, raffia
shelters one mannequin and curls across the window floor. Henri Bendel, New York. Close-up of
model sheltered by raffia, partially hidden, adds a
touch of mystery.

Three mannequins supported by pillars, two, partially hidden. This window at Lord & Taylor, New York, has the feeling of a stage setting. Masses of plants and flowers, foreground, soften what would otherwise be a too-stark display.

heads; heads were considered unrefined! The high fashion store usually showed one mannequin in a window, and the mannequin was always placed in the exact center of the window, creating a precisely symmetrical effect.

A trend in fashion window display ignores symmetry and makes use of groups of mannequins, or single figures.

Mannequins are made so that they can be placed in more active poses; they no longer stand rigidly, one foot forward, one foot back, one hand on hip. The flexibility of gesture makes it possible to show clothing in different ways. A mannequin in a tennis dress swings her racket. A mannequin in an evening gown is posed like a film star. A mannequin in an at-home caftan lounges languidly on the floor of the window, or on a couch. There is mood and emotional intensity in these poses, heightening the dramatic effect of the windows.

Mannequins are no longer limited to vapid, well-bred faces. Their faces may be copies from the faces of well-known models, and may express definite personalities. They can be life-like, or exaggerated, or abstract. Bendel's, in New York City, stuffed mannequins with straw so that they looked like elegant scarecrows in burlap, and the

"Indian Summer" themes a traditional window display, Bonwit Teller, New York. An Indian hanging is the background for a dressed mannequin. In the foreground, a "carefully careless" pile of clothing and accessories.

Elegant western sportswear in a window at Bergdorf Goodman, New York. Model gets in action with lariat. Wooden corral fence is background prop.

result was a stunning fall sweater display. The possibilities for arrangement of fashion mannequins, like other aspects of display, conform less to pre-fixed rules.

But rules have not disappeared entirely; there are still elements of display that should not be ignored.

Cluttered windows, like cluttered ads, fail to communicate. Usually, the more merchandise shown, the less visible each piece becomes. Merchandise needs to be surrounded by space.

Props and background should accent and dramatize merchandise, but should not overpower it.

Lighting can turn an ordinary window into a dramatic window.

Most display managers think windows should be changed every week, or every two weeks. When left in too long, windows go stale. People get tired of seeing the same merchandise in the same setting over and over again.

Ingenuity can count for more than money. Inexpensive materials like egg boxes and wooden packing crates can make interesting props.

Different kinds of merchandise call for different settings. Designer merchandise has enough interest to stand on its own. Less expensive merchandise may need dramatizing. Lighting, props, backgrounds, and fashion accessories all help.

There are ways of displaying fashion without mannequins: pinning, draping, flat cut-out "paper doll" figures, and hangers. These are best in small windows of small stores. In standard window displays, most clothes look best on a mannequin.

All clothing should be completely accessorized if it is shown on a mannequin.

Mannequins should always be completely dressed from head to toe. A display of ready-to-wear is not complete if the mannequins are not wearing shoes, belts, jewelry, and any other appropriate accessory. In a large store, accessories will come from another department. In a small store, they must be borrowed from another retailer and credited.

Mannequins should be contemporary; their hair, especially, should reflect changing styles. Black mannequins are now available. Some stores have been quick to pick this up; others have dragged their heels. Adherence to old prejudices can create resentment and can lose business for a store whose management is insensitive to changing times.

Small accessories tend to disappear; they need to be grouped and spaced carefully. Lighting can dramatize groups of scarves, shoes and handbags, which can be mounted on ladders or steps, or wall-like arrangements of bricks or other materials.

Window display cards are helpful in a large store with many departments. Card messages should be brief. A theme, department name and floor are sufficient. The theme should be stated in a few words, for instance, "summer flowers," or "holiday glitter."

Each window in a group should be numbered, so the customer can refer to merchandise by window number when she is inside the store.

The display manager works under unending pressure because display calls for an endless supply of new ideas. Mistakes cannot be hidden away in a stockroom; they are right out front where everybody can see them. There are no peak seasons and dull reasons to explain ups and downs; windows are expected to be *great* all the time.

An endless supply of ideas calls for nourishment and renewal. The display manager must draw nourishment from as many sources as possible.

Gene Moore is a man who has found new ways of drawing unique ideas from his surroundings. Mr. Moore, is display director and divisional vice president of Tiffany & Co., one of the country's great jewelry stores. Mr. Moore pioneered in the use of extremely ordinary and extremely extraordinary props for jewelry. He used hardware and brown paper bags as well as original, fine art to dramatize jewels.

Mr. Moore's ideas start with his theory that a good display must have some kind of emotional appeal.

"A good window display makes the viewer feel a little bit the way one feels when one falls in love for the first time," he says. "There is wonderment, communication,

"Splashy beach news" themes window display, Lord & Taylor, New York. Models seem to walk, lounge and dress in a life-like way. Light wood, slatted doors carry out the cabana theme.

and hopefully, some humor. The elements of a good window are very much like the elements of a good painting; there is balance and contrast, light and shadow.

"It's difficult to create exciting fashion windows, because everything is on a deadline. But I do think that every store should do what I call 'theme' windows every year, windows that have nothing to do with cruise or spring. Why? To make people talk, and to keep them interested in the store as something vital and alive, something aware and growing, something that is part of the community.

"Try to plan windows with a change of pace. A topical theme, a seasonal theme, an elegant theme are some examples of different moods you can create. A touch of humor or wit provides a change of pace, too.

166

Eyelet and gingham-checked "country" fashions star in a window at Lord & Taylor, New York. Mannequins are grouped together. Picket fence divides space attractively and repeats the country theme.

"Keep looking for new ideas wherever you go, and keep an open mind about ideas. An object doesn't have to shout lots of money to create elegance. Don't be snobbish.

"Travel, films, theater and secondhand stores will give you ideas. Look for new young artists in your own community.

"Be prepared for emergencies; be ready to improvise if a plan falls through. Some people work well under pressure; others don't. If you don't, have a backup plan on hand all the time.

"Don't leave windows in more than two weeks. Things happen to objects in windows; sometimes they lose their spontaneity and freshness, and become stale.

"Plan ahead for the big times, like Christmas and Easter, but try to leave yourself some flexibility in between so you can change your ideas as you go along—they'll usually change for the better.

"Don't try to 'out-kook' everybody. The world may be crazier, people may be crazier, fashion may be crazier—that still doesn't mean your windows have to be crazier.

"Learn to look at the usual as well as the unusual object. Dirt and stones can be effective props.

"I make props myself. A display person should know all about construction; should be able to tinker and build. That way, you learn just what the possibilities of a given material are, and how it will work in a prop.

"Learn all about lighting—it's 50 percent of a window's effectiveness. It makes the difference between a good window and a bad window.

"Fashion merchandise calls for theatrical lighting. Natural daylight is not as effective, even if you can get it. Windows are theater and must be treated that way. Shadow is very important. If there is light and no shadow, there is no contrast. Mannequins are inanimate, clothes are inanimate. It takes light to give a feeling of drama, to give depth and emphasis. Of course, a window display is much more limited in space than a stage, so the range of effects is more limited.

"The one thing a good display person cannot be is lazy. There is always an easy way out. You put a potted plant in a window with a few mannequins around it and there you are. But that is not creative. That does not sell effectively, nor add anything to your store's image.

"You must have your own point of view, your own ideas, if you want to be really good, if you want to do a good job. That is much harder. You must see things in a certain way and communicate your special point of view to your audience. You must not be afraid. This takes confidence. You must have confidence in yourself and your management must have confidence in you.

"The display person must be backed by top management if he is going to do a good job. Then, when you disagree with the buyer, you can say to her, go see the president. Eventually, she will come to trust you, if you know your business. She will begin to feel that you are on her side. Then there is more freedom—even freedom to go into the market and see whole collections. I think anyone in display must see collections, must know all about clothes, must know all about everything."

Lighting is crucial to jewelry display, for diamonds and colored stones are the smallest of small accessories, and their color is at the heart of their appeal. Not surprisingly, Mr. Moore feels strongly about the role of lighting in jewelry display. Some of his ideas apply to fashion accessories and fashion merchandise in general, as well as to jewelry in particular.

"You can't solve every problem perfectly," says Mr. Moore. "Some stones, for instance, the iridescents like star sapphires and tiger's eye, can't always be lit so that shadows and bars are eliminated. You could have a problem like that with a changeable fabric in fashion merchandise, too. Do the best you can.

"Try to show colored stones in their natural colors. I don't think it's fair to make a green stone look greener than it really is by intensifying it with a greener light. Don't light diamonds with a yellowish light; use a natural blue daylight.

"Neutral blue is good for almost everything. It's good for silver. Don't use a warm light on silver.

"Don't assume that the jewelry has to be the most brightly lit object in the window. If you have an interesting prop, light it brightly, and place the jewelry in a shadow. By doing that, you make people stop and look for the jewelry; you create a mystery.

"Every good window must have a center of interest, like a good painting—jewelry or prop, it must be there."

The way a store approaches window display depends on the quality and price of its merchandise, its size, and its location.

Large specialty and department stores plan windows months in advance. Chains plan display, like advertising, from the flagship store. The display head will visit branches to supervise, and there will be a local display manager in the branch unit. The central store may have its own department where props are built; the whine of the electric saw can be heard as Christmas props are built in August.

The display situation is very different in *smaller* fashion stores.

Windows are planned more informally. There may be no mannequins and few props.

Perhaps the owner will "do" the windows, or window. Or, the task may be delegated to an employee with a gift for draping, an eye for color, and the so-called sixth sense of what looks right. No matter how small the store, some pinning, hammering, and tinkering is needed.

The display stems from the nature of the store itself. A shop that carries expensive designer merchandise will not be able to stock in depth. A few pieces of each style are ordered. One piece goes into the window. The customer of such a store knows she cannot depend on finding the brown cape, size 10, three weeks after she sees it. The piece in the window may be the only brown cape size 10 in the store.

The window is the store itself; the customer may buy merchandise that must be removed from the window.

Another kind of small shop carries less expensive stock in more depth.

If a store carries stock in depth, current stock affects the window display. Windows are dependent on shipment and delivery. Slow deliveries may leave a small store with insufficient stock to back up display. When a great deal of merchandise is received at once, there is too much to choose from; the store must consider what it will show and what it will hold back.

Many small stores with an image of quality prefer not to show price tags in the window. The absence of price tags is a signal to customers; if they are looking only for bargains or discounts, they will pass by and avoid the store, for stores that build their image on price alone will also feature prices in the window prominently.

From an aesthetic point of view, some merchants feel that little bits of paper with numbers on them are not pleasing to the eye.

One example of a store that omits price tags to signal "Quality—no price promotions here"—is Village Casuals, a small sportswear store on a downtown street in New York City. The store carries mostly casual separates; shirts, sweaters, pants, skirts, and jackets. In 1977, prices for shirts ranged from $24 to $50 with strength in the $30 range. A corduroy jacket was $52; a summer cotton skirt $24. While a few special outfits go into higher prices, the thrust of the store is middle to just above middle; a range that became increasingly more difficult to maintain in an era of inflation.

Owners Eve Cooley, Marion Lewis, and Virginia Palmer depend on their window displays to attract steady customers as well as new customers. Because street traffic is so heavy, the display is "watched" by customers who live in the neighborhood, who will know something new has come in when they see it in the window.

Ms. Palmer has a gift for display; it is her job, officially. Unofficially, her co-owners have plenty of advice and comments to offer.

Changing the window is a major operation. Friday is the usual day for change. Some displays stay in longer than a week, but once-a-week change is the goal.

Friday is a good day for display changes because Saturday is the busiest day of the week. Though the store is closed on Sunday, window shoppers may spot a new item and call up Monday to ask about it.

The six-foot square window has one wall and an open back. The open back is closed in partially by cinderblock "bricks" painted white. The bricks form a divider useful for background and security.

Props can be set against the bricks for display. In terms of security, the partial wall is a barrier against hands that might reach into the window and pluck out merchandise. Neutral fabric of beige, gray or white covers wall and floor. The fabric is changed occasionally; the floor consists of planks which must be occasionally recovered with fresh fabric.

No mannequins are used; all merchandise is draped and pinned.

Props are few but tasteful. There are some antiques that the owners have collected over the years—a weather vane, some wooden initials covered with gold paint. Flowers, potted plants, a few framed prints, and appealing stuffed animals from a neighborhood toy store complete the inventory. A tall rattan ladder is useful for displaying folded shirts.

Following is how windows are created at Village Casuals—and many other small stores that care about display.

It is Friday afternoon. Before a new window can go in, the old one must come out. Each piece of merchandise in the window is carefully removed and checked against a list before it goes back into stock.

The white felt floor is dirty. It is vacuumed after the merchandise has been removed.

As old merchandise is put away, new merchandise is pulled.

After years of emphasis on pants, skirts are staging a comeback. So the window will include at least one.

Merchandise is selected and rejected on the basis of number of pieces in stock, color, timeliness.

A shirt is rejected—its orange stripe would turn into a washed-out yellow under the ceiling spotlights.

A color scheme of red, black and beige is beginning to emerge. One red-and-beige shirt that would be perfect must be discarded—it has been a best seller; only a couple of pieces are left, and it cannot be reordered.

Black blazer jacket, pants and flared skirt are chosen. Beige pants and shirt and a red-beige-black-white striped shirt are checked off.

The rattan ladder will go in the window as a prop.

The framed print hanging on the window wall comes down and is replaced by another with dominant orange-red tones.

Merchandise is listed; style number, size and price of each piece is on the list.

Merchandise must look neat. Tags are clipped off or tucked inside the garment. If they are clipped off, they are recorded and put aside in a box, so that they can be re-attached after the garment comes out of the window. Any extra buttons are put aside in the same way.

Some garments are wrinkled, though they have just come out of their shipping boxes. They are pressed in back of the store.

Each garment is inspected carefully for loose buttons or hanging threads.

The store believes in displaying its best selling styles and colors. Beige is doing well at the moment; that was one reason why it was chosen for display. Also, the color scheme is cheerful for early spring, yet not too far ahead of the season. Three dominant colors are enough for this small window.

Coordinated displays also help sell basic styles. A plain, straight skirt looks like nothing by itself; when matched with shirt, vest and jacket, it can be visualized as part of a total sportswear look. (Clothes borrow interest from other clothes.)

"Is this merchandise just a little ahead of the season or right on top of it?" This is a test question for window display merchandise. Another is, "What is the competition doing?"

Another store is showing all white windows, Village Casuals does not want to echo it. A men's wear store around the corner has just begun to carry a small selection of women's tailored sportswear; Village Casuals will move away from a strict haberdashery look in its displays for the time being.

The store sees itself as part of the community—an attractive canvas shopping bag that a local committee is selling to raise funds for the public library goes into the window with a small, neat sign.

The small fashion store makes observations; its owners and staff members translate their ideas into action quickly.

At the other end of the retailing spectrum, Sears, Roebuck, the largest general merchandise chain store operation in the country, has made far-reaching, in-depth studies that affect all aspects of store policy, including window and interior display.

Sears must move large quantities of merchandise as quickly as possible. Every inch of space must be utilized scientifically.

What follows is based on an interview printed in *Women's Wear Daily* some years ago. Though time has elapsed, the conclusions reported by a spokesman for Sears are still valid. These conclusions were based on a consumer study made by Sears.

The average shopper spends less than thirty minutes in a Sears store each time he or she shops.

Sears estimates its customers make three and one-half trips a month to the store and spend, in effect, about one and one-half hours of shopping time there.

Sears has ten to twelve peak selling hours a week. During those peak hours, salespeople are outnumbered by customers, possibly by as many as twelve to one.

The store has four and one-half seconds to make a visual impact on the customer.

From these findings, it was concluded, "The customer must be able to find what she wants quickly, so that she can move on quickly to make another selling decision in our store . . . The Sears program is based on speed, and we believe selling will get even faster as time goes on."

In order to speed selling, Sears employs the following in-store display techniques:

General elimination of traditional window displays. When window displays are used, they are geared to reveal, not conceal, the interior of the store to the customer as he or she enters.

In-store displays change every ten to twelve days. This is because many Sears customers are repeat customers, and they do not want to see the same display twice.

Fixed displays of a merchandise line are out. That is, all displays are movable. (A counter stand is an example of a movable display; a wall bracket and a lighting fixture attached to the ceiling are examples of fixed or permanent displays that cannot be moved.)

General elimination of product identity. That is, Sears would rather mix brands and stress its own name and assortment then stress any one brand name.

The Sears experience provides an excellent analysis of customer habits in large general merchandise stores. This analysis, however, could not be applied to a mass fashion store that did not sell general merchandise, or to a better specialty store, or even

Burdine's, Sarasota, Florida, sets up permanent display in men's boutique called "The Depot," imitating an old silent film; the mannequin-heroine tied to the tracks, the mannequin-hero coming to the rescue. Sound effects accompany the display: a train in motion and a scream.

to a general merchandise or department store with a clientele of upper-middle class customers.

As soon as fashion merchandise moves away from staple and becomes more varied and less standardized, then speed is not the most important element the store has to consider. It is no longer simply a matter of directing a customer to a counter where she will find a particular pantie or hosiery style. The customer may be looking at something new and different, or comparing a familiar piece of merchandise with something unfamiliar. She may want to think for some time before she decides to buy.

The more time a customer spends thinking about what she is going to buy, the longer she remains in the store, and the more important presentation becomes.

A store that wishes to sell merchandise above the level of staple fashion must minimize shopping frustrations and difficulties. And even the store that sells only staple merchandise must make it easy for women to shop.

Let's go back to advertising and set up a chain of selling action. Let's suppose that selling action starts with the ad a woman sees in her newspaper. She decides to go to the store to look at the merchandise. When she gets there, she sees the merchandise in the store window and pauses to look at it. Is there a copy card in the window that tells her clearly on which floor she will find the merchandise?

The customer sees the copy card and enters the store. If it is a big store, she pauses again, wondering where to go next. Is there a sign on a nearby wall or counter that tells her again where to find the merchandise in the window? Or is there a shelf with a throw-away circular that gives her this information?

Now the customer heads for the elevator or escalator. Is there a sign on the elevator wall telling her what floor to get off? Is there a sign at the head of the escalator telling her that she has arrived at the right floor?

The customer reaches the department. Does she see the merchandise on display, so she can walk up to it and touch it? (This is one of the most important links.)

A saleswoman approaches her (hopefully). Does that saleswoman know about the new merchandise? Is a copy of the ad, mounted on an easel, standing on the counter? (This helps the saleswoman as well as the customer.) Is the merchandise in stock? One or two pieces? Or a range of sizes and colors that includes the size and color the customer wants?

We can see how many links there are in this chain of action. If one is absent, the chain may break. The customer may wander around the store and become distracted, tired, and annoyed. The effective ad and good window display are both wasted. The sale is lost.

Of course, this is strictly a large store problem. The small store that occupies less space can bring its customers close to its merchandise quickly and easily.

Window displays lure shoppers into the store. Once inside, store layout, design

174

Interior displays from Belk Stores Services, Inc. A jaunty mannequin posed on a dais and contrasting carpeting define a departmental area. Lighting is recessed in ceiling. Belk-Hudson, Sunset Plaza, Moultrie, Georgia.

Tie-in promotion at Saks, Bal Harbour, Florida, links live models, Ford Motor Company, and *Town and Country* Magazine. *(Photography: Iran Issa-Khan)*

and fixturing take over as selling tools; they can enhance merchandise and make it more appealing.

Trends in store layout and design have changed the appearance of stores. There was a time when heavy, ornate chandeliers stood for elegance. Expensive clothes were hidden away in the stockrooms of formal salon departments. Saleswomen brought out garments, one by one, for the customer's inspection.

In budget stores, there was little or no attempt at display. Tables and racks were placed on the selling floor in no particular order. It was up to the customer to find the merchandise. Strong colors and interesting materials were avoided; fashion retailers felt that they would detract from merchandise.

In the 1970's, many retailers feel that fashion merchandise may borrow drama and excitement from its background. Wood, tiles, strong colors, mirrors, stainless steel and all sorts of materials are used in store interiors.

Merchandise is *openly displayed*. Store layout and design has tended, more and more, towards fixturing and display that presents merchandise directly to the customer. The rod and the rack, in one form or another, are basic fixtures. Stores selling budget-priced fashions have cleaned up their interiors and present their wide assortments attractively. Some stores carrying better-priced merchandise began to adopt similar techniques by the mid-1970's. They swept out counters, island displays of mannequins and seating areas, replacing them with rods and racks.

It was no coincidence that counters disappeared as the shortage of adequate sales help became more acute. Where there is a counter, there must be a salesperson behind it to show merchandise.

The disappearance of counters, islands and seating areas also reflected a dollar-value approach to fashion. Counters, seating areas and island displays are attractive, the reasoning went, but they take up space that could otherwise be used to show and sell merchandise. Since the aim of the store is to sell, why not use every available inch of floor space for that purpose?

Some stores found that customers reacted badly to new layouts that seemed like mazes of racks and rods, with never a chair to sit down on, and hardly a salesperson in sight.

However, young people liked the idea of totally visible merchandise. It was, in fact, the youth stores that pioneered in this type of layout. But the youth stores were relatively small stores; such a layout, translated to a large store's selling floor, became quite different.

Women seemed to miss the element of surprise, an element they had hardly been aware of. If some merchandise is on display, and some is kept back, then there is a little mystery, a little something to look forward to.

If fixturing conceals part of the selling floor from view, then the shopper will make a discovery as she moves from one area to another. A totally open display eliminates all surprises and all mysteries.

Informal living room atmosphere, with sportswear displayed on table. Lowered ceiling grid echoes openwork design of chairs. Belk-Hudson, Westgate Mall, Spartanburg, South Carolina.

Bridal display in latticework pavillion surrounded by plantings, a garden-like setting that suggests spring and summer weddings. Escalators and exposed elevator, sides and rear, become handsome architectural features. Parks-Belk, Fort Henry Mall, Kingsport, Tennessee.

178

The trend towards more open display solved some problems and created others. It helped solve the problem of the disappearing salesperson. It eliminated some expensive permanent fixturing. It added more flexibility to store layout.

New problems included an increase in shoplifting. It is easy for a shoplifter to work between concealing racks. The absence of salespeople is another boon to thieves.

Housekeeping became more of a problem. The more merchandise on display, the more customers tend to pull it out and disarrange it. This creates a messy selling floor, unless there are employees who spend a good deal of their time rearranging stock.

Customers of some promotional stores do not care about atmosphere, but customers of stores carrying better-priced fashion merchandise expect neatness and order.

Different stores take different approaches to layout and design. Often, they turn to architectural firms specializing in store layout. Architects, like retailers, bring special points of view to bear on solving layout problems.

Sheridan Associates has a long history of working with retailers to meet their needs. George Frei, vice president of Sheridan Associates, has seen development of the trend towards utilization of every inch of floor space for selling.

As of the 1970's, says Mr. Frei, a typical store uses as little as 15 percent of its floor space for non-selling; years ago, the figure was as high as 35 percent.

"Retailers want to use every inch of space for selling merchandise," notes Mr. Frei. "We feel that the best way to make use of space is summed up in one word—flexibility.

"Fixed walls, fixed counters, anything that can't be moved around easily is out.

"The inside of a store is like stage scenery. It has to change constantly to accommodate new merchandise, new kinds of merchandise representing some aspect of today's way of life—whether it's tennis clothes or blue jeans.

"We use panels that move around like screens instead of fixed walls. We have ceiling grids from which merchandise is suspended. The merchandise arrangement can change easily. Panels don't have to touch the floor and ceiling, they can be suspended from the ceiling.

"Sometimes panels suspended to different lengths make an irregular pattern—and the pattern can be changed easily. Even the walls that form a department can be flexible, so that they can change when the store wants to change the department. For instance, we've used mirrors for a junior shop—they give an effect of glitter and sparkle. They can be replaced by fabric-covered panels for a women's clothing area, or dark wood for a traditional men's shop—though dark wood isn't as popular as it once was.

"There's a contradiction here—we're breaking up space and at the same time containing it in the total unity of the store.

"Transition and definition are necessary within the total store space. The store is like a home; you go from one room to another. There must be both continuity and contrast.

Evening clothes by Oscar de la Renta are the theme of an interior display at Saks Fifth Avenue, Bal Harbour, Florida. Live model, right, poses with mannequins, left. Plants in straw baskets add life and warmth. *(Photography: Iran Issa-Khan)*

180

Summer sportswear on an informal grouping of mannequins at Saks, Bal Harbour, Florida, is typical of natural, life-like arrangements of mannequins. *(Photography: Iran Issa-Khan)*

"That doesn't mean a store has to have complete room settings or a fireplace, as a home does, but a good store should give its customers a sense of place, of being somewhere. If customers are just left wandering about a huge open space with no differentiation, they will feel small and lost and frustrated—as if they were wandering in some foreign, bewildering, and not-too-interesting city.

"Transition and definition can be as simple as a panel, a screen, a row of tubes, a change of wall covering, a change of floor covering—say, from wood to carpeting.

"In spite of the variations, there must be an overall unity. It can be a repeat in the architecture, perhaps an angle in the wall, that carries through on all floors.

"This unity creates a sense of rhythm. The customer may not realize it consciously, but she *feels* something. She feels that she is in this particular store, even though she may be moving from one department to another."

Variety of merchandise under one roof creates another problem for retailers who must deal with the "stage scenery" of the store. Like a stage, a store must be illuminated. *Lighting* can enhance or detract from merchandise.

Store lighting breaks down into two categories; general and local. General lighting affects the overall area. Local lighting is focused on specific merchandise. Spotlights and counter lights are examples of local lighting.

"The best lighting is the most inconspicuous," says Mr. Frei. "General illumination concealed in the ceiling avoids an obvious fixture.

"When ceiling lights are placed under movable squares like tiles, the lights can be moved from one position to another for flexibility.

"Track lighting is another example of flexibility. Spotlights on a track 'can be arranged so that they move up and down, or from side to side.

"Lighting involves the materials used on walls and floors, too. We look for materials that will bounce light back instead of absorbing it. Tile and vinyl reflect light. Dark carpet and dark wood absorb light and make it disappear.

"Whether lighting is high- or low-key, it is part of layout, and it has one purpose, just as all store layout has one purpose," concludes Mr. Frei. "Merchandise should be visible and available."

Good, clear lighting, or "honest" lighting, as it is sometimes called, is associated with mass merchandise selling. These are the stores that want to create a strong value image. All effects are simple; no frills are needed.

Strong, direct lighting is quite different from the moody, low-key lighting of some high fashion stores and special shops. A mannequin may be partly in shadow; merchandise can be spotlighted, with shadow surrounding the lighted area.

Some youth stores have found that their customers like dim lighting and rock music. Such stores cater mostly to teenage customers.

Lighting varies from one merchandise category to another. Some merchandise, like fur, absorbs light because of its texture and dense pile. More light is needed; walls

182

and floors of fur departments should bounce off light so that the merchandise does not look dark or dull.

While a feeling of warmth is generally desirable in fashion departments, fur does not need warmth; neither does skiwear.

Casual sportswear, on the other hand, can be illuminated with a warm, rosy-orange light in keeping with the mood of the merchandise.

Lighting in fitting rooms has been neglected in many stores, even as lighting problems on the selling floors were solved.

Many stores with good lighting have fitting rooms illuminated by old-fashioned, bluish fluorescent lights that make women yellowish as they look in the mirror. The dressing room may well be the place where the sale is made or lost. A good, strong neutral light that does not change the color of the customer's complexion, or the merchandise, is best.

Lighting has come a long way from the days of the chandelier. New fixtures and materials are invented each year, and the stage and scenery of the fashion store benefit from this wider range of possibilities.

Signage in a large store is an important part of display. It is both useful and decorative. Departmental signage tells the customer where she is, and immediately sets a mood.

A neon-light sign anticipates funky young clothes. A wooden sign with etched letters may express the mood of country clothes or leathers.

A simple name may point the way to an expensive designer department. If the designer is well known, the name is all that is needed.

Signage became more important from the 1960's on when large stores began to break up their merchandise into shops. Some fashion stores change shops constantly; each new shop calls for a new name and a new sign.

Poor signage can confuse customers. One example of such a sign comes from a story told by a department manager who happily watched as a shop for tall women was refurbished. At first, the new shop was a total failure. Women passed it by.

One day, the manager approached a tall woman who walked past the new department, ignoring the tempting display of merchandise.

"Madam," he said, politely, "Wouldn't you like to see some of our new fashions for tall women?" He pointed to the department sign, which read, 5'7".

The woman squinted at the sign. "Oh," she said slowly, "Is *that* what it says? I couldn't see those little marks. I thought it said 57, and that meant it was a department for older women in their late fifties and sixties."

Business improved when the sign was re-painted, in words, instead of numbers.

There is no need to sacrifice clarity for decorative effect. The simplest sign can be attractive and functional. Often, well-formed letters on a contrasting background are all that is necessary.

Models lounge on furniture in elegant room setting for an at-home-wear department. Racks in background. Belk-Hudson, Westgate Mall, Spartanburg, South Carolina.

On a large selling floor, signs must be well placed, so that they can be read easily from a distance.

Signage is a map of the store that guides the customer. Like lighting, it does not sell directly. Rather, it helps create an atmosphere that will be conducive to selling. It is part of the stage and scenery of fashion promotion.

The stage and scenery of the fashion store are a background for selling, and also for special events, a form of theater-at-retail that sometimes involves selling directly, sometimes indirectly. We will discuss special events in our next chapter.

Special Events:
Fashion Is Show Biz

12

Layout, design, fixturing, and lighting are what a store is, the stage and the scenery. What a store *does* is also part of the show business aspect of retailing.

The *fashion show* is a form of special may stand on its own or be part of a larger store event, or a storewide promotion. While special events are generally associated with large department and specialty stores, they can be adapted to small stores.

Fashion shows can be as simple as informal modeling or as elaborate as a theatrical production complete with lights, commentary, music, and special effects.

Informal modeling is a pleasant, low-key way of introducing customers'to new styles. Models may walk casually through the aisles of a store restaurant, or, through the aisles of the department wearing the clothes. There is no commentary. Models usually carry a card with some basic information; the designer's name, or the name of the department selling the clothes.

The designer fashion show stars the designer plus a supporting cast of clothes—and the clothes are modeled informally. These are expensive clothes with high price tags. Specialty stores often will run an announcement ad in the newspaper inviting women to come in and meet the designer.

Prestige designers create goodwill and generate sales when they appear on the selling floor. Often, such designers go on the road, traveling from city to city with models and clothes. Women like to talk to them; they are interested in the designer's opinions.

A customer has a little story to tell about her new dress if the designer helped her pick it out.

If she is not sure of her own taste, the designer's reassurance helps her make a decision. A designer is not likely to tell a woman that a style looks well on her if it really looks terrible.

Interaction between designer and customer is good for designers, too, for they find out what their customers want, hope for and fear.

As for the store, it can only improve its fashion image by bringing designer and customer together.

If a designer, or any guest, is going to appear in a store, it is a good idea to make sure that he or she can do something. Just standing around a department makes anyone feel foolish. Here is where store personnel can be helpful. Buyer, fashion coordinator, special events director, publicity director—*one* of them should be on hand to ease over awkward moments, to introduce the designer to customers, or ward off eccentrics.

The designer making a store appearance becomes a performer on the stage of the store. This is true of all guests—from the hard-sell demonstrator whose deft fingers slice vegetables with a remarkable new gadget, to the glamorous celebrity.

Not all celebrities are gracious. Not all guests are cool and poised.

When a guest seems rattled by people, it is time for store personnel to move in and act as a buffer.

Some guests are outgoing; others are shy. There is a famous designer who is so shy, he runs from customers. Wherever he appears, buyers, fashion coordinators and whomever else is available will watch him carefully. If not watched, he will fleé to the nearest empty stock room, while women are waiting on the selling floor to greet him. A disappearing guest can turn a fashion show into a non-happening.

A classic fashion show is held in the store, on a fashion floor. Folding chairs may be set up around a runway or stage. There are models, and there is a formal commentary. Such shows require careful planning.

Picking a theme is the first step; this should be done months in advance so that all clothes can be assembled in the store. (That is the ideal situation; many retail executives wind up with last-minute schedules and uneven shows.)

The show may mark the beginning of a season, or some event typical of the season. June is for graduation. August is for back-to-school.

The theme will carry the show forward and give it the unity it needs to hold customers' attention.

Production and staging are other decisions that must be made. Is the show going to be elaborate or simple? How much money is available? How much talent is available?

Big city stores can count on a more sophisticated audience and should be careful to avoid the kind of frankly corny approach that seems to be a fashion show tradition.

Stores in a smaller community must decide whether or not their audience will be delighted with a bit of theater because they are so rarely exposed to a live performance, or whether they will feel uncomfortable, and will be unable to concentrate on the clothes.

If the show is to be staged, then it must be very well staged. If this is not possible, because of limited money or talent, the store had better play it straight and work towards achieving two essentials; well-dressed models and a well-written, well-delivered script.

187

In commenting on window displays and advertising, we noted that expensive designer fashions do not need the added drama of props. This is true of fashion shows, too. Accessories, discreet music, and brief commentary are sufficient.

Putting together a fashion show calls for organizational skill, an eye for fashion, imagination, and patience. There are many details that must be taken care of, often under pressure. Sooner or later someone will scream at someone else; a peacemaker is needed as time grows short, rehearsals lengthen, and tempers fray. At the last minute, some vital accessory will be missing. It may turn up just before the show starts, or it may not. Someone must improvise and find another hat or bag to go with the blue outfit.

The length of the show is another important decision that must be made. Too short a show leaves the audience wanting more. Too long a show, no matter how exciting, is just as bad. After a certain point, the audience gets restless. Half an hour is usually the maximum length that an audience's attention can be held, even if the show is staged in a big way. Some stores prefer 20 minutes.

Choosing models, accessorizing fashions, and keeping records of merchandise all require efficient follow-through if the show is to run smoothly.

The fashion coordinator will find it useful to make a large progress chart for the show. The names of the models are written vertically. The numbers of the scenes are written across the top. As each part of each costume a model is going to wear is completed, a note is made in the proper box. This gives the fashion coordinator an up-to-the-minute record of work done and work that remains to be done. This grouping of merchandise may also suggest subjects for different scenes.

Some fashion coordinators prefer to keep notes on three-by-five-inch cards, using one for each outfit. These cards can be shuffled around easily, as the show takes shape. The fashion commentator may use these cards as her script for the commentary.

The effect of each outfit must be judged from a distance, with the lighting that will be used on the day of the show. A color or combination that is effective close up may fade away when seen under strong light or from a distance. Effects that look overly theatrical in natural light may look dramatic and striking in the spotlight and from a distance.

A good rule to follow in choosing accessories is when in doubt leave it out. Too much is worse than too little.

Choosing the hour when the show will be held is important. Eleven to two will attract housewives in a community where children do not come home for lunch. Noon to one o'clock will draw working women. Luncheon or brunch will attract well-to-do women whose mornings are free. Five-thirty is another good time to attract women who leave their offices at five.

Top: Davison's, Atlanta, stages a fashion show to honor women in industry, including Eastern Airlines. Bottom: models take traditional walk down runway. Facing page: in a more lighthearted mood, a group modeling swimwear moves as if in a chorus line.

If the show is to be reviewed by the press, deadline hours of the newspapers must be kept in mind. Some stores in large cities give a separate press show.

Today, production and staging of fashion shows is often professional and·imaginative, yet there are some faults that occur frequently. One of these faults is a tendency towards affectation, mentioned earlier in connection with advertising. The same rule that we applied to advertising can be applied to fashion show commentary; merchandise should not be overwhelmed by adjectives or gimmicks. They are not necessary if the merchandise is attractive; if it is not, they will not compensate.

There should be a complete run-through of the show shortly before it is presented. This may be just before show time, especially if merchandise or props are arriving at the last minute.

The fashion coordinator should assign someone to mix with the audience and answer questions, if she is doing the commentary herself.

The script should always be read aloud in advance to eliminate any tongue-twisting words or phrases. Writing fashion commentary is not like writing an ad—the ad is meant to be read, the script is spoken. Some words and phrases that make good copy sound artificial in a script.

Some stores provide a printed program that includes a price list. There should not be elaborate descriptions, just a tag word and a number that will identify each fashion.

190

The runway show can be taped or filmed—this adds to the cost but extends the usefulness of the show. A tape or film can be used for sales training, or sent to branch stores, or shown in women's clubs as entertainment. A local television station might carry a segment of a fashion show as part of one of its regular programs.

The store that wants to do a very special job of production will go outside and look for an interesting background. A local art gallery or museum, an exceptionally beautiful private home, gardens or tennis courts, a beach—are some examples of dramatic backgrounds for fashion shows.

Small stores should consider pooling their money; if they cannot afford individual shows, they can collaborate and produce joint shows.

The fashion show combining live models with slides, tape or film can be interesting and effective.

There are many different ways of using slides and live models together. While the model walks down the runway, or poses on a stage, color slides are projected on a large screen behind the stage or runway. The slides show the outfit she is wearing in an enlarged picture; or, they may show a detail of her outfit blown up to a larger size. Accessories can be shown on slides while the model wears a dress or separates. The same dress can be shown in a number of different colors. Separates can be mixed and matched in different ways to show their versatility.

A film can run and merge into a live fashion show. As the film ends and lights are turned up, the models are spotlighted, and begin to move.

These are just a few examples of the ways in which live action and film or tape can be combined to create a total fashion show.

When shows make use of sound, film or slides and live models, they are called "multi-media" shows.

Special effects can heighten the drama of a fashion show. For example, a fur fashion show started off with models wearing fur coats covered with lightweight, attractive raincoats as "slipcovers." The show began with a dark stage. Sound effects of thunder and rain were heard. The models walked on to the runway and raised umbrellas. At that precise moment the lights went on and the show began.

This is an example of special effects used properly; no fashion show director should allow such effects to overpower the merchandise. The merchandise is always the star of the show.

The television fashion show as programming lies in the future. After a few dismal failures in the 1960's, retailers gave up trying. Yet, there seems little doubt that television is an ideal medium for presenting fashion news.

There are so many things cameras can do that it sometimes seems as if we were on the brink of discovering an entirely new kind of fashion show. Cameras can move in on clothes, or the clothes can move and a camera can follow. Or, both camera and clothes can move. One camera can show a full-length view while another camera

At Burdine's, Sarasota, Florida, actresses from the play, "Bubbling Brown Sugar" help launch "Bubbling Brown Sugar" lipstick and lip gloss. Luncheon was held in their honor. Actresses were made up at counter, then walked through store, talking to customers.

enlarges a detail. Tight close-ups can show the smallest details. If the pitfalls of loud music and chattering commentary are avoided, the fashion show on television will have a bright future.

There have been a few new ideas that seem like hints of better things to come; some of them have slipped by almost unnoticed, on local stations. One such show ran less than ten minutes and was based on the designs of a famous husband-and-wife team. The man and woman spoke together, answering questions put by an interviewer. The three-way conversation was used as voice-over; the speakers were unseen. Their low-key comments provided information but did not dominate the clothes. Against this background of voices, with no music or other effects models walked, one at a time, towards the camera, so that each fashion ended in a close-up view. The format was simple and effective.

The fashion show is one kind of special event. There are many others. Special events may be as modest as the introduction of a new shade of lipstick, or as ambitious as a *storewide promotion* that includes all departments, and is carefully orchestrated, with lectures and demonstrations every hour on the hour. Large department stores

192

sometimes run announcement ads scheduling demonstrations and special lectures, so that people can time their visit to the store as they would time themselves to go to the theater. The storewide promotion is indeed theater at retail, with a large cast, and an even larger cast behind the scenes, planning, preparing, and cleaning up afterwards.

Storewide promotions based on elaborate nationality or ethnic themes may be planned months or years in advance. Imported merchandise is ordered and it had better be in the store when the promotion breaks!

Less spectacular special events are based on *topical* and *seasonal themes;* bridal parties, Spring, boating, and cooking. Many department stores and some specialty stores have found a market for gourmet food specialties. *Demonstrations* of how to prepare fancy foods are always crowd pleasers, especially if the demonstrator is a chef attached to a well-known restaurant, or the author of a best-selling cookbook.

Whether large or small, the special event is useful in achieving short and long-range goals. It can generate traffic and sales. It can build store image in general and fashion image in particular.

Special events develop a store's identity; it becomes known as a place to come to and an exciting place to be. Special events that tie in with the community warm up a store's image and make people see it as more human, less cold, less institutional.

Image has a way of carrying over; a store that presents exciting gourmet cooking demonstrations somehow gains in prestige and authority; that prestige and authority can carry over into fashion.

Fashion shows and demonstrations answer a need; women are curious about new fashions. They want to learn. The more they learn, the more they are likely to buy.

Home sewing events draw traffic to department stores and offer many opportunities for service to the customer. Home sewing shows are created with the help of manufacturer representatives who come to the store and demonstrate their various products, talking to customers, and giving them valuable information.

Speakers at home sewing events—and others—often have to field sticky questions. Sometimes the questions turn hostile. A veteran speaker will know how to handle a difficult situation.

Stan Herman, the well-known designer, addressed a group of women during the course of a week-long home sewing event at the flagship New York City store of B. Altman & Co.

Mr. Herman spoke thoughtfully on the subject of patterns, and how to choose them. When he finished, and asked for questions, it became clear that many women had grievances. "Why don't they. . . ." and "Why do they always . . ." were the beginnings of questions that were really complaints.

Mr. Herman was adept at fielding the question-complaints. To a heavy woman who complained about the lack of interesting patterns in large sizes, he responded, "I know how you feel. I'm short, and I have a terrible time finding clothes that fit me. . . ."

By drawing attention to his own problem, he neutralized the woman's hostility. He then made specific suggestions about what kind of styles she should look for.

The biggest special event in the world of retailing has nothing to do with fashion at all, though it is staged by a store that carries fashion merchandise. It is Macy's New York Thanksgiving Day Parade, an annual afternoon of floats and fantasies that draws huge crowds, is covered by television, and has become, over a period of many years, a part of the city's life. A year without Macy's parade would be as unthinkable as Christmas without Santa Claus.

Fashion is often the focal point of special events, including some so special that they can never be repeated. Saks Fifth Avenue, the national specialty chain, celebrated its 50th anniversary in 1975 by going back to its own beginnings in 1925. Years of research and planning were needed to find and develop source material.

In 1925, art deco was the dominant decorative influence. Saks invented a simple geometric design and carried it out in display, packaging, and advertising. The logo was re-drawn. Old ads were examined; they had been done in so-called floating layouts. In the old-fashioned floating layout, merchandise is not shown on a woman's body, but is placed or "floated" on the page. It is not grouped or arranged in a composition. It is surrounded by white space. Hence, the term, "floating." The anniversary ads went back to this technique to create a feeling of nostalgia and set a style. Up-dating old formats and themes is very tricky; the old look must be identifiable, but it must also look contemporary. Any hint of a campy or exaggerated imitation would have spoiled the effect.

There were special exhibits in the store—one was of old photographs of the 1920's. Merchandise recalled the 1920's; there were chemise dresses, pearls, white flannels, silks and smooth, short hair styles.

The promotion ran from September till the end of the year. The format was flexible enough to accommodate fall and holiday fashion merchandise.

In the mid-1970's, Saks had 31 stores in 14 states. Carrying out a promotion of this scope called for cooperation between branch stores and the central store in New York City.

Stores started to work out their own promotions months before the break date; store managers in branch units had three months' notice of the break date.

The promotion was kicked off with parties which were carried out differently in different stores.

Saks—San Francisco opened a "speakeasy" on its lower level, recalling the days of Prohibition in the 1920's. A "best customer" list culled from store records became the guest list.

Saks—Houston worked with a core group of women six months before the break date, arranging a party to benefit the Texas Mental Health Association and the Houston Symphony.

Saks—Chicago worked with presidents of civic groups who had cooperated with the store over a period of years, and sent them invitations to the store party.

Within the framework of the overall plan, each store was free to develop its own plan based on its own needs, and its relationship to the community.

The elegance of the Saks 50th anniversary promotion suited a store with an image of high fashion. Home sewing and how-to-cook events are more compatible to the image of department stores with across-the-board assortments of fashion and home furnishings.

The character of a special event has to do with the needs and taste level of its customers. Again, we are back to the problem of store image, and store identity.

Who are the customers? What do they expect from the store?

In some stores, special events are as simple as one or two fashion shows a year. Such simple events and limited schedules can be handled by a fashion coordinator or a publicity director. In a store with a heavy schedule of special events, a separate department may be set up, with one person in charge.

A & S (Abraham & Straus), a northeastern division of Federated Stores, the national department store chain, stages special events continually.

As of 1977 A & S had ten stores, eight in New York, and two in New Jersey. Events are planned centrally in the flagship store in Brooklyn, New York, and carried out in branches.

Because A & S is a full department store, the special events department includes activities that relate to hard goods as well as soft goods. Some events involve both categories. Others focus on fashion.

Myrna Masoff, Special Events Director of A & S, often feels that she is involved in producing three or four plays for the stage at the same time. But she is not producing shows for the stage; she is producing events for her store. Her comments on what special events mean to fashion at A & S shed some light on the how and why of planning and coordinating.

Special events interpret and explain fashion to the customer, comments Ms. Masoff.

In the mid-1970's, clothes are simpler, less decorated, less complicated in cut. Yet, in a way, simpler clothes are harder to wear than the old, constructed clothes of the 1960's.

How do you drape a shawl? How do you wear a loose, voluminous dress? How do you arrange an off-the-shoulder neckline? Demonstrators show women how to wear clothes. In this sense, the guest demonstrator or designer interprets fashion, confers fashion prestige on the store, and helps the store move merchandise.

If a store decides to carry pareos and sarongs that are really just squares and rectangles of fabric wrapped and tied, display and advertising are not enough. A person must come into the store and *show* customers over and over again how to wrap and

all wrapped up
in anne klein's
south seas pareo plus

To the beat, beat, beat
of the tomtom,
Anne Klein goes native...
with all the pieces you'll
need to create your own
Island look...night and day.
Cotton pareos, squares
and oblongs in bold batiks
and Polynesian prints, and
Island solids. To wrap, tie, drape,
shape...play with and enjoy!
Anne Klein for
Robinson & Golluber.
The print pareo, 10.00.
Solid pareo, 8.00.
Print square, 7.00.
Solid oblong, 5.00.

Let us inspire you.
We're holding demonstra-
tions in New York and all
fashion branches.
New York:
Tomorrow 12-3.
Friday 11-3.
Saturday 1-5.
Bergen County:
Saturday 1-5.
Fresh Meadows:
Friday 11-3.
Garden City:
Tomorrow 11-3.
Short Hills:
Tomorrow 11-3.
Stamford:
Friday 11-3.
Tysons Corner and
White Flint:
Tomorrow, Friday and
Saturday 12-5.
White Plains:
Saturday 1-5.

The Pareo Shop, Bagatelle,
Escalator Level, New York
and all fashion branches.

bloomingdale's
it's like no other store in the world

Bloomingdale's, New York, invited customers to come in and learn how to wrap and tie pareos. Ad
announced times of demonstrations and showed some ways pareos could be worn.

196

tie. The demonstrator must demonstrate on herself and on the customers. (Demonstration on customers is something films and tape cannot do.)

A woman will not buy a fashion she does not understand.

She will not buy a fashion she is afraid of.

She must be convinced that she can wear the new fashion correctly; that she will not look or feel foolish.

Demonstrations are one kind of fashion event; others are more complex and call for more planning.

A week-long promotion called "New Energy at A & S" was really built around a physical fitness theme, but it related to fashion. A flyer handed to women read, "Slim-down food and recipe ideas! Exercise classes! Hair and beauty tips! Meet 'New Energy' experts all this week! Get a burst of 'New Energy at A & S.' Get in shape for revealing maillots and sundresses."

Posters on the walls of fashion departments carried the message. The flyer opened up to a list of slimming recipes.

It helps when you can give the customer something to take home with her; something that she will remember after she has left the store. It does not have to be fancy. It does have to be useful.

Keep things moving. If the "Hustle" is the latest dance, hire a dance team to

Rich's, Atlanta, teams up with *Glamour* Magazine to stage a series of workshops for young career women. Shown here, exercise class.

demonstrate and teach it in the junior department. You will attract more than juniors —women of all ages will be interested.

Hire a gymnast to demonstrate exercises. Maybe the demonstration is in the sporting goods department, but that department is right next to active sportswear, and that is where the warm-up suits are. You will sell warm-up suits.

Use elevator cars as well as flyers, posters, and cards on the restaurant table. Every announcement draws your "audience."

Presentation of a theme can change from department to department, depending on the merchandise and the customer who buys the merchandise.

A special event that calls for romantic music may be set up with different music in different departments. What is "romantic?" In a junior department, romantic music may have a strong disco beat. In a misses department, more traditional popular music will be played; perhaps Cole Porter. This "shading" of music and other aspects of presentation from department to department is pure theater; essential because it helps create the proper mood and atmosphere.

But no matter how carefully music and other ingredients are put together, no event pleases everybody. If a store attracts 3,000 people and gets one complaint, the event was a success. If there are 3,000 people and 200 complaints, something was wrong.

Every event, even the simplest, is difficult to plan. Letters must be written, publicity releases must be sent out. An ad must be prepared. Signage must be designed and created. Central plans must be made that will include all branch stores. Store managers must be alerted. If there is merchandise involved; it must be in all stores.

Then pray for good weather.

Special events represent one kind of store promotion. There are even events that take place outside the store, including fashion shows, that are associated with and sponsored by the store. All these events are theatrical; it is that quality that gives them excitement, and it is excitement that draws traffic.

Other forms of promotion rely on service rather than theatrical excitement. For example, prestige fashion stores often provide shoppers who will help a woman pick out a wardrobe, or buy gifts for everyone on her Christmas shopping list. Such services are available to men, too.

There was a time when special shoppers were assigned to men, to help them pick out gifts for women. Some stores held "For Men Only" nights before Christmas. The "For Men Only" idea was based on the theory that men do not like to shop and do not know how to shop. As men have become more aware of fashion and more relaxed about it, the need for this service has diminished.

Gift wrapping and shopping bags are promotion and can be a source of publicity. Stores may offer special courses and classes in beauty, grooming, and exercise. Branch stores in shopping centers often have a community room that can be used for community activities—classes, art exhibitions, and organization meetings. All these services are part of the store's total promotional effort.

Charge accounts are a personal service. Store charge cards seem to be losing ground to major credit card companies, but the individual store that controls its card can provide some special services.

Some customers want two charge accounts for personal reasons. Husbands and wives with joint accounts may want to surprise each other with birthday or Christmas presents. The present must be delivered before the bill arrives—otherwise the surprise will be given away.

Personal shoppers assist foreigners who do not speak English. Prestige fashion stores offer the shopper-interpreter as a service to such customers, who are usually wealthy women visiting the United States. They often spend large amounts of money on clothes. The profits they bring to the store justify the special service that the shopper-interpreter provides.

Some stores maintain travel agencies that help customers plan trips. This is an image-building service; it may not result in sale of merchandise. On the other hand, the woman who plans a trip in the store may shop for a travel wardrobe in the store.

Fur storage, jewelry repair, gift certificates, bridal registries and planning of clothes for bridal parties are other services that stores may offer customers.

Personal services are a form of promotion. They enhance the image of the store as an organization staffed with helpful people who care about the customer. In some cases, as with bridal consultants and bridal registries, personal service increases sales.

Packaging is a promotional tool used by retailers, but created by manufacturers, who prepare and ship merchandise in packages, which are displayed and sold on special fixtures in the store.

Packaging should not be confused with gift wrapping. Gift wrapping is a special service. The store can gift wrap any merchandise that the customer selects, but this service is performed at point of sale.

National brands of bras and pantyhose and cosmetics are among the most familiar merchandise categories sold in packages.

As self-selection and self-service increase, packaging becomes more important as a selling tool, for the package is imprinted with vital information. Packages can be attractive, as well as useful. Color, shape, and size as well as any picture or copy are ingredients of packaging for fashion merchandise.

Packaging is a convenience for the customer; or should be. She can pick out what she wants, much as she would pick up a can of tomatoes in a supermarket, and take the package directly to a cashier who will ring up the sale.

From the store's point of view, a good package must be more than attractive and informative.

It should be well-sealed, so that it cannot be opened casually and spoiled. No customer wants to buy an opened package. The package should be easy to display on a standard fixture. It should protect the garment and give it a long shelf life—that is, the merchandise should not deteriorate in the package over a period of time.

Sometimes it is not the fault of the package when merchandise deteriorates. The merchandise itself may not have a long shelf life.

When spandex fiber was first introduced as a basis for stretch fabrics used in girdles and bras, it had a tendency to lose its white color and turn yellow. Packaging could not change the characteristic of fiber and fabric.

But packaging can keep fashion merchandise clean and neat. When merchandise is standard, and need not be tried on, packaging simplifies shopping.

A useful package containing fashion merchandise tells the customer everything she needs to know.

Size, color, price, style number, care—how to wash or dry clean—those are all facts the customer must know.

In the case of pantyhose, size charts telling the customer how to choose her correct size are also important. Any special feature, such as a gusset or a reinforced closing, should be described, and, if possible, illustrated on the package.

While all this information adds up to a complicated message, the message must be conveyed in words and pictures that are easy to read and understand. The customer should be able to absorb all the information she needs at a glance. Too much copy or too many pictures may confuse the customer and "unsell" the package.

Although packaging may enhance the merchandise and attract customers to a counter or display fixture, there are limits to what it can do.

A woman may buy a dozen pairs of packaged pantyhose in different shades, but the sale ends with pantyhose.

It takes a person to suggest another merchandise category and build another sale. A package can sell another package like itself, but it cannot sell additional merchandise.

From the biggest, splashiest store event down to the smallest gift certificate, everything a store does to pave the way for selling is promotional. Building image paves the way for selling by creating positive attitudes; the customer likes the store and chooses to shop *there*, rather than someplace else.

It takes more than fashion to sell fashion. It takes more than people to sell fashion. If merchandise is to acquire that special appeal, that special sheen that makes it irresistible, lights, color, wrappings, packaging, display, special events—all those theatrical trappings—must be used to the hilt. Promotion may not be an art form, but it is theater, and everybody who wants to sell must get into the act.

Publicity: Reaching Your Maximum Audience

13

Publicity is attention. It is a spotlight turned on the store. It may happen accidentally, but usually, it is planned.

Publicity is something that makes news—perhaps a fashion show, or a designer appearance. A news story is printed in a newspaper or magazine. Perhaps the event is mentioned on radio or shown on TV. The link with one or more of the communications media is essential. Publicity *material* does not become publicity until it has been reported by media. It is the act of reporting that brings the event to the attention of the public; that turns on the spotlight calling attention to the store.

Why does a store bother to seek out publicity? Doesn't it get enough attention through advertising? The answer is that the attention a store gets through advertising is quite different from the attention it attracts by publicity.

An ad is a paid message; it represents the store's point of view, which appears in the advertising columns of a newspaper, or in the radio or television commercial. The public knows it is reading, listening to, seeing a paid message when it reads, listens to, or sees advertising.

News based on publicity represents the ideas and opinions of reporters, columnists, editors, talk show moderators, and guest lecturers. This is a different kind of message. It does not come directly from the store. It is persuasive because it is the voice of someone with authority or prestige outside the store. Or, its persuasiveness may derive from the prestige of people mentioned. "Name-dropping" can create prestige. If a newspaper columnist mentions in her column that Ms. M., the bank president's wife, was seen shopping in Store X, that is good publicity for Store X. The store's image is improved through mention of its name, and through association with Ms. M., a woman who commands prestige in her community.

While publicity may increase sales, its main purpose is building store image by presenting the store to the public in a favorable, positive way. Special events, like those discussed in Chapter 12, generate good publicity.

There are many ways in which stores court the goodwill of newspaper columnists, so that they will remember to drop the store name into a column when there is an opportunity to do so.

Getting and keeping the goodwill of newspaper editors, columnists, reporters for radio and TV is the job of the publicity director. (Publicity director is just a title— in some stores, this job may be handled by a fashion coordinator, or special events director, or the sales promotion director.)

Publicity directors, or whoever fills the job, must, first and foremost, supply editors with useful material. They must be able to angle stories and pictures so that they meet the needs of different editors. One may want a photo taken against a background, so that the background will be part of the story. Another editor may want photos taken against a plain background with no detail, because the photos are reduced in size, and background turns into blur.

Two rival newspapers will not want to use the same photos. Each one will want a different story angle.

One may want an "exclusive" story that will break before it appears in any other publication. This usually does not serve the needs of the store, for it will antagonize the paper that is shut out.

The timing of an event may favor a morning or an evening paper. Sometimes this can be adjusted, but the event must be geared to the needs of the customers. A fashion luncheon will favor the evening paper. An evening event will favor the morning paper.

In such a situation, the publicity director may give the newspaper that loses out in time an even break by releasing an advance story.

When publicity is planned for an event that is also going to be advertised, the publicity director must make sure that the release is sent out before the ad breaks. No newspaper worth its salt will run a news story on material that has already appeared in an ad. The pattern is, news story (based on publicity) first, then the ad. This pattern works most effectively for the store, as well as for the newspaper.

There are many things publicity directors can do to please editors, and assure the use of material. A great deal depends on the size of the store, the community and the readership of the publication. This also applies to radio and television coverage.

Efficient publicity directors in large communities keep card files listing the names of all editors and reporters whom they might contact. When they send out a release, it is sent to the right person. The name is spelled correctly.

The release is written, as nearly as possible, like a news story.

The most important facts should be in the first paragraph of the release, as they would be in a news story. The shorter the release the better; newspapers have limited space. Publicity should be geared to the convenience of editors. A release of one page is desirable; the longer the release, the more work for the editor who has to "cut" it to fit.

Adjectives should be kept to a minimum; this is a problem with fashion. Many fashion releases are far too flowery.

If a designer is quoted, the quote should be meaningful. Quotes like, "I feel this is the new look now" do not mean anything. "I believe in longer lengths for daytime," is a statement of opinion.

Releases should always be typed and double-spaced.

A contact name, address and telephone number should be listed at the beginning of the release, so that the editor can call up for additional information, if necessary.

The last paragraph on the page should end at the bottom of the page.

If a kit containing release and pictures is sent out, the pictures should be properly captioned. Slips of paper pasted on the bottom of the pictures are best. Only essential information should be given in captions; price, fabric and color are usually sufficient.

Most newspapers prefer 8" × 10" glossy, black-and-white photos. Some papers will ask for color, especially for a feature in the Sunday edition. Some papers can use smaller photos, or can even use Polaroid photos.

A newspaper may want to combine publicity photos with artwork; sketches done by its own artist. In such a situation, the publicity department will make sure the merchandise is available to the artist.

If the store does not wish material used before a set date, this is indicated on the release, and is known as the "release date." Otherwise, the release is tagged, "for immediate release."

Sending out releases and photos is not the end of the publicity director's job. There must be a follow-up call; at least one. Can the editor use the material? Is anything more needed? When will it appear? Such inquiries are proper, but the publicity director must be careful not to push too hard; editors dislike high pressure tactics. Sometimes the answer is "no," and that negative must be accepted graciously for the sake of future relations.

If a store is sending out one general release to all media, and a designer or other personality is involved, the publicity department may want to send out a "fact sheet" on the designer including biographical data.

It is also the publicity department's job to arrange interviews with visiting celebrities, designers and others.

It is usually not necessary to send a covering letter with a release, but if a letter is sent, it should be properly addressed to the editor. Editors do not appreciate receiving letters that start out with the wrong name, or worse yet, with a false greeting, like, "Hi, there."

Some publicity directors mistakenly assume that editors want to see what other publications have done with the material, and they send along copies of news stories that have already appeared. That is a mistake. The editor then feels she is being treated in a secondhand way. "Why didn't I have it first?" she wonders.

Many small store owners ignore publicity and lose out on valuable opportunities to gain recognition in their communities. While they cannot stage major events, or send out pictures and impressive stories, they can get their name into a local newspaper. The important thing is to put information down in writing; a task many small store owners would rather avoid.

Still, small stores receive new shipments of merchandise, and that merchandise may be newsworthy. A few typewritten lines of information on a sheet may result in a short paragraph in the newspaper; editors are always looking for very short stories to use as "filler."

Other types of information rate a paragraph or two; a remodeling or refurbishing, for example. Perhaps a women's wear store will begin carrying some men's wear.

The small store that creates a stunning window display might invest in a photo and send it to the editor of the local paper. All these efforts are risks—but worthwhile for the publicity they might bring.

The small store may ignore publicity, the large specialty or department store cannot. Sometimes publicity directors have in-store problems because an overly enthusiastic buyer will push for publicity for merchandise that is not really newsworthy. Or, the store president may insist that the release start off with his name, a structure not likely to please newspaper editors.

Some problems start in the store; others have their roots in situations that develop outside the store, for example, in relationships with the advertising departments of newspapers.

Because newspapers and magazines are supported by their advertising revenues, the store that advertises regularly will have little difficulty in getting editorial coverage. Some newspapers and magazines withhold editorial coverage from stores that do not advertise as a way of pressuring them to advertise. Some stores insist on striking a bargain; they will advertise if they also get editorial mention.

Suppose that two stores in a community are giving fashion shows that will feature two prominent designers. Store A and Store B both send a release to the local newspapers. Store A does not advertise in the morning newspaper, but Store B does. Therefore the morning newspaper does not use the release sent out by Store A.

Several things may happen. Another paper may run the release. Or, Store A may inform its customers by direct-mail announcement of the designer appearance, enclosing an invitation with charge account statements, or sending out a separate postcard invitation.

In any community, small or large, there is a group of fashionable women who know what is going on in all the fashionable stores because they shop regularly.

Word gets around. Women will know that Store A is sponsoring a fashion show even though it has not been announced or reported in the morning newspaper.

Newspaper readers will eventually grasp the relationship between advertising and publicity. They will begin to question the newspaper's editorial judgment—can they really trust a women's page or fashion writer who is not free to cover all the news?

In the long run, the newspaper, as well as the store, loses out. Loss of credibility eventually loses readership. Circulation is based on readership. Advertising is based on circulation.

Top newspaper executives are sometimes indifferent to the fashion pages. Most newspaper executives are men. Some men do not feel that fashion is really news; they do not treat it with the respect they give to other subjects. They may allow the advertising department to exercise more control over fashion than over other sections of the newspaper, for if fashion is unimportant, it follows that it does not matter how it is handled.

The handling of fashion publicity through editorial credits in magazines is different. Most magazine advertisers are manufacturers, rather than retailers. Still, merchandise in the editorial columns of magazines is credited to stores, so stores are involved.

There is a definite tit-for-tat relationship between magazine advertisers and fashion editorial credits. For example, cosmetic manufacturers advertise heavily in fashion magazines. Therefore, there are many editorial features in those magazines that give publicity to cosmetics. Sometimes magazines are top-heavy with cosmetic features, when editorial space could better be devoted to other aspects of fashion or other subjects.

This kind of restriction is damaging to all parties involved, in the long run.

There are many reasons why magazine readership has declined. But if we were to list all the reasons, we would have to include restrictions imposed by advertisers.

As readers become aware of editorial limitations, they lose faith in the magazine. The publicity, or store credit, means less. The short-range gain is a long-range loss.

The question of store credits involves store policy. Publicity directors cannot shape store policy, though they may sometimes influence it. They must work within its limitations as best they can.

There are other problems with store credits. For instance, Store X may get an editorial credit for a sweater and skirt in the September issue of a magazine. But the sweater and skirt are shipped to the store in July, or November. Customers are frustrated and disappointed. The faulty timing involves the store's buyers and delivery dates. The publicity director cannot control delivery dates, but often gets the blame for bad timing.

Though publicity is often hard to pin down, it is worth pursuing. Stores can survive without it, but most stores do better when its spotlight touches them, reminding customers that the store exists, building image and drawing traffic.

Changing Patterns in Fashion Merchandise

14

Fashion experts are fond of saying that every fashion returns eventually. It does and it doesn't. The pinched-in waist, the short skirt, the low neckline are recurrent themes in fashion, yet each time they appear, they appear in a different form.

A woman of the 1970's could not wear the loose chemise of the 1920's or the old "New Look" of the late 1940's. Something happens to life, customs, values, and environment that makes fashion obsolete.

In this chapter, we will examine some fashion trends of the 1970's, dipping into the past to show how they evolved. A knowledge of the past helps us to understand the present, and sometimes, to predict the future. Fashion is after all, just another way of looking at history.

Our story will not be consistent, because fashion is not consistent.

In the 1970's, women were freer than ever before, and their clothing reflected their condition.

The supreme authority of the fashion establishment faded. But freedom goes hand in hand with responsibility. Women who are free to wear what they like must decide what they like. Their range of possible decisions has expanded. For many women, freedom to choose is a mixed blessing.

Clothing reflects the increasing freedom of women, though if we said that clothing is less restrictive because women are freer, that would be an oversimplification. Less restrictive fashions are a result of many events, trends, and even disasters.

During World War II, American designers came into their own for the first time. Cut off from Europe, Americans had a chance to show their talents. Designers like Tom Brigance, Bonnie Cashin, Tina Leser, Claire McCardell and others pioneered in colorful, comfortable separates, swimsuits and dresses. They created original styles that were quite different from anything that had come out of Europe.

During the 1970's, the silhouette softened and loosened gradually. Skirts dropped below the knees. *(All pictures in this chapter courtesy of Eleanor Lambert.)*

Bill Blass, Spring, 1972. Low-flaring chemise silhouette recalls the 1960's. Hemline, still above knees.

John Anthony, Spring, 1973. Silhouette, more fitted. Skirt is fuller, with pleats. Hemline hits about mid-knee.

210

Right after the war, Paris reclaimed its position as fashion leader of the world.

Freedom took a step backwards. Dior's New Look, with its long, full skirts, petticoats, corseted, pinched-in waist and padded hiplines, was the last major restrictive fashion silhouette of the century—so far.

It did not last. By 1950, skirts were inching up again, and the padded hipline was gone. By the mid-1950's, the narrow waist eased and the silhouette began to evolve towards a more natural, less restrictive look.

All this was background for the sportswear revolution; an event that affected the way women dressed all over the United States, and, eventually, all over the world.

The phenomenal growth of sportswear was related to a population shift from city to suburbs. In general, suburban life was more informal than city life. The suburban way of life called for simple, informal clothing.

By the 1960's, city women, as well as suburban women, were wearing sportswear, which had expanded far beyond the old categories of skirts and sweaters.

Sportswear as a term covered separates of all kinds; blouses, skirts, sweaters, pants and jackets. It also included clothing made of leather and of knitted fabrics; two sub-classifications which were expanding rapidly. Sportswear manufacturers and designers produced coats and dresses as well as separates.

Sportswear represents a combination of many foreign fashion influences, yet it is uniquely American. It is casual. It says, "Let's take it easy." Even when it is elegant, it does not consciously strive for a drop-dead look.

Many countries have contributed their characteristic costumes to American sportswear. The Mexican poncho and peasant blouse, the Japanese kimono, the Middle Eastern djellaba, the Norwegian sweater, the Irish sweater, the British Norfolk jacket, the Polynesian sarong, African tunics and robes based on tribal dress—are just some of the international influences that sportswear has absorbed.

The Italian attitude toward sportswear played an important role in its development in the post-World War II period. Italian designers had a knack of using color and fabric with dash and flamboyance; it was an informal flair quite different from the formal reverence of the French couture. Italian designs, and Italian and French knits, of the highest quality inspired Americans to continue their own explorations.

As sportswear diversified, the barriers between traditional markets fell. The coat and suit market was no longer separate from the dress market. The blouse market disappeared.

Disappearance of separate markets was one result of the sportswear revolution. Only formal evening wear, bridal wear, and some special categories like maternity wear remained as distinct markets.

Housedresses vanished.

Sweaters and other knits multiplied. There were short and long sweaters; sweater coats and jackets, sweaters for evening and sweaters for beachwear.

Jim Baldwin, Fall, 1973. Left, tailored pantsuit, classic of the 1970's. Right, dress with matching shawl, new cover-up. Some skirts are still above the knees.

Adri, Spring, 1974. Loose jersey dresses can be worn belted or unbelted. Shoulderline and sleeves are softening. Skirt hits about mid-knee.

Ilie Wacs for Wacs Works, Fall, 1974. Silhouette is loosening and softening, though armhole is still high. Waist, left, shows beginning of blousing above belt. Hemline covers knees.

214

Oscar de la Renta, Spring, 1975. Soft dress is coming back. Shoulderline, rounded and dropped, waist marked with wide sash with gathering above and below. Hemline covers knees.

Knit dresses, once considered dowdy, became fashionable. There were textures and patterns of all kinds. Knits were comfortable for everyday wear, and ideal for traveling because they were easy to pack.

The Pucci silk jersey dress, with its unique prints, and almost hidden signature, was an early status symbol of the post-World War II period; often imitated, but never quite equalled.

Active sportswear expanded as more women played tennis, skied and sailed. Some active sportswear fashions, like the jogging suit and the tennis sweater passed into casual separates for street wear.

Summing up trends from the late 1940's to the 1960's:

- The post-war Dior New Look had come and gone.
- Sportswear, including beachwear, leathers and knits, was flourishing.
- The growth of sportswear was breaking down barriers between markets.
- A new silhouette, based on the architectural designs of the great French couturier, Balenciaga, was emerging. It eased over the body without nipping in the waist.
- The evolution of a new silhouette marked the beginning of two more decades of fashion change, including some first-time-ever developments.
- Skirt hemlines moved up higher than ever before in the 1960's.
- The change in outerwear brought about changes in inner wear, which almost disappeared.
- Women could not wear gartered stockings under mini-skirts. They wore pantyhose instead.
- Corsets and foundations disappeared. Some young women gave up bras.
- Slips and petticoats could not be worn under the very short mini-dresses of the 1960's.

While women were shortening their skirts, the next major fashion development was in the making, though it did not have major impact until 1970.

Pants became standard daytime wear in 1970.

Pants and the pantsuit were an innovation of monumental significance (think of the old cliché, "Who wears the pants in the family?").

As early as 1963, Courrèges, the prominent couturier of the 1960's, was showing pants for street wear, but they were considered extreme at that time. In 1965, Yves St. Laurent showed more elegant pants and pantsuits for street wear. Still, their acceptance was limited, and there were places that would not admit women wearing even the most elegant pantsuit. Expensive restaurants frowned on them. Women made news by exiting from restaurants in tunics over pants, removing the pants, and returning in the tunic, which had become a mini-dress, and, as such, was perfectly acceptable!

216

Kasper for Joan Leslie, Spring, 1976. Two-piece dress with new bloused waistline. Soft silhouette hangs away from the body. Hemline hits almost at mid-calf.

Albert Capraro, Fall, 1977. Right, smock dress with peasant look. Loose silhouette again, but much softer than chemise of the 1960's. Print dress is layered over solid-color skirt; is worn with boots. Left, quilted vest worn over blouse and long skirt for evening.

James Daugherty Ltd., Fall, 1977. Softened silhouette in two evening dresses, both with gathered tiers, loose bodices bloused over the natural waistline.

Young women and men had been wearing jeans for years, but jeans were quite different from street wear pants of more conventional cut.

It was the crisis of 1970 that did it. That was the year of the midi, a mid-calf length for dresses, skirts and coats that came as a terrible shock after the thigh-high lengths of the late 1960's. Though the midi was endorsed by the fashion press, and some stores, it was a failure, and a total disaster for stores that stocked it heavily. American women were not ready for so sudden a change. This was not 1947, when a war was over and everybody wanted to "get back to normal." There was, in fact, a nasty war going on in Asia. Women declared their own war against the midi. Some clung to mini skirts. Others turned to pants as a way of solving the length problem. (In Europe, there was more acceptance of the midi than in the United States, but less than enough acceptance to establish it.)

By the end of 1970, women across the country were wearing pants almost everywhere. There were dressy pants for evening, which sometimes turned into full, floating evening pajamas. There were straight-leg and flare-leg pants. If they were not made of double-knit wool or synthetics, they were made of flannel or tweed or light-weight synthetic blends for summer wear.

Heavy women wore pants, with a jacket or vest covering the buttocks, and found the combination flattering as well as comfortable. Pants gave new life to short coats and pea jackets as well as heavy sweaters worn like coats.

Every fashion creates a reaction. In the case of pants, there were very short pants, known as "hot pants." They were as brief as the briefest of micro-minis. They were a short-lived fashion, a farewell to brief lengths. Often, they were worn with boots and full-length "maxis," coats that swept the ground. Maxis were also a short-lived fashion; they were warm, but the length was not practical. ("You can't catch a taxi in a maxi" was a slogan of the time.)

Skirt lengths started to come down, slowly but surely, in the early 1970's. From thigh-length, which was always extreme, even in 1969, skirts dropped to just above the knee. By 1974 they were at knee length. By 1976, they were covering the knee, and designers, in Paris and the United States, were showing dresses and skirts at lengths only slightly above the ankle.

This time around, longer lengths were less of a shock. The change was not so sudden. Nobody *had* to wear them; in fact, across the country, many women, oblivious to fashion, were still wearing slightly longer versions of the old mini skirt.

The silhouette had changed, too. In 1970, manufacturers took their minis and cut them longer, instead of working out a new silhouette. By 1976, and even before, the silhouette had loosened and softened, so that longer lengths looked entirely different from the midi.

The silhouette of the 1970's emerged as a pleated or dirndl (gathered) skirt with perhaps a bloused top on a knitted waistband, suggesting a sweatshirt or jogging shirt.

Natural shoulders and waistline; natural, rounded hipline declared freedom from old-fashioned corsetry. Skirts stopped below the knee—perhaps at the top of the calf, perhaps at mid-calf, or at an even lower point. High-heeled shoes with oval-shaped toes or boots, completed the silhouette.

The layered look grew out of coordinated separates, starting in the 1960's and gaining momentum in the 1970's. Ready-to-wear designers like the Missonis, Sonia Rykiel, and Kenzo invented new ways of wearing one separate over another that added to the versatility of sportswear. Shirt over sweater, vest over sweater, scarf over shirt over T-shirt—these were just a few examples of layering.

The striated-stripe slinky knit sweaters, skirts and dresses of the Missonis were status symbols of the 1970's as Pucci silk jersey prints had been status symbols of the 1950's and 1960's. The Missonis used rayon, rather than silk.

Clothes were loose and free-flowing, with a minimum of seams and detailing. There were few trims; what trims there were were machine-made. There were fewer collars and cuffs and even fewer sizes. Features like drawstrings and elasticizing simplified sizing. There were more clothes in small, medium and large, or, even in one size for all sizes.

Economic factors turned manufacturers and designers towards simplified styling and sizing, for their costs were rising, leading to higher retail prices. Many women complained of higher prices and declining workmanship at all price levels.

Simplified fashions represented changing consumer taste as well as economic factors. After the frenzy of costume looks and the extremes of minis in the 1960's, there was a need for calmer, more relaxing fashion.

As mini-fever subsided, some old favorites that had been abbreviated beyond recognition during the 1960's re-emerged.

The trench coat is perhaps the most durable fashion of all. It started as a British military uniform, was popularized by early Hollywood films. Humphrey Bogart, Ingrid Bergman, Marlene Dietrich and many other glamorous stars wore trench coats in their "golden oldie" films.

The blazer jacket has never really gone out of fashion. Single- or double-breasted, summer weight or winter weight, it continues as a classic separate.

The short, tailored jacket with an inset waistband has been known, through successive generations, as the Eisenhower jacket, battle jacket and peace jacket. Call it by any name—it is a classic.

The kimono and the bathrobe wrap, both jackets without any fastening except for a self-belt, disappeared only to reappear, as jackets, dresses, blouses and coats.

The dirndl skirt is popular whenever skirts are popular. It may be narrow or full. It may be sophisticated, or peasant style.

The wrap skirt is a favorite in everything from denim to velvet.

Straight-leg pants must now be added to this list of classics.

The tailored shirt survives.

The survival of the T-shirt is still undetermined. It was done and re-done and overdone in hundreds of versions during the 1970's, until it began to look like anything but a T-shirt.

The sweater keeps returning in new forms; it is not a question of survival, but rather a question of, what next?

The cape turns up every few years; it has its devoted friends, and it has its enemies who complain that they cannot carry handbags and shopping bags when they are wearing a cape. Still, it is a good way to finish off a layered look.

Shawls followed long scarves as an important accessory.

Other trends of the 1970's, with perhaps a shorter life, included sundresses and gypsy peasant separates; laced bodices, ruffled blouses and full skirts.

New kinds of pants were designed towards the end of the 1970's, fulfilling a rhythm of fashion that never seems to change.

1. A fashion comes in strongly.
2. It is adopted by some women.
3. It is protested by many women and men, who call it indecent, immodest and totally unacceptable forever.
4. It becomes universal fashion.
5. It becomes unfashionable through over-exposure.

(The late, great fashion historian, James Laver, wrote in his book, *Taste and Fashion* that a fashion is shameless five years before its time, daring one year before and dowdy one year after.)

Between steps four and five, universal fashion and decline into unfashionable, a new trend is shaping up. It replaces the "old" fashion that is declining because of over-exposure. These separate stages are not so clearly defined as they once were. If women are free to wear what they wish, "dowdy" is in the eye of the beholder, as beauty is.

We can follow pants through these stages from 1970 on.

In 1970, pants were fashionable. By 1974, they had become a cliché, especially double-knit polyester pantsuits. That is, they had passed through stages one through four, and had arrived at five—unfashionable through over-exposure.

Skirts looked "new" again because they had not been fashionable since the late 1960's, and then, in such short versions, that they were hardly skirts.

By 1977, new versions of pants appeared, and, in their turn, looked new again.

There were styles that tied at the ankle, and others suggesting draped and pegged pants worn by men back in the 1940's. There were also boxer shorts and longer walking shorts for summer.

In spite of flurries of interest in so-called fantasy clothes, the overall trend was towards what was comfortable and easy to wear.

Formal, full-length evening gowns were worn less frequently.

Bridal wear continued to attract a following. Some young brides chose simple cotton dresses rather than laces and taffetas. During the 1960's, there was a brief vogue for barefoot brides, carrying daisies and wearing pastel cottons or lace-trimmed Mexican wedding dresses. However, the traditional, elaborate bridal gown was still a popular choice.

Maternity wear became more fashionable every year. The popularity of the full, tent dress for all women made maternity dressing easier. The old convention of navy crepe with a touch of white near the face disappeared. Maternity fashions became as smart as any other clothing. There were swimsuits and party dresses as well as daytime dresses and separates. This versatility reflected changing attitudes toward pregnancy, which was no longer a period of isolation and inactivity.

There was a dearth of clothing for heavy women who wear sizes 18½ and up.

While retailers talked about expanding large size departments, little was actually done. The ideal of the slim figure so dominated clothes, that heavy women were ignored; few clothes were designed to meet their needs.

More interest was shown in the petite size range; small, short women, some under five feet tall.

Rainwear was a growing category. Beside the trench coat, there were rain capes, lightweight synthetics, poplins, and styles that packed into small envelopes.

Swimsuits showed little change, except for bikinis, which diminished into even scantier suits. One style, called "the string" was little more than a few triangles of fabric. Some beaches began to accept nudity and/or toplessness, though they were exceptions. Still, Rudi Gernreich's topless suit seemed less sensational and more prophetic than when it was first introduced in 1964.

Active sportswear, including accessories, continued to grow. Women were breaking new barriers; they were becoming jockeys and racing car drivers. Little girls fought their way onto the previously all-male Little League baseball teams.

On the whole, it seemed that women were wearing fewer clothes per outfit. Yet they were buying more kinds of clothing, even if all the new kinds of clothing were sportswear, one way or another.

On the minus side, there was intimate apparel.

The recent history of intimate apparel is a continuation of the disappearing act that started in the 1960's. A new category, called bodywear, took over some of the functions of intimate apparel.

Leotards and tights based on dancers' practice clothing appeared in stretch fabrics—another example of how work clothing passes into everyday fashion. Leotards were worn with skirts and pants. Dancers' leg-warmers became leggings. Socks and

In 1970, confused by skirt lengths, women turned to pants, and, eventually, wore them for all occasions. Following photographs are just a few of the many pant styles that were shown and worn.

223

Anne Klein, Fall, 1970. Gauchos worn with a low-slung belt, and typical Argentine-Far West accessories, including boots.

224

Donald Brooks, Fall, 1972. Straight, loose, cuffed pants; with sweater and shirt, under fur-lined poplin coat. Pants gave new life to the short coat.

knee-highs were worn over tights. The layered look moved to legs.

In the late 1970's, a bikini pantie might be the only undergarment a young woman wore. If she wore tights, she might also dispense with the pantie.

Whether this trend would reverse itself remained to be seen. The late Sylvia Pedlar, whose lingerie designs were copied even after her death, once remarked that lingerie was useful because it gave women a certain feeling of fastidiousness and attractiveness underneath their outer clothes.

But as of the 1970's, the importance of traditional lingerie had dwindled.

An exceptionally cold winter in 1977 created a reverse trend. Stores sold out of "woolies" and old-fashioned long underwear. That development was based on weather rather than fashion.

There were many changes in accessories during the 1970's. Some were the result of pants, others of the softer silhouette. Some were new, others had started in the 1960's.

Boots went back to Courrèges and his 1960's silhouette. They were mid-calf high and flat-heeled. Later, the film, "Dr. Zhivago" ushered in a romantic Russian period look, with long coats, fur collars, muffs and boots. Pants were worn with ankle boots, skirts were worn with taller boots. Women spent hundreds of dollars on boots, buying several pairs at a time in different leathers, heel heights, and colors.

Shoes became more expensive as leather prices increased sharply. Young women took to sneakers and clogs, and to the Earth shoe, and other styles designed for comfort. Such shoes spurned fashion and were absolutely sexless. At the same time, other women were wearing the most unhealthy, high-heeled, sexy boots and shoes that money could buy!

Wedgies and platform soles returned. High heels and platforms evoked warnings from podiatrists followed by sprained and broken ankles incurred by women who ignored all warnings. These shoes seemed an exception to the general rule that clothing should be comfortable.

Philip Johnson, the famous architect, remarked by way of explanation that high heels make women look impressive and monumental, like tall buildings.

Shoes, like handbags, were often made of canvas or other fabrics. Straw, rope and burlap substituted for expensive leathers. The espadrille, formerly a beach or play shoe, was worn on city streets.

Handbag styles went in several directions. Large, soft pouchy bags, often with shoulder straps, were convenient carryalls. The flat envelope of the 1930's was revived, usually with a wrist or shoulder strap. Little flapped bags were worn over the shoulder, more for decoration than function. Briefcases and attaché cases were carried by women, as well as men. Men began to carry simple shoulder bags as a matter of practicality.

Status accessories based on European names were prized and often imitated. The Gucci loafer was perhaps the most copied shoe style. Gucci striped luggage and Gucci chains were also copied. Vuitton luggage expanded into totes and other accessories. The famous initials were copied by other designers; the idea of interlocking initials as a print was used on many accessories. The signature scarf was a popular gift item. It seemed almost impossible to buy a shoe, bag or scarf without a signature or initials.

Sunglasses continued to be fashion. Were women imitating film stars or looking for privacy? Perhaps a little of both. Tinted lens, abstract shapes, metal frames and no-frame effects tempted women to buy more than one pair.

Hats and gloves were worn mostly for warmth. Wide-brimmed straw hats gained some following as summer accessories, but their appeal was limited. Scarves were tied around the head for protection against the sun. The long, rectangular scarf evolved into the knitted muffler, which in turn evolved into the shawl.

Jewelry and furs are two very special categories of fashion, part clothing, part decoration, part status symbol. From the most ancient times, men as well as women wore both. They were frequently regulated by sumptuary law—law that decreed what kind of clothing people could wear, according to their rank in society. Nobility wore the best—the furs, the jewels, the gold; as well as the best of velvets, laces and other precious fabrics.

Yet, by the 20th century, men had abandoned rich clothing, giving up furs and jewelry almost completely, so that both became women's clothing, women's decoration, women's status symbols.

By the 1960's, when men were just beginning to reclaim their peacock role, they were laughed at when they put on gold chains and bracelets, fur coats, and hats. It has taken some time for men to re-state their rights to both furs and jewelry, but the statement began to come through in the 1970's.

It was, actually, the other side of the coin of women's liberation. If a woman did not have to dress up to the role of slinky, man-entrapping sex goddess, then a man did not have to meet the challenge of the sex goddess by offering a complete contrast— short hair; stark simple clothing, no decoration. Men began to wear furs and jewelry, as they had during many periods of history.

This crossing over of fashion echoed ready-to-wear markets. Many of the classic fashions we mentioned earlier—the trench coat and the blazer are two examples— started out as men's wear and crossed over into women's wear.

Furs, which had lapsed into dowdiness during the 1950's, caught up with fashion. Jackets, coats, ponchos and capes of short and long-haired furs were so well designed that they appealed to men and women of all ages.

There was trouble in the fur market when conservation groups agitated against the killing of fur-bearing animals for the sake of their skins. Certain endangered species of animals, notably the leopard and other spotted cats, were banned in the United States.

Oscar de la Renta, Fall, 1972. Evening pajamas of satin crepe, loose and easy. These were called palazzo pants.

228

Halston, Spring, 1973. Classic jacket and straight-leg pants in white linen.

Calvin Klein, Fall, 1974. Camel hair boy coat, sweater and full pants. Note loosely draped muffler and beret.

continue
/

Without going into the pros and cons of conservation, it seems fair to say that many people accepted the idea that animals can be bred or hunted for their skins, if they do not belong to an endangered species. Women who could afford furs wore them with pleasure; fur has always had an emotional appeal.

Fur styles were smarter and followed ready-to-wear silhouettes more closely. Though mink was still in demand, it did not dominate the market; it shared the spotlight with many other furs, from lavish sable to modest squirrel. Long-haired furs, the foxes, and raccoon, were fashionable again. New techniques of working skins led to interesting textures and patterns.

In jewelry, there were strong ethnic influences. Good American Indian jewelry was highly prized. African, Middle Eastern and Oriental antique jewelry rose in value. A good string of turquoise or amber was more fashionable than a string of real pearls or a diamond necklace.

Pearls passed out of the fashion picture during the 1970's; perhaps they had been too popular too long. Towards the end of the decade, there were signs of a pearl revival.

Though the diamond engagement ring was universally desired and owned by women of all classes, expensive diamond necklaces and bracelets were not fashionable. Perhaps the eclipse of traditional "real" jewelry had something to do with the times; it was unfashionable to look rich, and it was easy to become a victim of burglars or robbers.

The most widely accepted jewelry came from a new designer; Elsa Peretti, whose "diamonds by the yard" were very much imitated. The idea of tiny stones strung along fine gold chain had its roots in classic antique designs. But the merchandising concept was new, the look was smart and young, and the idea caught on.

Other influential Peretti designs included sculptured pendants, belt buckles, and molded cuff bracelets.

In gold, Aldo Cipullo created his famous "love bracelet," which fastened with a "permanent" closure incorporating an idea based on hardware. Cipullo's way with simple, tailored motifs like the knot gave his designs a distinctive look that was very much in harmony with contemporary fashion.

Watch styling diversified; women often owned four or five different styles. The Cartier tank watch, with its rectangular face, Roman numerals and simple gold setting became a status symbol, and was undoubtedly one of the most imitated designs of all time.

A small, but increasing number of people began to look to individual craft designers for one-of-a-kind jewelry, collecting it as art.

Attitudes towards jewelry changed. The same women who wore real jewelry might also wear bright, plastic bracelets. Costume and real jewelry were often combined, an idea going back to the 1920's and Coco Chanel.

Improvements in ear-piercing equipment paved the way for pierced-ear earrings.

Amulets and good luck symbols were worn as rings and pendants. The ankh was popular even before a revival of interest in Egyptian art inspired jewelry designs based on Egyptian motifs.

Some young women collected "original" plastic and rhinestone jewelry of the 1940's; this was part of their fascination with old and antique clothes.

A fascination with the past was just one way in which young people declared their independence of the fashion establishment. Many young people refused to buy expensive clothing, and reserved their strongest criticism for the couture, which to them, represented the establishment.

Paris was the center of fashion from the mid-19th century on. One hundred years later, Paris ready-to-wear was still an influence, but couture power had declined.

The couture, a term often misused, refers to those houses or organizations headed by one designer who creates models for clothes that are produced, one at a time. Each garment is made to order for an individual woman. Custom-made is another term for this process, though it does not necessarily imply the backing of an illustrious designer.

By the 1950's, the private clientele on which couture houses (maisons de couture) traditionally depended was dwindling. Store bought couture originals and had them copied at different price levels.

Many copies of couture originals were poorly made. This had something to do with the decline of the couture, but it was not a decisive factor; it was more effect than cause.

Couture prices had gone up; one dress cost well into the thousands. The supply of cheap labor available to the couture declined as working conditions improved. Little girls who worked fourteen hours a day sewing or embroidering were sent to school, instead of to the couture workrooms.

When couture prices rose, fewer women were able to afford couture clothes.

There were other reasons why the great couture houses lost their private customers. Each garment was a work of art, carefully constructed and fitted. Such fashions were made for ballrooms, drawing rooms and elegant restaurants; they did not meet the needs of women who worked in offices, played tennis and golf, and participated in community activities. As more women, even wealthy women, led active lives outside their homes, they found couture clothing heavy and cumbersome. They needed things that were lightweight and easy to wear, easy to pack for traveling, and easy to keep clean.

Clothes had been a woman's chief status symbol, as the expensively dressed woman had been man's chief status symbol.

As sex roles changed, clothing needs changed and clothing simplified.

The word "unisex" was coined to describe clothing that could be worn by men and women, like jeans.

232

But the word was an oversimplification. Women's clothing was different from men's clothing, even if the styles were the same, because women's bodies are different from men's bodies. Young girls with slim hips and boyish figures may prefer boys' jeans, but most women are more comfortable in jeans that conform to their figure needs; wide hip, narrow waist.

What did happen was that women's clothing became less alluring, in the old sense of the word, and men's clothing became more colorful and individual. Men were no longer confined to sober navy blue suits and white shirts and striped ties. Women emerged from corsets, frills and ruffles—into sober navy blue pantsuits and white shirts! Both sexes had more freedom of choice.

There can be no changes in merchandise without corresponding changes in the way stores sell fashion.

The dominance of sportswear and the merging of the markets broke down traditional departmental structure.

Retailers struggled to bring their clothing departments into line with the new structure, which was really an absence of structure. Inevitably, there were stores with coat departments, and more coats in sportswear departments. There were dress departments with suits and suit departments with two-piece dresses.

One solution was the department based on use of merchandise, or style of living. Retailers turned departments into shops with names that included the words, "young" and "contemporary" among others. One shop might carry avant-garde clothing, another might appeal to more conservative customers. Famous designers had their own shops or departments. The result was some duplication and confusion.

It was unfortunate that many retailers moved away from mannequin displays, for clothing of the 1970's was so simple that it looked like nothing on the hanger; women could not visualize how it would look "on."

Ingenious display directors found space-saving substitutes for mannequins. They cut out semi-abstract body shapes from clear plastic or wood, and stood them against walls, dressed in shorts, T-shirts and other separates.

Rainwear departments grew. Some stocked umbrellas and boots along with coats and hats.

Millinery departments virtually disappeared, except for main floor "hat bars" selling inexpensive styles.

Accessories were often grouped together in main floor departments; this was the last gasp of the boutique movement of the 1960's.

As furs became less formal, fur moved closer to ready-to-wear departments, and was often sold with ready-to-wear. Fur and leather coats and jackets were often sold in the same department, carefully partitioned off in an effort to stem increasing theft.

The old main floor hosiery department disappeared, replaced by counters of packaged bodywear—tights, leotards and socks.

Calvin Klein, Fall, 1974. Flared, full flannel pants and coordinated top, worn with belted trench coat;
Note low armhole on coat; high-heeled shoes.

234

Albert Capraro, Fall, 1977. Survival clothing: rubberized poplin coat, shirt, drawstring pants, full and bloused over rubber boots.

Department and specialty stores set up inexpensive sportswear departments on their main floors, which had been traditionally reserved for cosmetics and accessories. Such departments were often unsuccessful; from the customer's point of view, racks on the main floor had a bargain basement look, and the merchandise was all too similar to what they found upstairs.

Special departments carrying jeans and jean-related merchandise were aimed at young people, or, as retailers called them, "the youth market."

In our next chapter, we will examine the nature and influence of the youth market. Influential it was—it shook up the whole world of fashion and changed it forever.

Youth Sets
the Fashion Pace

15

The youth movement revolutionized fashion in the 1960's, and its reverberations echoed on through the 1970's. Before the 1960's, women docilely followed fashion as dictated by the fashion establishment. After the 1960's, women began to feel that they did not have to take up every new fashion that the establishment decreed.

There were other reasons for this change in attitude, but the slogan of youth, "do your own thing," was a tremendous influence on women of all ages. If they did not follow youth's slogan to the letter, they were, at least, influenced by its spirit.

It was not always so, it may not always be so, but in the 1970's, everyone wanted to look young. "Mature" became an unflattering word.

The youth market grew out of the youth movement and the general rebellion of the 1960's. The term, "youth market" generally refers to teenagers, and sometimes includes young people up to twenty-five. Young people turned away from what was accepted, and invented their own fashions, as they invented their own standards of behavior and their own political ideas.

They proclaimed a fashion message that went something like this: "We do not want to wear expensive clothing. We do not want to throw out clothes every year because some designer tells us to. We want to accept our bodies and show them. We do not want restrictive clothing. We want our own clothes, and we want them to be different from the clothes our parents wear."

The hope of being different from their parents was only partly realized, as older people followed their children into jeans and a series of other youth looks.

Recycling, patchwork, antique clothes, army surplus clothing—were ideas that came from young people. But first and last, they glorified jeans, the all-American work clothes invented in the 19th century. It was true that "pure" Levis gave way to "pre-washed" jeans and even imported French jeans, but those variations came later,

A typical Gap store. Entrance, opening directly onto mall in shopping center. Lettering, top and sides, is large and poster-like. Front, sign on a rack reads, "What's New!"

in the 1970's. So did jean skirts, which were made of cut-up, patched jeans.

The interesting thing about jeans, aside from their universality, is their combination of two totally opposite qualities. They are a uniform, and yet, they can be, and often are, the essence of individualism. The shape of an individual body gives shape to jeans, especially when they are worn tightly.

Then there was the patch. At first, the patch was a symbol of I-don't-care poverty. No two patches were alike.

Patches became decorative. They were stitched, embroidered and appliquéd. A pair of jeans told a life story. Some of the needlework was so skillful and creative that a pair of jeans or a denim jacket could be a work of art. What is more individual than one's life story? The uniform had made a full turn.

Of course, not all young people enriched their jeans; many opted for the poverty look: frayed edges, patches and holes, and a lack of interest in cleanliness.

As the rebellious 1960's continued, a new word entered the fashion vocabulary: *funk*. We referred to funk in Chapter 4, and noted that there are some funky fashions for women. But basically, funk is of young people, by young people, and for young people.

Funk is protest and escape. Funky clothes express rebellion against the fashion establishment and a desire to escape from the harsh realities of present life.

It is not nostalgia. Women who grew up in the 1950's do not wear clothes of the 1950's in the 1970's. They do not turn back to what they knew. It is younger women and girls, who never knew the 1950's firsthand, who escape to fantasies of the past— a past they can only see filtered through old movies and music. They may choose the 1920's or the 1930's. Some of the youngest girls, in the 1970's, began to "discover" the 1960's. Each new generation creates fantasies of its chosen past.

Funky clothes, at their best, show flair, imagination and taste. Funk combines the most disparate elements—an evening skirt and a denim jacket, a lamé blouse and a seersucker skirt.

Not all funky outfits depend on old clothes; they can just as well be new. The best funk is individual; it is an improvisation, like jazz.

Sometimes funky clothing seems wistful as well as mocking. Who is to say if shabby velvet expresses a contempt for luxury or a longing for it?

Why pay so much attention to funk? Isn't it a passing fad? It may be just that, but it is important because it acted as a catalyst on mainstream fashion. Clothes worn in the 1970's would have been unthinkable twenty years earlier.

Who could have foreseen conventional people wearing black velvet blazers with jeans to formal parties? Challis dresses with leather boots? High-heeled shoes and pants? These are just a few examples of fashion themes that were accepted after young people introduced them. Gypsy costume looks that started "on the street" wound up in designer collections. The circle closed. The unthinkable became the desirable, and the acceptable.

As the mainstream caught up with funk, young people moved on to clothes that imitated the costumes of current rock musicians. There was glitter rock, with its sequins and satins; and punk rock, with its cult of torn T-shirts, chains, razor-blade pendants and brightly dyed hair.

Though the thrust of the youth movement was away from mainstream fashion, there were some ironic echoes of the mainstream.

Young people developed *status symbols* based on brand names. Their parents prized Vuitton and Gucci. The younger generation wanted Frye boots and Adidas sneakers.

It did not take manufacturers and retailers long to realize that young people had developed their own tastes. In the 1970's, there were iron-on patches and letters and patch kits. When young people boiled and bleached their jeans, pre-bleached jeans appeared in stores, followed by pre-washed and pre-faded jeans. Flare legs, straight legs, hip-huggers, double-zipped jeans, and jeans with all sorts of pocket detailing turned the uniform into fashion.

In the 1970's, the hippie, with one pair of jeans to her name, disappeared. Her younger sister was cleaner and neater. If her hair was long, it was washed. So were her clothes. She collected a wardrobe of jeans, tops and accessories. She even discovered the skirt, a brand-new, revolutionary fashion!

The fever of funk dropped. There was less of the bizarre and the outlandish, though young people still reserved the right to make their own fashion judgments for themselves and their peers.

Large department and specialty stores set up youth departments to meet these new needs. Independent retailers pursued the growing youth market. Some independents evolved into chains.

The Gap is an example of a national chain of youth stores, larger than most, that was born of the youth revolution. Starting with one unit in California, in 1969, and a stock devoted exclusively to Levi Strauss merchandise, The Gap moved eastwards, and eventually widened its scope to include other brands. Its name came from the phrase, "the generation gap." (In 1976, there were 167 Gap stores.) Early stores located in shopping centers. Later, the chain penetrated downtown metropolitan shopping areas. The Gap advertised in print, on television and radio.

A simple design idea provided a motif for store layout, advertising, and packaging. It was a diagonal line. The store logo was always shown on a diagonal. In stores, racks were placed on a diagonal. The diagonal design motif was carried through on the store's plastic shopping bags.

Salespeople were young, and dealt with customers in a straightforward manner. Merchandise was openly displayed on racks or shelves. There was some pinning of merchandise to walls. Signage was clear. Sizes and categories were easy to find.

Dressing rooms were numbered and painted with different motifs: a sunset, a moon, a rainbow. Lighting was high-key. Racks of shiny silvery metal added to the bright, clear atmosphere.

In the mid-1970's, management of The Gap began to build a second chain of stores under the name, Logo. This second chain aimed at an older customer group, picking up where The Gap left off.

Not all youth chains were national; some were local, and some were regional. No Name was an example of a regional youth chain with its own approach to the youth market. As of 1977, No Name had twenty-six units in New York, New Jersey, Pennsylvania, and Maryland. Stores were located in shopping centers; they did not penetrate downtown metropolitan areas. No Name did not advertise.

No Name established a distinctive decor based on low-key lighting, rock music, and merchandise hanging from the ceiling in an organized clutter that appealed to young people. At the front of each store, there was a raised dais supporting a mirror surrounded by light bulbs. The effect was theatrical; the dais looked like a stage.

There were communal dressing rooms; one male, one female. About 85 percent of its customers were female.

Another view in a Gap store: open shelves display folded merchandise. Lighting fixtures hang from ceiling. At right, behind cashier's desk, the diagonal store logo.

Dressing room doors are painted in bright colors to simulate poster-like drawings of work shirts. Dressing rooms alternate with mirrors along entire wall.

Salespeople were young.

Like The Gap, No Name started with heavy emphasis on jeans, and then branched out into jean-related merchandise and more diversified sportswear.

Towards the end of the 1970's, youth stores were on their way towards becoming specialty stores emphasizing sportswear, rather than jeans stores. They were also attracting more customers over twenty-five—men and women.

In spite of changing merchandise, youth stores and youth departments maintained some features that were an essential part of their appeal. Retailers had learned what young people wanted.

They wanted merchandise displayed simply, as in a supermarket. They wanted to reach out and pick size, style and color from a rack or a shelf.

They appreciated decor, but not decor in the old sense. They did not care for seating areas and plantings, for island displays or chandeliers. Sometimes, they liked the moodiness of dim lighting. Or, they might prefer clear, strong lighting that illuminated merchandise clearly.

They liked loud rock music.

They wanted dressing rooms just off the selling floor. They did not like department stores with dressing rooms half a block away from the selling area.

They did not want old-fashioned service. They did not seek the opinions of mature salespeople. They were interested in the opinions of their peers. They liked to shop in groups, and advise each other. They wanted to buy from young salespeople who would present merchandise without imposing a point of view.

They regarded shopping as an informal group experience. They wanted to come into a store with an ice cream cone or a slice of pizza and eat as they shopped. They were rarely desperate for clothes. Shopping was a casual experience, not a ritual.

Girls often bought boys' jeans and shirts. Boys did not buy girls' merchandise. Boys and girls—and young men and women—shopped together. Men were just as interested in clothes as women; sometimes, more so.

Often, the right brand name was important.

Customer age dropped. Twelve-year-olds shopped like adults, with their own money.

The meeting and mixing of the youth market and the fashion establishment was inevitable. But young people had a way of striking out on their own. Retailers could only shrug and wonder what would come next. Would it shock? Would it astonish? Would it last?

We cannot tell if we are in for shocks and astonishment, but we can say that as long as society worships youth, young people will have a strong claim to fashion leadership.

Customers List
Their Pet Peeves

16

T he following list of customer complaints was compiled by informally interviewing women of different ages and incomes. No attempt was made to conduct a scientific survey.

Almost all the interviews started off in the same way: *salespeople are at fault.* Other complaints had to do with *the merchandise itself,* and some with *the way merchandise is presented and handled in the store.*

Considering all these difficulties, it is a wonder women ever find the courage to go shopping at all. Retailers may well wish to ponder this question: If some of these problems were eliminated, or at least minimized, would women buy more?

The author, an inveterate and enthusiastic shopper, says yes, we would. Here are some of the problems that hold us back. *(The they" in these statements refers to salespeople.)*

If you ask for a specific brand, or style, and they don't have it, they pretend it doesn't exist.

They give meaningless answers because they don't know the real answer. I ask, how do these fit, and the saleswoman says, they're designed by Anne Klein.

They don't let me look around. One after another, they come up and insist on asking if they can help me.

As soon as I walk into a department, a saleswoman comes up and says, My name is Ms. Brown, let me know if I can help you. Then she walks away. She doesn't want to help me at all—she just wants to ring up the sale.

If you ask them if they have something, they say, everything we have is on display.

I hate the ones who try to wait on three customers at once in fitting rooms when it's clearly impossible. Then you're left high and dry in the fitting room. I'd rather wait my turn and have enough attention. I think they just want to make sure they get all the sales.

Once the sale is made they couldn't care less about helping you get your package and receipt.

Some saleswomen get you into the dressing room and look at your underwear to see if it's expensive.

I tried to buy some scarves that were on display at a corner of one counter. There was no saleswoman at the counter. There were, however, two down the side of the counter, who were just talking. They didn't have anything to do. They said they couldn't wait on me because they weren't in the scarf department and went on with their conversation.

They try to tell you a dress doesn't need much alteration when it practically has to be taken apart and put together again.

They encourage you to place a special order; you wait, and it never comes.

If they'd only stop calling me "dear" and "sweetie" and "honey"! Those words really bother me!

If I say I don't like something they look at me as if I were a fool. Then they say, "*All* our customers bought that dress." I always tell them I don't want to see myself coming and going, so show me something all your customers *didn't* buy.

They are very glad to take your money, but when it comes to returning it, or exchanging merchandise, you have to move fast to catch a saleswoman. I have learned never to approach a counter with an open package in my hand. When I used to do that, they would scatter to the wind. Now I hide it in a shopping bag, and I start to talk first and then pull out the package quickly. Sometimes they escape, anyway.

If the service manager is always busy, why don't they have two?

I hate it when they say, we haven't had any complaints about this from anyone else. I don't care about anyone else. All I care about is that it went wrong for me.

I think they purposely ignore you when they are having a private conversation and you interrupt them to ask a question or to get waited on. It's almost as if they had to show you that they're independent, and that they're not at your beck and call.

Do they have to talk about their operations and other personal affairs at the top of their lungs?

Sometimes, when a customer says "they," she is referring to store management. She does not know the name of the president or the vice-presidents, so "they" sums up all the unknown people way up there, who shape the policies of the store and are responsible for the problems the customer encounters in the store. Sometimes, a problem involves the manufacturer, rather than the retailer. But to the customer, the store is responsible, for "they" take her money.

Too many tags. They get caught in the zippers.

In the shoe department, you can't win. If you take an average size, they tell you they sold out of that size right away. I have a friend who takes an unusual size, and they tell her they hardly ever carry it.

Shoes do not fit.

Shoes wear out too fast, even expensive ones.

Boots are made for women with calves like toothpicks.

Whatever happened to good-looking leather slippers for at-home wear? And those mules with rosettes?

I wish somebody would invent a strapless bra that really stays up.

Sizes are mis-marked. I tried on a dress marked size 12 and then another, and I know the second one was really a 14.

I wish they would all make the same size 12.

Buttons fall off. And they are poor quality.

Seams are unfinished. There are hanging threads on everything. Why should I have to finish sewing a garment?

Why doesn't someone invent a good leather cleaner?

Those labels about how to wash or dry clean clothes don't mean a thing. You have to experiment and find out which fabric does what.

Spots don't come off synthetic fabrics the way they come off cotton and other natural fabrics.

A lot of things that are called wash-and-wear dry with plenty of wrinkles. And they aren't easy to iron.

I hate silk. If you just get a little drop of water on it, it dries and leaves a ring.

Cotton knits either stretch or shrink. I never know what size to buy.

Why don't tailored shirts come in sleeve lengths the way men's shirts do? Sleeves are all too short for me.

I am short-waisted and nothing fits me.

I am long-waisted and nothing fits me.

Why don't cosmetic manufacturers make small sizes of lipstick and tiny compacts that would fit into a small evening bag?

Whatever happened to cake mascara? It was almost as easy to put on and it lasted much longer. The wands are very expensive, considering how often I have to buy a new one.

I see something I like in a newspaper or a magazine and it says what store to go to, but I can never find it in the store.

Demonstrators are too gushy and push too much.

I love the demonstrations. I wish they had more demonstrators so more than one woman at a time could get a chance to be made up. I'd love to learn to use cosmetics really well.

I know this sounds unbelievable, but it really happened. I had trouble with my charge account bill, and I kept getting letters from a Mr. Jackson in the store. So I called up to make an appointment to come in and see him. His secretary said he was in conference. After I got the same answer about ten times, I finally insisted on making an appointment. It was for Saturday. I asked the secretary if Mr. Jackson came in on Saturdays—she said yes. When I got to the store on Saturday, he wasn't there. No one knew where he was. Finally I made a scene, and you know what? There was no Mr. Jackson. It was a made-up name they used for sending out letters!

There's a woman whose name is exactly the same as mine living in Philadelphia. I keep getting her bills, for hundreds of dollars every month. My husband has a fit. I called the store a dozen times, but they can't seem to straighten it out. I guess she's getting my bills. Now I'm afraid to buy anything in the store.

Fashion and Retailing
in the Future

As planes travel faster, as television brings far places closer, and as science prolongs youth and life, our society is changing.

Where do we go from here? No one knows for sure, but we can make some guesses, more or less serious, about the stores, shopping habits, and fashion merchandise of the future.

Looking into our crystal ball, we see:

Big stores will grow bigger. Most customers will shop in big department stores that sell everything, including food.

There will be a few small specialty stores that will be patronized by the rich. They will be the exception, rather than the rule.

Shopping will be international. *National* chains will become *international* chains. Foreign retail organizations will have branches in the United States.

American retailers will object to free trade because imported merchandise competes with American merchandise, but consumer demand will overcome these objections.

Women will order merchandise by phone, calling Paris and Hong Kong directly.

Women will spend the day shopping in London or Rome and be home in time to make dinner.

Shopping centers will turn into small towns with more recreational facilities, such as libraries and museums.

Streets in downtown city areas near stores will be closed and will be converted into parks, with swimming pools, skating rinks, lawns, and landscaped gardens. Downtown will resemble shopping centers.

17

Traffic will be underground or confined to the outer edge of cities. Customers will leave their cars just outside the city, and commute by bus, above or underground, to the store itself.

There will be parking facilities and service stores underground. And repair stations for helicopters.

Instead of subways, there will be conveyor belts with or without seats.

Underground activities will make lighting more important. Greater use of artificial lighting will change attitudes towards color. Men and women will wear more bright colors to compensate for the absence of natural light.

Machines will take over or share tasks now performed by people. More psychological tests will be used to hire and assign store personnel. The tests will be graded by computers. Employees will resent this use of computers and will develop a special computer neurosis.

Some eager job applicants will try to rig the computer so that it will decide in their favor.

A woman will be chosen as president of a department store. She will buy her clothes secretly in a specialty store and change the labels.

A man who scores low in a computer-scored psychological test will be hired as a clerk and will eventually become president of the store.

Machines will not only re-order fashion merchandise, they will also place initial orders. Buyers will fight this development and will claim that machines have no taste or judgment. Management will find that machines are more efficient.

Instead of traveling to market, buyers will look at manufacturers' lines on television. When machines take over ordering, the machine will be programmed to react to the picture on television screens.

Machines will also make decisions about new store locations, when information about population and geography is fed into them.

Display personnel will change store decor by pushing buttons and changing the lighting, which will change the overall color scheme.

In addition to visual display, there will be sounds and odors that will stimulate customers to buy. For instance, in the skiwear department, there will be a scent of pine trees and a sound of wind. Sound effects will be substituted for piped-in music. This will add to the theatrical quality of the store.

There will be fewer live shoppers. Women will be able to shop by means of phones with built-in television. They will be able to see merchandise in all parts of the world. Customers will also watch fashion shows from all over the world on television.

Customers will not have to go from department to department in a large store, looking for a particular type of merchandise. When they enter the store, they will "tune in" each department on one of many television screens. They will be able to see immediately if the store has the merchandise they want.

Because so many fashion shows will be televised from stores themselves, display and decor will become more theatrical and will be geared to the home viewer as well as to the "live" shopper.

The trend towards shopping from home by television-phone will help compensate for disappearing salespeople.

Inner circuit television will be used to police salespeople and detect theft. Salespeople will rebel against this. The status of selling as an occupation will sink lower. Fewer people will want selling jobs.

Self-service and self-selection will become more sophisticated. If a customer does not find the merchandise she wants on display, she will feed a punch card into a machine. There will be a signal that will tell her if the store has the merchandise in stock or not. If the store does have the merchandise, it will move from stockroom to customer on a conveyor belt.

Billboards will finally be outlawed. New promotional techniques that are more sophisticated versions of skywriting will be developed for outdoor use.

Machines will wrap packages. Customers will pick up their packages as they leave the store. The machines will break down at the height of the Christmas rush. Old folks will reminisce about the good old days when packages were beautifully wrapped by skilled people.

There will be many new packaging developments. One will be a sealing technique that makes it possible to open a package and close it again so that no one can tell it has been opened.

The package will be merchandise. A dress will come "packaged" in a matching handbag.

Weather will be partially regulated by science. When there is a water shortage, local governments will decree three or four days' rain at a time. Men, women and children will have complete wardrobes of rainwear. There will be handbags, gloves, and dressy dresses made of waterproof synthetics. The synthetics will really be waterproof.

Shortages of energy will lead to new fabrics with insulating qualities. Miniature transistors will create individual climate controls attached to clothing that will keep people warm or cool, as the weather requires. This will alleviate the effects of a series of energy crises. This clothing will be universally worn. The price of oil will drop.

There will be fewer regional differences in fashion.

A woman will be able to pack three or four disposable paper or synthetic dresses in her handbag and travel with a minimum of luggage, discarding the used dresses as they become soiled.

Swimsuits will dry in five minutes.

Buttons will be completely replaced by zippers that never catch or stick.

Zippers will be replaced by a chemical that is invisible and harmless to fabric. When this coating is applied, it will create an adhesive surface. Zipper manufacturers and workers will put pressure on legislature to have it declared illegal.

Skiers will fly to Alaska for skiing weekends in the summer. They will catch cold when they return to hot weather. There will be more pressure on scientists to develop a pill that cures the common cold.

Someone will invent a chemically treated brush that brushes spots and stains off fabrics. Laundries and dry cleaners will pressure legislature to declare the brush illegal.

There will be no more innerwear and outerwear; the two will merge, as will all the other fashion markets.

The one-piece jumpsuit will become a universal utilitarian fashion for both men and women. It will be varied by adding tunics, skirts, jackets, and pants.

Both men and women will wear pants and skirts.

Increased leisure time will call for more leisure wear.

Almost all clothing will be made of fabrics with some stretch. Rigid fabrics will virtually disappear.

Electronic developments will reveal a new spectrum of colors, hitherto undiscovered. Dyes will be invented that will apply these new colors to fabrics. The fabrics will be made up into fashion merchandise. The merchandise will be described as the "New Look." Women will protest the change, but eventually they will throw all their old clothes away and rush to the television-phone to order new clothes in the new colors.

Fabric developments will provide variety in fashions. Synthetics will reflect light in new ways. There will be printed synthetics with patterns that shift and change color depending on environment; for instance, sitting on the grass will turn a synthetic fabric green.

A harmless, appetite-killing pill will make dieting easy. Women will have better figures. Old women will tell young women, "You don't know how easy you have it. I remember when we had to starve to stay thin."

It will be possible to order clothes "cast" in plastic that will conform to individual figures. This will revolutionize sizing.

Long before the 25th century, the comic strip world of Buck Rogers and Flash Gordon will be with us with its fashion and gadgets. Everyone will have a flying belt —a small motor worn across the back. We will be human helicopters. We will need clothes that allow freedom to fly in. Metal helmets, high boots, jumpsuits, tunics, and tights are tomorrow's functional clothing for inner and outer space.

Index